NO LANGUAGE!
NO NATION!

Gerard Cairns

NO LANGUAGE!
NO NATION!

The Life and Times of
The Honourable Ruaraidh Erskine of Marr

GERARD CAIRNS

First published 2021
by Rymour Books
with Hog's Back Press
45 Needless Road
PERTH
EH2 0LE

© Gerard Cairns 2021

Cover design by Ian Spring
Typeset in Garamond
Printed and bound by
Imprint Digital
Seychelles Farm
Upton Pyne
Exeter

A CIP reord is available for this book from the British Library
BGH: Biography: historical, political and military
HBJD1: British and Irish History

ISBN 978-1-9196286-0-8
EBOOK 978-1-9196286-4-6

The paper used in this book is approved
by the Forest Stewardship Council

FSC

CONTENTS

ACKNOWLEDGEMENTS

I am very grateful for the help and assistance of the following: I received generous assistance and patience from the staff in the reading rooms and special collections departments of the National Libraries of Scotland and Ireland; in Edinburgh and Dublin respectively. Whilst in Dublin, I would also like to thank Donal and his enthusiastic team in the Irish Labour History Museum on the site of the old Beggars Bush barracks. Back in Scotland, I am also hugely grateful to the staff in the special collections rooms of the universities of Glasgow and Edinburgh. It was also great to catch up again with Carole McCallum and the team in the Glasgow Caledonian University archives as they had also been a great help when I was researching John MacLean. The staff at the Mitchell Library in Glasgow were always patient and helpful. In cyberspace, the British Newspaper Archive was invaluable.

A huge thanks are also due to two fine historians of the Irish national movement: Stephen Coyle and Dr. Máirtín Ó Cáthain. Both very kindly made their own notes available to me and Stephen also gave me access to the radical Irish newspaper archive which was an absolute gold mine. I am also grateful to Stephen and Mark Stewart for proof reading and comments on the text. Any mistakes or omissions are, of course, mine. The eccentricities, if any, I share with the subject of the book.

For the sharing of knowledge, ideas, as well as positive challenge and friendship I would like to thank Donald Anderson, Peter Urban, Jim Clayson, Allan Armstrong and Dr Martin MacGregor who has been a great encouragement to me with regard to the Gaelic language. Dr Catriona MacDonald and Professor Richard Finlay are due particular thanks for giving me some leads into the spiritual side of nationalism. Malcolm Erskine, the current Earl of Buchan, kindly provided family information.

Finally, to the forbearance and patience of my wife, Shirley, and my daughter, Lucy, as I ploughed into all things relating to Erskine of Marr. They were immensely supportive and understanding. Lucy proved her worth as a fine research assistant when called upon to help her old dad!

Mòran taing a h-uile duine!

Gerard Cairns   Glasgow, June 2020.
Gerri Mac A' Chùirn   Glaschu, An t-Òg Mhios, 2020.

Introduction

Indeed, in all national movements the role of the writer is a vital one, because it is to him that the nation looks to give it all the trappings which the Romantic Movement taught Europe to expect of a nation: a glorious past, a distinctive culture, a national language.

H J Hanham[1]

I believe that this is the first, full biography of a largely forgotten figure in Scottish history.[2] There have been numerous articles and references to the man and I hope to do this justice in the book. The interesting thing is that for someone who is so little known, he has been written about by quite a lot of people. There is something in Erskine of Marr that draws in writers and scholars of Gaelic and of Scottish nationalism. Maybe it is his eccentricity, maybe it is his boundless energy and commitment and maybe he had and has something to say. Erskine has his supporters – most notably the historian and Gaelic language activist, Seumas Mac A' Ghobhainn who hailed him as, 'a forgotten Gaelic patriot'.[3] He has his critics too – the BBC's Andrew Marr, wrote that, ' …in colloquial terms he was a bit of a nutter'[4] – although he does not deny the contribution of the eccentric Earl to a period of Scottish history. It is also worth noting that most modern histories of Scottish nationalism give him his place in that history; a contribution that was first acknowledged by the New Zealand academic, Harry Hanham.[5]

Erskine led a life very much on the move. He has left us no personal papers, although his stamp is across the personal papers of many others. It was intriguing tracking these down. Among others, he current incumbent of his clan seat, the Earl of Buchan, kindly sent me additional information on his great uncle.

Back in the 1970s, a group of radical nationalists produced a set of papers on an independent Scotland. The editor, Gavin Kennedy, wrote a fine positioning introduction in which he set out his vision:

Radicals approach independence with a great deal of optimism and a granite determination to influence the future of their country. Independence for Scotland is on the agenda and nationalists intend to keep it there until we pass over to the post-independence reconstruction of our country. This is no job for faint hearts serving trivial ends. Neither is the SNP a place for opportunists and carpet baggers. Our country requires more of us than we can give but independence will give our people more than they can hope for.[6]

Erskine himself is not mentioned in this book – a forward-looking, progressive set of papers written by leading nationalists at the time – yet their radical nationalism owes so much to him, making it hard to understand why so few are aware of his contribution. Hopefully, I will address that neglect in the course of this study and strive to give Erskine back his deserved place in the nationalist movement.

As Hugh MacDiarmid said regarding Erskine, 'Justice will be done to him yet with a biography'. This is it and it is long overdue.

Finally, I should point out that I am a Gaelic learner and am by no means fluent in the language. I have consulted Erskine's Gaelic publications and have tried to do them justice in the book. Any quotations used are reproduced as they would have been written in the original Gaelic with an English translation in the footnotes. This does justice to the language. If I have not given Erskine's Gaelic output the full credit it deserves, I hope that a Gaelic scholar may take up that mantle in the future.

Chapter One

Learning Gaelic from Your Nanny

Genealogy should be easy when you are an aristocrat. There are various peerage books and *Who's Who* anthologies to find out which line one has descended from. The first-born son will go on to become the next Baron or Duke or maybe even King while the other children will make up the other runners and riders in the national aristocratic race.

The town of Erskine in Renfrewshire gave its name to the family name of Erskine and it was Henry of Erskine who was the first recorded person of that name during the reign of Alexander II at the start of the thirteenth century.[1] By the late fourteenth century, the family had married into the Keith family which had descended from the Mormaers of Mar and became Earls of Mar. It was John Erskine, Earl of Mar, who built Braemar Castle in 1628.[2] Unfortunately, an attainder or forfeiture was placed on the earldom and its property after the 1715 Jacobite Rebellion as this was led in Scotland by John, 23rd Earl of Mar who was exiled in France after the rebellion. This remained until King George IV removed it under the influence of Walter Scott in 1824. By this time, Thomas Erskine, the third son of the 10th Earl of Buchan, had been made the first Baron Erskine in 1806. Erskine had made his name as a radical lawyer. At the height of the sedition trials in England in 1794, Thomas represented leading radicals in England such as Thomas Hardy, John Thelwall and Horne Tooke. Such was the nature of his defence that when the London crowd believed that Hardy had been acquitted, they took the wheels from Erskine's carriage and carried him through the streets in celebration.[3] However, he did not receive his baronetcy for his service to English radicalism. Instead, his career saw him move in a different direction and this included representing the reactionary Proclamation Society in its prosecution of a printer who had published Tom Paine's revolutionary *The Rights of Man*.[4] Thus the young radical lawyer would become the British Lord Chancellor in the same year as he became the first Baron. This would begin a line of attachés and diplomats and soldiers although his contribution in supporting those who planted the liberty tree in England should be remembered.

The Honourable Stuart Richard Joseph Erskine was a second son.[5] His father was the 5th Baron Erskine. This allowed his father, or William Macnaghten Erskine, to sit in the House of Lords as his forbears had done. Being the second son made Stuart the Earl of Marr. Or did it? As we go through Stuart's journey you will note the extra 'r'. He liked to refer to himself in later years as the Honourable Ruaraidh Erskine of Marr and as we shall see, indirectly, there was an Earl of Mar who frequented similar circles. How did this come about?

His direct line of descent goes back to the British government's creation of a baronetcy in 1806, not to the historic line of the earls of Mar. There is, of course, a line to the Earls of Buchan through the first baron, Thomas. The point, however, is not in the lineage but in the timing. The Honourable Stuart Erskine became the Honourable Ruaraidh Erskine of Marr. We will trace this journey in due course. Just for the record, Ruaraidh is the Gaelic name for Roderick, or Roddy. This does not make him a fraud or a trickster. It was a journey of his own identity with a piece of self-invention thrown in that suited some radical – even revolutionary – purposes; both for the Gaelic language and for Scotland. He may have aligned himself dubiously – or rightfully – with the Scottish branch of the Erskine clan but his direct lineage would suggest otherwise. It is not my place to quibble – but through his life, he arguably brought things back full circle to his great, great, great grandfather by planting a twentieth-century liberty tree in Scotland.

So, for our purposes, the Earl of Marr was born on 5th January 1869. The great Liberal, William Ewart Gladstone was Prime Minister at the time. His mother, Caroline Grimble, appears to have been a commoner, although there was nothing common in his sibling's names – there was an elder brother, Montagu; his younger brother, Standish as well as a younger sister called Margaret.

While the genealogical line may be easy to trace, it is not so easy to fill in the gaps. We know that the Baron had been a captain in the 9th Lancers before going on to become a barrister at Lincoln's Inn in 1873. They appear to have been an itinerant family which would be a factor throughout the Earl's life. The Honourable Stuart's birthplace was Brighton; at 1 Portland Place. However, by his own admission, he was raised in Edinburgh.[6]

This brings in one of the interesting parts of the Erskine of Marr story. The family hired a nanny who hailed from the Isle of Harris.

Erskine does not name her but states that he learned Gaelic from her. While there is no reason to doubt this story, it is quite incredible. Yes, he would have been very young and could easily have soaked up phrases and songs like a sponge. Yes, being in Edinburgh would have felt different and hearing the beautiful native tongue of Scotland may have felt exciting for a child. However, there is no doubt in my mind that Erskine was constructing a bit of mythology around himself; namely that he 'learned' Gaelic from his nanny.

It is not my intention to debunk myths nor to re-write history but it is important to look at the facts soberly. I am no language expert and may be way off the mark. Yet in my mind, to retain the language learned so young would have necessitated usage either at home, in school or with friends. There does not seem to be any evidence of this. Indeed, as a teenager Stuart was sent to be educated in the private boarding school of Uppingham.

Uppingham was, and is, an exclusive school in Rutland in Leicestershire. It had been founded in 1594 and is proud of its Elizabethan roots. The school caters for teenage boys and girls. In 1883 the school opened the first school swimming pool in the UK while Erskine would certainly have still been there as a pupil.[7] There is no documentary evidence as to when he left the school but if I make an assumption that he was there from about 12 to 18 then he would have left around 1887. The family appear to have been back in the south of England by this point. It may be fair to say that some of his nanny's Gaelic may have seemed a bit distant by this point and he would not have been using the language on even a semi-regular basis.

As we shall see the language did not feature in his first journalistic adventure at all. Something else happened that re-kindled a belief in and a desire to learn the old tongue of his country and the nanny from Harris had certainly lit a spark in him. My belief, backed by some hard evidence, is that he went back to learn the language sometime around the end of the nineteenth century. At least he fondly remembered this childhood experience which is more than can be said for his memories of his Leicestershire education.

Erskine did not go on to university. After leaving Uppingham he stayed in Northampton close to his family. Journalism would be his first venture in the big world. His professional intentions were confirmed when he entered David Anderson's School of Journalism in Northampton when he was just 19.[8]

There is not much to go on by way of material for his young life. His own family appear to have been comfortable financially as would be expected. The great aristocratic fear was democracy and from this fear the young Erskine was not exempt. Two years before he was born the Reform Act was passed which enlarged the electorate; while by no means giving the vote to the masses at this stage, the fear was that it would eventually. The historian, Eric Evans, tells the story of the Liberal Chief Whip, George Glyn, telling Gladstone, 'all is new & changed & large & I fear I must say in some respects dark.'[9] This fear of democracy would crop up time and again in the older Erskine.

Young Stuart also met the Grand Old Man of Liberalism. No date is given. He recalls defending the memory of the Jacobites' own James VIII who had been 'traduced' by historians. Gladstone sat in silence before stating that James was 'ruled by favourites'. Erskine felt that Gladstone suspected in the young Erskine that he was part of, 'an anti-Reformation cabal… a popish plot to blow up the memory of Buchanan.'[10]

These formative years certainly instilled an identity in the young Stuart. He was an aristocrat, he felt Scottish with romantic Jacobite sympathies and was an exile for a lot of his life. At this time, he embarked on his first literary project. This was to be a short biography of his great grandfather, the second Baron Erskine. The young author had amassed letters from Charles James Fox, the Duke of Wellington and George IV and promised to have some insights into the Caroline affair in 1820 when the king tried to divorce his wife, Caroline of Brunswick, to prevent her becoming queen. To my knowledge this book was not published although it did receive some pre-advertisements in local newspapers.[11]

Political activity would have to wait for a couple of years. While he was schooling there were political movements in Scotland for Home Rule. As Erskine set out on a personal, career path after school so too did Scottish nationalism set out on its own path. The paths would merge of course yet it is interesting to note that as Erskine set his sights on career and the future, the new Scottish Home Rule Association (SHRA) published its manifesto in late 1887.[12] Two of the signatories had been real driving forces in the early nationalist movement – the renowned academic and Celtic scholar, J S Blackie and Charles Twaddie.

The document strikes a very moderate and devolutionist tone. There were three stated objects focussing on a Legislature and a Scottish Executive for purely Scottish affairs while maintaining the 'integrity of Empire'. They also wanted 'parity' for Scottish political business within the Imperial parliament. The manifesto is trying to distance itself from the Home Rule all round argument by claiming that Scotland's claim has nothing to do with Irish demands.

Indeed, the only nationalist tone of the document is in the calling for a Scottish Party (similar to the Irish Party of Parnell and Redmond one would presume) and in its statement that Scotland's claim, 'since the Union of 1707 has never been lost sight of by a small patriotic band of our countrymen'.[13] Although, the new Party would be above the 'ties and trammels of party politics' and seek to get an equal share of home rule as would be afforded to England and Ireland. The manifesto ends with the surprising claim that they would prefer Unionists in the Party than 'any merely Irish home ruler.'[14]

Yet the SHRA was young and raw as it had only been formed a year before in 1886 and it did have the remnants of John Murdoch's radical and original Highland Land League in tow. The Chair of the Land League was also President of the SHRA as well as being a Crofter MP and it was Mr Gavin B Clark who would introduce four motions for Home Rule between 1889 and 1893.[15] It should also be noted that this early incarnation of the SHRA had two early Labour pioneers. Ramsay MacDonald – future first Labour Prime Minister – endorsed Keir Hardie who was the Labour candidate in Mid-Lanark in the 1888 election. MacDonald was an Honorary President of the SHRA in London and believed that the cause of 'Labour and Scottish Nationality would suffer' if Hardie withdrew from the election.[16] Sydney and Olive Checkland have explained this late nineteenth century development: this confluence of the causes of labour and nation in the Lowlands was mirrored by a combination of language and land activism in the Highlands. 'Thus', they argued, 'could Gaelic revivalists and Lowland radicals come together, especially over crofters' rights.'[17]

These political visions would inform political nationalism in Scotland for a long time. It would not be long before the young Earl of Marr would be informed by them too.

Chapter Two

A lively and eccentric young journalist

Ruaraidh Erskine of Marr's life was long and full. He entered the public arena when he was only 21 as a journalist and newspaper editor. On 21st June 1890 the first edition of *The Whirlwind* came out. It was subtitled as, 'a Lively and Eccentric Newspaper' and the 'Organ of the Honourable Stuart Erskine and Mr Herbert Vivian' (at this time he was still using his given Christian name). The newspaper was printed in London. Herbert Vivian was four years older than Erskine and had been schooled at Harrow and graduated from Cambridge University.

These young editors proclaimed their intentions in the newspaper's slogan: 'De l'audace, de l'audace toujours de l'audace.'

Their opening editorial asserted itself as a manifesto covering everything from politics to literature to religion through to philosophy and sport. It was not a very progressive manifesto. Students of the Scottish nationalist, Gaelic activist would not recognise that young Stuart Erskine was the same person (other than the obligatory Honourable prefix). *The Whirlwind* would be 'individualist' in politics; that is if individualist means rabidly reactionary!

In politics Marr and Vivian wanted to re-establish the old Manchester school of economics meaning that they would be, 'unswerving advocates of nationalism, peace and free trade.'[1] They elaborated by committing themselves to the notion of monarchy as well as to frequent parliaments and referenda although while claiming to favour 'real representation' for the people they oppose, 'female, childhood or doghood suffrage.'[2]

To be fair, the dogs and the children didn't pose the same threat to these two young toffs as the Suffragettes did. It was Erskine who explained his reasons in his personal piece inside the first edition and in doing so brought the other enemies of *The Whirlwind* to the fore. They opposed female suffrage because 99 out of 100 women support 'State Socialism'. It has a claim to be the most outrageous statistic ever published! Yet Erskine believed that they could forsake any notion of individualism if women obtained the vote – and to make matters worse it would open the door to socialism – 'the greatest national danger of the day.'[3] Thus began Erskine's tortuous relationship with the great ideology of working-class liberation. In 1890 socialism was a heresy against all laws of political economy. It wouldn't always be so.

There were other noteworthy points from their manifesto. Jacobitism was one such point. In history the newspaper would be legitimist and Jacobite while in religion they would be, 'eclectics searching after the truth'. These points would come out time and again in the thirteen issues of the paper and it is important to state that they were radical in certain things. In line with their audacious slogan, all great men would be 'interviewed or lampooned'. The newspaper would also make a significant artistic contribution through the sketches of Walter Sickert, initially, and then James McNeil Whistler. Perhaps the aristocratic well-wisher, the Honourable Auberon Herbert summed it up in his contribution when he said that: 'Whirlwinds are constantly needed to clear both religious and political atmospheres...'[4]

This particular *Whirlwind* blew in certain fascinating directions. It was a whirlwind that would blow away the House of Hanover. The young editors had their own heir apparent in waiting in the form of Mary, the wife of Prince Louis of Bavaria who was born in 1849. By their reckoning it was only her Catholic religion that kept her from the throne.[5] A table of genealogy was produced for this 'legitimist' succession in the very first issue. As Erskine grew older, he adopted a love/ hate relationship with the House of Stewart, but he was very much in love with them at this time. Erskine and Vivian had been the founders in 1889 of the Legitimist Jacobite League of Great Britain and Ireland. As we shall see the inclusion of Ireland is significant.

This organisation was a spin off from a previous incarnation – the Order of the White Rose. This organisation (which also included our young whirlwinds with Vivian as the president) had sought to organise a grand Stuart exhibition in London in 1888. A later Stuart claimant, the self-styled HRH Prince Michael of Albany, relates that the White Rose organisation was infiltrated by government agents and when the Exhibition did go ahead in 1889 it was a celebration of the Whig 'glorious revolution' which put William of Orange onto the thrones of England, Scotland and Ireland. Queen Victoria was the patron of the exhibition. This was too much for Erskine and Vivian who resigned to form their own Legitimist league.[6]

With not much public support for a Stuart restoration, Erskine used the pages of his newspaper to keep the flame alive including birthdays, tables and the reprint of a manuscript charting bonnie prince Charlie's 'miraculous' escape after Culloden.[7] It must be noted that their Jacobite loyalty did not stop them from fraternising with loyal Hanoverian aristocrats against the socialist enemy. The editors attended the annual banquet of the Liberty and Property Defence League where Lord Wemyss made 'many good points' against, 'the ridiculous Fabian Society.'[8] For the sake of liberty and property they could live with Victoria as queen!

The newspaper lived up to its name in the language that it used. There was no holding back against the great and the good even if it was borderline defamation. At times the language used was of an immature, undergraduate nature while there were times when it was quite vociferous. The younger editor was the main culprit. A good example was Erskine's report of a visit by the Dunfermline expatriate millionaire, Andrew Carnegie, to Dundee. By way of background, it should be remembered that both Erskine and Vivian sought from the outset to lampoon celebrities through open letters entitled, 'Letters to Absurd People'. These were meant to be witty and satirical.

In one such, Letter to Carnegie, Erskine held nothing back. It was a tirade inspired by a republican speech delivered by Carnegie on Tayside. To Erskine, ' …he is a rebel against the monarchy… vermin,' who should be pursued as he, ' …spreads sedition while accepting the freedom of cities in gold boxes.'[9] In inverted racist language he suggested that the rich Fifer should go back to America. It is not pleasant as an author to recall such language but it cannot be ignored either. Young Stuart would mature in time. However, this whirlwind of intemperate language is part of his story.

In the very last edition of the newspaper, Erskine wrote a piece on 'Revolution'. The backdrop had been the rise in trade unionism and fears of socialist infiltration in to the armed forces. Erskine saw the danger of a 'universal Republic'. At the end of a bitter industrial dispute, Erskine wrote: 'We are glad that the Southampton Dock Strike has ended disastrously for the labourers.'[10]

The gladness at the defeat of working-class people with no other redress than strike action displays an utter lack of empathy and a conceited prejudice born of his own class lifestyle at that time. Thankfully, Stuart Erskine grew up.

The island of Ireland was a conundrum for the British political establishment in the late nineteenth century. Everyone of a progressive hue knew the answer to the question or so they thought: Home Rule.

The Whirlwind was no different. The positive line on Irish Home Rule was one of the few progressive aspects of the newspaper. In fairness, it was Vivian who pushed the line. He used one of his 'Letters' to critique Arthur Balfour, the Tory Prime Minister, over his treatment of Ireland.[11] Vivian made special reference to an 80-year-old called Alexander Lumsden. Vivian alleges that Balfour rack rented him after 40 years of loyalty, taking his possessions and sending him to the poor house. The wider political point was that it was 'incongruous' for the Tories to appoint, 'a dreary Scotchman without religion, sentiment or sense of humour as despotic ruler over the liveliest, most sentimental and most deeply religious nation on earth.'[12]

Not only did Vivian have pro-Home Rule sentiments; he had contacts too within the Irish National League in London. Vivian was a supporter of the Irish Party and used *The Whirlwind* to give his personal reminiscences. He knew all the leaders including Charles Stewart Parnell and John Redmond. These contacts also brought him into contact with the nationalist left. He recalls Michael Davitt accurately as a republican and socialist who was a 'charming man' but 'a dangerous politician'. The anecdote is quite revealing as to how far removed this Legitimist and Jacobite was from Irish political reality:

> I remember on another occasion, meeting him at a banquet of the Irish National League in London and expressing my surprise that the toast of 'the Queen' appeared upon the list. 'Well, I won't drink it', he said defiantly. 'You had better join me in drinking it over the water', I suggested, but he shook his head and said that would be still worse.[13]

These motives and Vivian's other contacts opened the door to an interesting part of Erskine's political journey. It is a fascinating aspect of his career which Erskine kept quiet until a throwaway line years later. It was June 1922 and Erskine was giving his Presidential address to the Scots National League. He posed the question of Home Rule or Independence? Marr cited Charles Stewart Parnell as someone he knew well as he had accompanied him on his final tour of Ireland: 'The great Irish leader had said to him on one occasion, 'Mark my words, sooner or later, the question of Home Rule will be set aside and that of Independence raised'. Recent history had proved Parnell right.'[14]

This last tour would have been in 1891. The Irish Party had split in November 1890 after the revelation of Parnell's affair with Kitty O'Shea and public court case. In December 1890 Parnell lost his

Kilkenny constituency. He did fight two other by-elections in 1891 before he died after becoming ill with rheumatic fever on 6th October. Ironically, he died in Erskine's birthplace of Brighton. It is perfectly plausible with the ending up of *The Whirlwind*, and with Vivian's contacts, that Erskine could have gone to Ireland. Yet it seems an outlandish claim. Did it happen?

Erskine waited 31 years before passing on this information. He did corroborate it with his book, *King Edward VII and Some Other Figures*, which he published in 1936. This is the closest we have to an autobiography of Erskine of Marr. Marr has a chapter on Parnell.[15] From this we can fathom that Erskine toured Ireland collecting information on the Home Rule cause in the entourage of a frail, politically broken Parnell. Erskine does not recall him as a great statesman or political genius but rather as a good Party organiser and leader. He first met Parnell after the divorce and when his political friends were deserting him although John and Willie Redmond did stand by him. The first meeting was on a packed train to Roscommon although no specific date is given.

It is interesting that this account corroborates his 1922 address:

> He was used then to make no secret of the fact that the 'constitutional' agitation for Home Rule on which the parliamentary party of Ireland was engaged was but pretence, in the sense that the true design of the whole national movement was absolute independence.[16]

A lot had happened in those 45 years. Ireland was a partitioned Free State. Marr mentioned that Parnell's words might not sound like much ' ...but in those days it was tremendous, and, had it been declared, would have set all political England in a fury, I imagine.'[17]

Erskine's account ties in with an account given by the Irish Party supporter and solicitor, John J Horgan. Horgan's father had been Parnell's election agent for the Cork seat since 1880. He recalls a conversation in his home shortly before Parnell's death:

> He told my father that night that he foresaw the failure of Gladstone's Irish policy and, in that event, he said, the only course for the Irish representatives to follow would be to return to Ireland and, by organising a policy of civil disobedience, make the government of the country impossible.[18]

I believe that Erskine was in Ireland in 1891 and was witness to a radicalisation taking place; Parnell's radicalisation. Was this radicalisation borne of political defeat? Or was it his true Irish nationalism coming to the fore – his heart's desire? The truth could be somewhere in the middle. Careerism can suppress the political passions of the holder and by then the great Irish nationalist parliamentarian had nothing left to lose. The experience certainly had an influence on the young eccentric journalist. Ireland caught him, as it has done with so many progressive Scots, and he started to apply some lessons to his own country.

Sometime around his trip to Ireland in 1891, Stuart Erskine joined the Scottish Home Rule Association (SHRA). In all probability he would have joined the London Branch and it may have been before the trip. This branch had been run by the future Labour Prime Minister, James Ramsay MacDonald, only a short time before. Harry Hanham notes that, by 1892, the SHRA was already a broad church of provincial left/ crofter radicalism and a right-wing Liberal base in Edinburgh.[19] Young Stuart, as we have seen, had no grounding in Scottish politics apart from a few Jacobite references in his newspaper and a piece on Lord Roseberry.[20] This letter criticised the Scottish Secretary for becoming 'imbued with democratic ideas' and speaking in two tongues: 'Scotch and English'. In other words, he was playing to a Scottish gallery when back home.

On 18th July 1891, Stuart Erskine got married at the age of 22. His wife was Muriel Lilias Colquhoun, who was the daughter of a British Army major general (G Irving Graham.) They were married in the little Italian Catholic Church of St Peter's in Eaton Square in London. It is not known for certain where the young couple stayed but it is fair to say that it was in the south of England. However, Erskine's gaze and his heart were being drawn back to the old country.

Chapter Three

Rejected by the Liberals of Bute

By the 1890s, the Jacobite dream was well and truly over. For a hundred years, since the songs of Lady Nairne, Jacobitism had survived as a safe, historical curiosity which posed no threat to the British Establishment and its Hanoverian monarchy. Two audacious young journalists intended to change this through their Legitimist League of Great Britain and Ireland. In the very first edition of *The Whirlwind*, they had traced a line of descent which placed a young lady, Mary, the daughter of Prince Ferdinand of Modena, next in line as the Stewart heir apparent.[1] In their line of descent, it is the English nomenclature that is used which would indicate that their target audience was English.

Arguably, the English language had created a gulf between the real Jacobitism and its sugary, sentimental imposter. The Gaelic bard, Alasdair MacMhaighstir Alasdair (Alexander MacDonald), had been Prince Charles' Gaelic tutor during the '45 Rising. It was MacMhaighstir Alasdair who had captured the excitement that he was coming, 'O hi ri ri, tha e tighinn, O hi ri ri, 'n Righ tha uainn.'[2] Charlie was coming, the exiled King who would save the martial, literary and cultural traditions of the Gael including their dress (the tartan). MacDonald was a scholar who understood where his culture fitted in with European culture. He also knew his history. 'O Charles, son of James, son of James, son of Charles', penned MacDonald citing the reasons why the Gaels supported Charles as faith and reason (creideamh us reuson) which meant that this was not some ragtaggle army of reactionary, backward serfs but a force for rationalism, culture and right. To place him in historical context, Charles was the 'beautiful jewel of the race of brave Banquo'.[3] It was from Banquo's son, Fleance that the Stewarts were descended.

So many Gaelic bards wrote in a similar vein. After Charles' death in Rome in 1788, a poet from Skye named William Ross composed, 'the last genuine Jacobite poem in Scotland'.[4] This was the view of John Lorne Campbell, a Gaelic writer and collector from Canna. He was no Jacobite apologist as he believed that the Rising was a disaster for the Highlands and Islands. Yet, he understands that Ross' poem,

An Suaithneas Bàn (*The White Cockade*), was the Prince's 'only true elegy':

Soraidh bhuan do'n t-Suaithneas Bhàn,
Gu Là Luain cha ghluais o'n bhàs;
Ghlac an uaigh an Suaithneas Bàn,
Is leacan fuaraidh tuam' a thàmh.[5]

Jacobitism had died with the Prince. When one understands the authenticity of the concepts and ideas held by the Gaelic bards and scholars, one will also hopefully understand that the appropriation of these concepts by English language writers such as Walter Scott and Lady Nairne was a gross misrepresentation which took rational, radical even spiritual concepts and made them safe and sickly sweet to a later audience.

Blissfully unaware of the true nature of Jacobitism, Erskine and Vivian embarked on an audacious plan to put the young lady from Modena on the throne in London. The Legitimists held what was widely reported in the English press as the first public meeting to be held in England or Scotland since the 1745 Rising in support of the cause of the Stuarts.[6] (that is, if we discount the public gathering of the clans at Ruthven after the battle of Culloden in April 1746) to discuss the way forward. There were two speakers that evening. The first was the Reverend J C Fillingham who spoke on the effects of the Revolution of 1688. The second speaker was Erskine and his topic was the Union of 1707 between England and Scotland. It is probably safe to say that Erskine reminded his English audience of the Scottish nationalist sub-text to historical Jacobitism as both James VIII and III (on landing at Peterhead in 1715) and Charles, in a declaration in October 1745, repealed the parliamentary Union between the two nations. They did not repeal the regal Union established by James VI and I in 1603.

The Legitimists moved a motion to 'restore the House of Stuart to the throne of England.' There was an amendment moved by the chair of the local school board (more a direct negative really) that the present dynasty should be maintained and he argued that the speakers had the liberty to speak as they did because of the liberties bestowed by the Revolution of 1688. The mayor of St Ives seconded and their amendment was carried with great enthusiasm. This probably put paid to any national speaking tour.

Back in Scotland, the *Glasgow Herald* also reported on the St Ives meeting. The Honourable Stuart Erskine was called a 'leading spirit' of the Legitimist League who was himself 'a sprig of nobility'. His 'short lived print' – *The Whirlwind* – was mentioned as it showed that there were, 'real, live Jacobites outside of Bedlam.'[7] This article is suggestive of a little-known part of Erskine's story. The correspondent asserts that the Jacobite leading spirit came to light after an, 'abortive candidature in the county of Bute for Scotch Home Rule'. So what made him want to stand for Parliament? And why Bute?

Rothesay is a pretty little town – the capital of the Isle of Bute on Scotland's Cowal Peninsula. As I write, it's town centre has a visual representation in the form of a signpost of something that would loom large in Erskine's later musings – that is the Highland/Lowland line. This line cuts through the town and the island. The town itself looms large in the working-class story of Glasgow. At Wemyss Bay train station, which adjoins the ferry terminal, there are photographs of hundreds of happy working-class Glaswegians waiting for the train to take them on a day trip or holiday to Bute which was a favourite destination during the Glasgow fair holiday. This would still have been the case as Erskine made his designs to be the new Member of Parliament.

We only have scraps to go on from the newspaper archives. The first indication of Erskine's intentions was in a south Yorkshire newspaper in January 1891:

> The latest election intelligence. The Honourable Stuart Erskine will, at the next general election contest Buteshire in the Scottish Tory Home Rule interest. This young gentleman is of 'Whirlwind' fame – being one of the famous proprietor-editors of that erratic little sheet. Mr. Erskine, if successful, will have a free hand. As a 'Scottish Tory Home Ruler' he will be able to fraternise with any or every political party.[8]

A 'Scottish Tory Home Ruler' requires some explanation. Erskine was not standing as a Tory. Mr Andrew Murray was the Tory candidate. Erskine's epithet, I would suggest, has more to do with eighteenth-century, High Tory Jacobitism with his own pro-Home Rule stamp. Indeed, as the story got out, he was getting called the Jacobite candidate but this is not the full story. It should be borne in mind that at this time Erskine was wearing two hats.

We have seen that young Stuart toured with Charles Stewart Parnell sometime in early 1891. It is highly probable that he was in Ireland as an observer from the Scottish Home Rule Association (SHRA). It is not clear exactly when he joined but is fair to say that it would have been sometime in late 1890 as his articles in *The Whirlwind* were becoming more aware of Scottish politics. His candidature, therefore, would have raised the profile of both the Legitimist League and the Home Rule Association.

It is also fair to say that Erskine had no ties with the island so it is an intriguing choice which throws up some nice lines of enquiry. *The Whirlwind* certainly irked so many snobbish mainstream newspapers. This election gave the former editor a chance to gain some invaluable front-line political experience and simultaneously raise the banner of the SHRA. There is also a Jacobite angle. The heir to the British throne is the Prince of Wales and the Duke of Rothesay. The banner of a Stuart revival could be raised in the dukedom of the heir apparent, Edward. There also may have been an aristocratic link. The Marquis of Bute may have been a personal friend and did show an interest in Scottish cultural affairs. Primarily, the reason was that there was a by-election in October and that would certainly have raised his profile. Yet he dropped out of the race.

Erskine announced this at the SHRA's Conference in the Music Hall, Aberdeen on 29th September. The Caithness Crofters' MP, Gavin Clark, was in the Chair. Charles Waddie, James Reith and some Liberal MPs were in attendance. Proceedings were delayed a little as the delegates awaited the contingent from Glasgow and the west who were themselves delayed on the train. When they duly arrived, led by Keir Hardie, the Music Hall captured the joyous sound of applause and cheers.[9]

Elections were held for the office bearers with Erskine being elected as vice-President. In his contribution, he thanked the Conference for this vote and it was at this point that he announced that he was withdrawing from the by-election in Buteshire as Mr McCulloch had committed to 'Home Rule all round'. This was a reference to the Liberal candidate, John McCulloch. So that was that!

The Conference itself is indicative of where Home Rule style Scottish nationalism was at this time. A motion was passed which was pretty much the party line of the 1886 manifesto. Scotland would obtain a legislature and executive and only candidates who supported Home Rule should receive the support and votes of the SHRA – all this while, 'sacredly maintaining the unity and supremacy of the Imperial Parliament'. The prospect of Scottish Home Rule was slipping away – almost flowing down a drain of Liberal disinterest. The choice of the word 'sacred' may have been an attempt to ingratiate the Liberal interest again within the British Parliament especially as another Home Rule bill was planned for 1892, to be moved by Clark.

It was Waddie who summed up the mood of frustration. In

his report to the Conference, he bemoaned Gladstone's attitude to Scotland's case for self-government. The Liberal leader's attitude seemed to be, 'Ireland, Ireland alone'. Waddie's feelings toward Liberal policy had been expressed the year before when he delivered a protest on behalf of the Association (as honorary Secretary) against official Liberal policy in Scotland. As Naomi Lloyd Jones put it: 'With a general election fast approaching and Scottish Home Rule still missing from the Party programme, the SHRA began to express its doubts as to whether the support avowed in past SLA conference resolutions was sincere.'[10]

The conundrum was that the SLA (Scottish Liberal Association) was still their biggest supporter and indeed this conference piggy-backed the SLA conference which took place in the same venue in the afternoon. The contingent from the socialist movement was not yet strong enough to make any impact.

One Thursday morning, Stuart Erskine braved the April showers and arrived at Glasgow's Central Station. His destination was Rothesay. He was too early to be going 'doon the watter' on holiday. There was other business in mind that took him to Wemyss Bay for the short ferry trip. We do not know if Muriel was with him but we can take poetic licence and assume that she was taken along to savour the charms of Bute. They were booked in to stay at the Royal Hotel which could be seen prominently from the ferry.

The local newspaper, the *Rothesay Chronicle and Buteshire Advertiser*, reported that, 'The youthful looking hero of *The Whirlwind* visited Rothesay.'[11] It was Round Two of his political engagement! With the general election looming in July, Erskine was still keen to stand for the Buteshire seat. In fact, the Conservative and Unionist victor of the by-election in October past, Andrew Murray, was now the Solicitor-General for Scotland in Lord Salisbury's government. This time, Erskine went in person to woo the good people of Bute.

Word had got out in February that the Legitimist League were standing four candidates in the general election including Herbert Vivian for East Bradford and Erskine for Buteshire.[12] Their plan was to leave 'no stone unturned' in their plan to overthrow the House of Hanover. So far, so good. The problem was that Erskine did not arrive with pro-Jacobite literature to hand out on the shore front. Instead, Erskine had an appointment at Beechwood to meet the local Liberal Association. If successful, he had assured the local Party that he accepted the Gladstonian Newcastle programme of 1891 'but making Scottish Home Rule the principal feature of his political faith'.

The headline for the article said it all – 'Rejected by the Bute Liberals.' The local Party were having none of it and gave him no encouragement. For his part, he was unable to work his magic and convince them of his new found Liberal credentials. By way of consolation, they intimated that they probably would not stand a candidate anyway as they were reluctant to stand against the sitting Solicitor-General. (This turned out not to be the case as the Liberals chose Robert Earle Smith as their candidate).

Erskine could conjure the bizarre at different stages of his life. This trip to Bute was certainly up there in his list of bizarre acts. He was no natural Liberal nor did he show any inclination in his whole life, except on this Thursday in Rothesay, to be a parliamentarian. The other times that he intimated an interest to stand in an election, namely the year before and again in 1917 against Churchill in Dundee, he withdrew of his own accord citing a noble reason. On this occasion, he did not withdraw. He sought the Liberal nomination and was turned down. Of course, it is highly probable that he was on the island at the instigation of the SHRA; to boost the number of pro-Home Rule candidates standing in the election. Yet it is still out of character for the audacious, Honourable Stuart Erskine to arrive cap in hand at the Bute Liberal Association. Incidentally, he did not stand as a Jacobite either. He left the next morning to return to Edinburgh.

Erskine went back to what he knew best. He was a journalist and his heart was set on editing a new journal. He temporarily moved away from politics and into satire writing a piece for *Vanity Fair* on a recent meeting of the International Society for the Propagation of Cruelty to Animals. This was a 'report' on the said meeting passing a motion supporting a donkey race between Edinburgh and London.[13] This led to a very short-lived periodical with an inexplicable name.

Houyhnhnm, taking its name from Swift's *Gulliver's Travels,* was subtitled 'A journal for Yahoos'. However, it seemed to be *The Whirlwind* all over again. Erskine's intention was simple. It was to be, 'the propagation of polite learning and the diffusion of gaiety and wit'.[14] Not much is known about this short-lived publication. Occasional reviews appear in the press at the time. However, for all of his satirical intentions, he was still involved in Scottish Home Rule politics and this came across in his new publication. The pro-Home Rule *United Ireland* newspaper was very complimentary of a piece he wrote denouncing the Unionists as 'Obstructionists'.[15] Although there were signs that he was becoming a bit disillusioned with the direction of the SHRA – hinting that the office bearers were pursuing the wrong course in backing the Liberal Party and that, as a result of this, there may be a split in the Association 'greater than imagined'.[16]

Happiness and tragedy would strike very soon. The happiness was the birth of a baby boy, Alison Colquhoun Erskine, on 20th August 1893. However, the infant died just over a year later in October 1894.[17] It is hard to comprehend the personal impact on the young couple of losing their baby so early. Erskine would have no more children in his long life. Alison was buried in Christchurch, Hampshire.[18]

Within less than a year, Muriel was also dead. She died in April 1895, aged 24 while in Torquay and was buried in Newton Abbott in Devon.

This was real personal tragedy and there is no written record of how Stuart dealt with this. He makes no mention in his writings. What is clear is that there is a change of direction for the young aristocrat. We cannot correlate this change in direction with his own tragedy as that would not be a fair assumption to make. We can only say that there was a change in writing style; a change in politics; a change even in his very name.

Chapter Four

Goodbye Stuart, Hello Ruaraidh

There are so many Erskines in the aristocracy, some of them with similar initials, that the Honourable Stuart Erskine has gone in for a mild form of protection against confusion. He announces that he intends to discontinue the use of his Christian name of Stuart in the future, and to be known as the Honourable R Erskine.' *Northampton Mercury*, 1[8th] December 1903.

The journalist became a full-time writer. He would never abandon his love of periodicals and newspapers but for a spell Erskine concentrated on books. The transition had already begun. Over late 1894 and early 1895 the *Perthshire Advertiser* carried a serialised piece of political romance entitled, 'The Protector'. It was a dramatic account of the breakdown in political relations between Scotland and England. A revolutionary 'Committee of Safety' had been formed in Scotland but not of Jacobins or the masses. Rather, this committee consisted of earls and dukes battling out a Jacobite re-match! This would have summarised his own political romantic vision at that time, although it was more significant as a precursor to a period when history and tradition were to focus heavily as he threw himself into writing.

It would be 1897 before his first published book came out and it was about his Jacobite, High Tory, aristocratic hero. It was an anthology of the writings of Lord Bolingbroke.[1] His intention was to publish excerpts to make 'that great man's writings' accessible to the wider public'.[2] Erskine must have used the year before, while getting over his loss, to read over Bolingbroke's many works to bring them into an accessible volume and while the contents are not of much present concern, the subject matter is significant. Bolingbroke was his hero and if you care to plough into Erskine's writings in English you will find how he constantly uses him as a point of reference and anecdote. His very writing style (in the English language) borrows from this source too.

A couple of things were significant about Bolingbroke. In the mid eighteenth century he was the quintessential, High Tory, Catholic Jacobite. Erskine would have been drawn to this as a cultural starting point but would have seen that there was more to the man. He was a thinker and would not tie himself to any one system of government, whether it was absolute monarchy or rule by aristocrats. Bolingbroke was a believer in balance and into this balance was added the democracy or commons. Checks and balances ruled by his 'patriot king'. This appealed to the young Stuart. The appeal was summarised by another biographer: 'Bolingbroke touched life at many points: he was at once a statesman, man of letters, and citizen of the world.'[3]

At various points in his life Erskine sought to be these things too. The first book led quickly to the second which was also based on tradition: a satire of his own aristocratic stock. The tale is fictional and is a send up of an aristocratic family – the Heavisides. The noble rearing is evident in their family motto: 'Je ne pense rien du tout!'[4] So, they weren't thinkers nor were they achievers. The hero is called Gilbert and his journey through aristocratic circles is told in an understandably dated, humorous manner until he eventually becomes Lord Dullborough with his own coat of arms of two donkeys.

This is not a tale that has passed the test of time. It is, however, fascinating in suggesting a starting point for Erskine's new direction. There is a sudden break in the fictional narrative. Erskine as narrator tells of visiting Gilbert and travelling from Scotland to London. It is probably disingenuous to suggest that Gilbert was someone he knew. The point of visiting London is revealing. The narrator seeks to regale Scotland's disadvantages within the Union and the narration itself tells us exactly where Erskine's politics were at that point in time:

> Without wishing to undo the Union – a thing my father and some of my ancestors were much set on in their lifetime, and which the former endeavoured, without much success, to persuade me to also to put a hand to, – I have always thought it a pity that our forefathers when they undertook the affair of a union between the two countries of England and Scotland did not settle it in such a manner… as might have contributed a little more to the ease and dignity of my country.[5]

'My country'! This was the first affirmation in print of his political allegiance and statement of his national identity. It was never fully asserted in *The Whirlwind*. His political work through the SHRA was low key although it was taking him in a definite political direction; while at this time, if we take his own words, he was still a Home Ruler of the Unionist mould. The physical part of Gilbert's journey would suggest that he was relating a real trip and informing us that he was based in Scotland at that time. The lack of personal papers and physical evidence makes this only summation on my part. A summation based on his writings and the continuing political journey that would lead him to radical nationalism.

His country was catching him in its thrall. Stuart set about capturing its history and dress and language from the starting point of his new location – the North-east. There are not many fragments of evidence to go on but, circumstantially, why else would you write a tour guide and history of Braemar if you weren't acquainted with the place? Why else would you explore your ancestral pile of Mar if you were not exploring your own sense of self – and this is especially pertinent in the light of the personal tragedy that he had come through. *Braemar: An Unconventional Guide Book and Literary Souvenir* was his strongest work yet. The book came out in 1898 when Erskine was 29.

Erskine showed an appreciation of the geography. Aberdeenshire, he asserted, was split into Mar and Buchan. Two things struck him in this part of Scotland. Firstly, a reading of the history of the area's involvement in the Jacobite struggle led him to question that movement a little bit more. After a great hunting match in Aboyne, the Earl of Mar left hastily to raise James' standard at Glenlivet in 1715. Yet, his portrayal of this event in the first part of the book is certainly not romantic and he questions the intrigues in England of the former Hanoverian turned Jacobite. He could see that the Stewarts were not always the friends of the Gael and argues that the Highlanders' support for that House who had, 'systematically oppressed them most…' is worthy of closer attention from philosophers and historians.[6]

Secondly, this was an early statement of the part that Marr's faith would play in his writings. Despite the animosity of his own clan and the Farquharsons, the majority of the people of Braemar had stayed loyal to 'the old church'. Prior to the Rising in 1715, about '500 souls' were ministered by a Jesuit priest. His Catholic faith would always come across in his writings, although not always in a positive manner. Braemar's faith in adversity drew him in just as Scotland was drawing this Brighton-born aristocrat in.

His Jacobite sobriety didn't last all the way through the book. The last chapter is called 'A Jacobite Reverie' and is a creative piece of literature, a dream sequence as Stuart is visited by the Earl of Mar who is his cousin in the dream. He is carried away with romanticism in an entertaining way revelling in the way the Earl introduced him to a gathering of the clans as: ' …a true patriot, and as much for King James and a Repeal of the Union as we are ourselves.'[7]

Erskine was clearly thinking about the 23rd Earl who had raised the standard for James at Braemar in 1715 and welcomed the exiled King over the water at Peterhead. History has not been too kind to him. His enemies knew him as 'Bobbing John' for his propensity to change sides. He had been a loyal supporter of Union in 1707. Nor do his actions come across well during the '15 where he is portrayed as indecisive. Erskine clearly saw his dotted line relative in a different light and, to his credit, produced a piece of revisionist history for the Scottish History Society. Recent documents had shown the Earl of Mar in a favourable light as a statesman. Erskine praised his 'Scheme for Restoring Scotland its Ancient Military Spirit'. This showed John to be a, 'politician with remarkable foresight.'[8]

He was entering the field of politics again. A political odyssey that had begun touring Ireland with Parnell, led him next to Wales to a Pan-Celtic Congress in Cardiff in 1899. This congress was under the guise of the national Eisteddfod. It has been argued that at this congress Erskine probably met a young Patrick Pearse, who would go on to become the first president of the Irish Republic, and Arthur Griffith who would form Sinn Féin.[9] This would not be their last collaboration.

It is perfectly plausible that Erskine was at the congress mingling, listening, learning. His future course shaped by a basic observation: namely, the chasm between the language movements of the three Celtic countries in the British Isles. Welsh was by far the strongest numerically, with Irish having a strong political content. Pearse addressed the Congress followed by Count Plunkett and both specifically represented the Gaelic League.[10] Opening his address in Irish, Pearse then reverted to English and told a receptive crowd that the Welsh and Irish were two parts of the one great race and he was over to study the 'ways and methods' of teaching Welsh that he could take back to Ireland. (Pearse would go on to set up an Irish language school called St Enda's in Dublin so he was true to his word).

Scottish Gaeldom was represented by John MacKay from the 'Highland Mod'. His opening was in Gaelic but he didn't read it He told the audience that while the Scots were 'trying to reconstruct the mother tongue' they would not ignore English lest 'they would fall behind in the race of life'. Compare and contrast this to Pearse who called English the 'language of the foreigner.'

Erskine did compare and contrast and drew some conclusions. The first conclusion was to learn the language. It is my belief based on the gap between his tour guide of Braemar and his next output in 1901 that he used this time based in Scotland to learn Gaelic. New evidence has borne this out. The *Highland News* reported in September 1900 that the Honourable Stuart Erskine had been studying Gaelic for some time by attending the classes of a Mr Cameron in Beauly – commenting that he had, 'considerable fluency already.'[11] This also indicates that he was staying in and around the Inverness area at this time to attend his classes. He would also publish his next book there.

As the nineteenth became the twentieth century, Stuart became Ruadri. It was not the correct form of Ruaraidh that it would become but he was in transition. Ruadri is a more Irish form of the name that he would adopt which may have been due to his own misunderstanding. It is not surprising that he would make mistakes whilst learning the Gaelic language. However, he was learning and changing.

Goodbye Stuart, hello Ruadri! And Ruadri would shortly become Ruaraidh as his appreciation of Scottish Gaelic grew. Ruaraidh is not the Gaelic name for Stuart; it is the name for Roderick. Nor was he the Earl of Mar. Yet he became the Honorable Ruaraidh Erskine of Marr. Self-invention was taking place. A personal invention that would have a huge impact on language activism and political nationalism in Scotland. We do not fully know the reason for the adoption of his nom de plume. Living in the north east with an awareness of his family background rooted in that of the Mars' and the Buchans was a contributory factor. Increasing readings of Scottish history would have helped. In later years he claimed that it came from his father.[12] The defining reason, I would argue, was his learning of Gaelic. He was swept away by the horizons that it opened for him. He was personally distinct as Ruadri/Ruaraidh just as Scotland was nationally different as a Celtic and Gaelic country. We do know that this personal transformation would define him more than any other thing.

In May 1900, he gave an interview for the *Dundee Evening Post*. Erskine was promoting the grand Celtic Congress due to take place in Dublin the following year. This interview is his first statement of intent of his support for the language:

There are words in Gaelic which express sounds and sensations only to be rendered in the English by tedious circumlocutions... Believe me we are all in deadly earnest to relieve the many years of neglect and persecution under which the ancient language has groaned. Scotland is probably more determined in her effort than Ireland, but both countries are likely to make the language problem a political question. Nor can I conceive a more promising and engaging plank for any political platform.[13]

In his new guise he published *The Kilt and How to Wear It* in 1901. The kilt is 'Scottish Celtic dress.'[14] He was trying to latch on to its ever-increasing popularity and to construct more a suggestion on how to wear the garb than a dictat. The main point is that Erskine saw the book as part of the 'Celtic Renaissance'. As we have seen, this view did not come out of a vacuum. He believed the Scots were not alone so, significantly, he was looking to the Irish for inspiration: 'Our dress and our language, though not threatened with extinction, yet comprise a faith, as it were, whose tenets and principles require all the emphasis and advertisement they can command.'[15]

Here we see the evolution of Erskine's political thought process. He is back in Scotland, thinking about her culture, learning the language and taking a harder line as each year passes. This book is his first debunking of the notion of a Highland line splitting the country into Lowland and Highland. He saw one Scotland and one language. Patrick Pearse would approve and Erskine was ready to step up to the challenge.

In late 1901 the Honourable R Erskine of Marr attended the Pan-Celtic Congress in Dublin as the Scottish representative. He had also started to edit a new bi-lingual newspaper, *Am Bàrd* subtitled Ar Tir agus ar Teanga or The Poet – Our Land and Language. This was a major undertaking for a learner and it is fair to say that it was a major achievement for Erskine personally and a major milestone in Gaelic publishing and activism.

MacTalla was the first Gaelic language newspaper. It was published in Cape Breton and ran for 14 years from its publication in 1892. The crofting activist, John Murdoch, published *The Highlander* and sought to give Gaelic prominence in the paper. However, as Donald John MacLeod argues, all serious political articles in Murdoch's publication were in English.[16] Erskine's publication raised this bar – giving Gaelic equal footing. For MacLeod, this meant that Erskine was, 'a more serious catalystic influence.' The fact that he was a learner worked to his advantage and he could deploy: ' …his own capital and his remarkable resources of ideas and of energy to rid Gaelic literature of the influence both of its 'peasant origins' and the new 'enthusiasm for the music hall' and so to raise it to the same level as the best of English literature.'[17]

He could not and did not fully achieve this with *Am Bàrd* although that would come later. He did, however, set out his stall. His bilingual periodical would have the preservation of Gaelic as a 'national aim'.

The first page of the new paper didn't feature politics or religion or high culture; it featured Remington typewriters! A bit of shameless, bilingual commercialism that, at least, gave parity to the two languages in its advertisement.

His own Gaelic was advancing and the journal was enhanced by contributions from other Gaelic writers including J G MacKay who contributed a Gaelic idioms section and also serialised an old poem, *Diarmaid na Feinne*. Erskine relied heavily on serialisations including long articles on the Jacobite poet, Alasdair MacMhaighstir Alasdair, the Jacobite Wars and a Gaelic play – *Iseabail no ri Linn do Sheanair*. These provided originality and purpose for the fledgling journal as well as a progressive, consistent cause that was a world away from *The Whirlwind*.

However, he still had his *Whirlwind* moments. For instance, his series on 'The True Spring of the Jacobite Wars', saw the beginning of what would be a protracted intellectual war against the Reformation. With a turn for inappropriate language that he had honed in his early days of journalism, he began his assault. John Knox was, 'a gloomy Geneva bigot of the most absurd and offensive description.' He was not the worst though. That epithet fell to the earls of Murray and Morton who were 'clever rascals'.[18] With echoes of his fusion of faith and nationalism, he stated that the worst crime of the Reformers was to introduce an 'English party' into Scotland.

That was the 'old' Stuart. The new Ruaraidh was making some positive contributions for the language and the Gàidhealtachd. He used an editorial to call for a capital for Celtic Scotland.[19] (He suggested Oban. He was most definitely looking across the North Channel and learning from his Irish brothers and sisters and learning that sentiment was not enough. Economics was required to 'fix people to the soil'. Regeneration of the language required regeneration of the Highland economy and a capital such as Oban was a good start. Inverness was ruled out as it was moribund and Glasgow was as good as degenerate under 'the sway of the gall'. He clarified what he had in mind for the jewel of Argyll:

We do not of course mean a capital smoking with factory chimneys and disgraced by slums and whisky-brothels such as, seemingly, the Gall of the towns delight in. We would rather that mill-stones were put about our necks and ourselves summarily cast into the Clyde than that so melancholy a fate should overcome the 'pearl of the west'.[20]

He was developing a better sense of humour and temperance activists would, I'm sure, have loved his description of pubs as 'whisky brothels'! His Celtic capital would need investment but would be endowed with, 'morality, lofty aims and natural endowments.' There no loftier an aim than the language and he believed that the arbiters of the language were letting it down. Ireland had a thriving, politicised Gaelic League. Scotland had the inaction and bureaucracy of An Comunn Gàidhealach.[21] Over the next couple of decades this valid critique would see Erskine come into his own as a language activist. His own language was still developing. Most of his contributions were in English with more and more Gaelic coming from his pen as the journal developed.

His personal brand was growing and in April he was part of the Celtic Union series of lectures and he spoke in Edinburgh on 2nd April on 'The Place of Jacobitism in the National Life of Scotland'. In July he was contributing to the Spanish journal, *Nuestro Tiempo,* on closer cultural relations between Scotland and Spain due to Spain's Celtic roots. There were romantic reasons why Erskine had access to a Spanish journal. For present purposes, suffice to say that his literary reach was growing at a personal level while the reach of *Am Bàrd* was contracting. Throughout volume two, it was noticeable that contributors were drying up amid accusations of 'Popery' in the letter's pages. Erskine was characteristically unapologetic stating that he didn't care if he had only one reader.[22] Ironically, the only advertiser was Red, White and Blue Coffee which poses a nice juxtaposition of the cultures of Orange and Green in Scotland that the young aristocrat would not have been unaware of.

Am Bàrd was wound up in July. But it was the beginning of Ruaraidh's political journey that would see him emerge as one of the foremost Gaelic nationalists in the country. He even gave the language movements in Scotland and Ireland a new battle cry: "'No bishop, no king' was a favourite maxim of Charles I. We go one better and say, 'No language, no Nation".[23]

No language, no nation – gun chànain, gun chinneach! It was the start of a sojourn that would shape political nationalism in Scotland – a journey that would radicalise the movement, radicalise Ruaraidh himself and give to Gaelic Scotland one of its finest periodicals that would be a benchmark for others to follow.

Chapter Five

Gun Chànain, Gun Chinneach!

Would you say the year's voice? Or would it be the voice of the year? It doesn't seem right does it? Neither the imagery nor the grammar sits right in the English tongue. As the new Gaelic speaker appreciated, it sat just right in the language of the Gael: 'Guth na Bliadhna'. It was perfect. And it would be the banner heading for one of the most influential Gaelic publications ever to be published and *Guth na Bliadhna* has continued to make its voice heard down through the years.

As a publication it is arguably Erskine's finest achievement and spanned an incredible 21 years of his life from 1904 until it went out of business in 1925. It was bi-lingual until the last three years when it became an all Gaelic publication. More importantly, it is still recognised for its cultural achievement by modern Gaelic scholars. Derick Thomson, who would go onto edit a worthy successor publication in *Gairm*, argued that *Guth na Bliadhna* heralded, 'a clear move towards journalistic and modern writing in Gaelic.'[1] This view was supported by Donald MacLeod who saw the magazine as the 'true beginnings' of Gaelic journalism. Not bad for an adult learner from Brighton! MacLeod cites the employment of Angus Henderson, who plied his trade in journalism, as a key factor and an impressive example of the subjects covered: 'Free trade, the fishing industry, Gaelic drama, Land Reform, education, deer forests, Belgian neutrality, the Treaty of Versailles, the Russian Revolution, Scottish Nationalism and Gaelic publishing'.[2]

Nobody else, as we shall see, was doing this sort of thing in the medium of Scotland's two main languages and MacLeod acknowledges the way that Erskine, 'set his sights uncompromisingly high'. The only subject missing from the list was the significant omission of Ireland although that country would play a major part in his political life over the next ten or so years. There is one final piece of Gaelic recognition. In June 2019, a young academic based in Prague, Petra Johana Poncarová, gave a lecture on, 'Ruaraidh Erskine and Derick Thomson – Gaelic Innovators' at the University of Glasgow.[3] Petra made the point that native speakers closely associated with the journal, and what really struck a chord for this author – made as it was by a fluent researcher – was that Erskine had no reason to publish his output in Gaelic other than his passion.

It is an appropriate and lovely word. Erskine was getting his passion back for life. After *Am Bàrd* wound up, Ruaraidh Erskine of Marr married again. His new love was Dona Maria Guadeloupe Zaara Cecilia Heaven y Ramerez de Arellano. She was the only daughter of Mr J R Heaven and the Marquesa de Braceras. Mr Heaven owned a lodge and some land in Aboyne in the Aberdeenshire hills. It is probably a safe assumption to make – in the absence of hard facts – to state that their meeting and courting would have had a lot to do with Erskine's time spent in the North-east from 1898 onwards. Their marriage on 6th August 1902 was a big affair. They were married in St Mary's Cathedral in Aberdeen with a choir and a full orchestra performing Lambillottie's Mass. Many well-wishers gathered outside as they made their way to their reception in the Grand Hotel just off Union Terrace.[4] After their marriage, Aboyne would be home to the couple for most of the next 15 years although Ruaraidh was always itinerant and would use a townhouse in London for business. The father of the bride's income and means would ensure that they would never struggle financially, although Erskine would blow some money on his political and literary schemes.

They would be together until death parted them and it is a pity that not more is known about his exotically named Spanish wife other than the snippets that come across in his letters. Marriage signalled an interregnum; a period away from public life. Probably they went on honeymoon. Certainly, he used the time to perfect his Gaelic and acclimatise to Aberdeenshire. When he came back to public life it would be as editor of *Guth na Bliadhna*.

The first edition came out in Spring 1904. It is important to put Erskine's journal into context. We cannot appreciate Erskine's revolutionary approach without a brief compare and contrast. Let's take 1903; while Erskine was on his interregnum. A leading nationalist and former leader of the SHRA, Charles Waddie, edited *The Scottish Nationalist*. This paper probably symbolised the Jekyll and Hyde nature of Scottish nationalism. The leading editorial proclaimed: '*The Scottish Nationalist*, as the name implies, is a journal that will be exclusively devoted to the vindication of the political and social rights of the Scottish people.'[5]

In other words, it had the same equivocation that all nationalist groups had had since the 1850s with the Association for the Vindication of Scottish Rights through to the Scottish Home Rule Association. Namely, pragmatism and federalism. The British Parliament was overloaded with work and a Scottish Parliament would be a practical way to alleviate this burden. This journal was not separatist but rather supported Home Rule all round as, 'the true historical terms are Federation versus Incorporation'.[6] Also, there is an inordinate amount of time in the paper given to reports on Westminster business.

However, even this very loyal journal had to incorporate some nationalist radicalism. The best exponent was John Morrison Davidson. Morrison Davidson, as he was better known, had pedigree. Ironically enough he was born in Aberdeenshire in 1843 and had been secretary of the Edinburgh Republican Club in the 1870's. He was a trained solicitor whose passion was radical journalism. He was hailed as the, 'the Grand Old Man of Fleet Street' in a pseudonymous pamphlet entitled *Highland Patriots* in 1909 as well as being, 'the chief exponent of the people's rights in Britain'.[7] He had also stood for Parliament in Greenock as a candidate for the Scottish Land Restoration League in 1885.[8]

While he lived most of his life in London – and died there on 18th December 1916 – his heart was still in Scotland. Socialism may have been an all British affair for him but it did not negate Scotland's claim to Home Rule. It is Morrison Davidson's article which stands out in Waddie's short lived journal. *Juvenescat Scotia Invicta!* Literally translated: 'Automatic Grows Young Scotland! 'While he argues that since the 1860s the Union of 1707 had become anathema, his argument is still for federalism. His tone, however, is thoroughly nationalist. He agrees with that other famous socialist and nationalist, R B Cunninghame Graham, that Britain is, 'a cross between a rich man's pleasure ground and a sweater's hell'.[9] While a self-governing Scotland could focus on, 'plain living and high thinking'.

What stands out in this article and indeed in the politics of Davidson and Cunninghame Graham, and even Keir Hardie at this time, is that federalism was a British Socialist Party line. Their hearts were for independence even then – at the turn of the century when Socialism was seen as the only hope of the world.[10] Scotland, they felt, could play a part in that transformation. His heart spoke at the end of his article: '[he has] hope of a brighter era when Scotland shall cease to be a Northern County of England, systematically drained of her wealth in men and money, and resume her ancient and honoured place among the Independent Nations of the World.'[11]

The *Scottish Nationalist* went out of business due to lack of support in August 1903. It never did commit itself to independence. Despite its name it wasn't all that nationalist at all.

There was a gap in the market, so it was timely that *Guth na Bliadhna* appeared in the Spring of 1904. Erskine of Marr had to enter the stage in his own inimitable, and sometimes unfathomable, style: 'In that general progress of the Catholic religion which is, happily, observable through Great Britain, the Highlands of Scotland are bearing a proportionate part.'[12]

The opening sentence of Erskine's new venture meant two things. Firstly, he wasn't looking to fill the nationalist vacuum right away. Secondly, he saw faith and language as the building blocks to setting Scotland on the right path: 'We have a love for our country, which cannot be gainsaid, and cannot be denied. To see it considerable and respected, to see it prosperous and glorious, to see it happy and contented; but above all, to see it re-united to the one true Faith…'[13]

This view was genuinely held by Erskine for most of his political life and he practised, devotionally, his faith. Yet he was so out of kilter with, not only mainstream Scottish thought and society, but Catholic thought also – as most Scottish Catholics had little belief and less interest in a twentieth-century Counter-Reformation taking place. You would have thought that such an opening issue would have been its death knell and still it survived and prospered for 21 years.

I think the key to this lies in the building blocks that I have alluded to. In terms of faith, *Guth na Bliadhna* was quite unique. It would be wrong to ignore the bigotry that underpinned some of Erskine's views. There were some quite distasteful anti-Protestant comments and throwaway lines which did not come from any other source than Erskine of Marr himself. The pity is that it clouded a historical critique of the role that the Reformation played in Scotland's history. He could not help his side swipes at Knox, 'the Scots' idol', who had, 'feet of clay but has the heart of a scoundrel as well'.[14] Surely, historically, he was on more solid ground when he argued that Hume, Burns and Scott had, in their own distinctive ways, led a kick back against the 'Knoxian revolution'. The solid ground of debateable, living history as opposed to personalised sentiment. Erskine did both well and, to be fair, opened the pages of his new journal to historical debate.

His Catholic faith had a positive contribution to make to Catholic Gaeldom. There are some quite beautiful Catholic prayers in Gaelic contributed by native speaking writers and essays on such subjects as, for example, the legendary priest, Maighstir Ailean (Father Allan MacDonald) of South Uist and Eriskay fame.. Pictures and drawings were in short supply in the periodicals of this time and *Guth na Bliadhna* had only one in all of its years of publication: a quaint and rather quirky drawing of St. Columba of Iona. This was accompanied by an article in Gaelic by 'A Scottish Priest' who finished with a little prayer to Iona:

I mo chridhe, I mo ghraidh.
An àite guth Mhanach bidh geum bà;
Ach mu'n tig an saoghal gu eirich
Bidh I mar a bha.[15]

As the Gaelic language has declined over the twentieth and into the twenty-first century so too has the practice of the Catholic faith in the language. There are reasons for this which are outwith the scope of this book. It is only fair to point out that for those of all Christian denominations who practice their faith in Gaelic, Erskine's *Guth na Bliadhna* has a treasure trove of prayers and graces. This is because language is the true, most important building block. There are untold treasures that still deserve to be explored by Gaelic scholars. This learner cannot do them justice. Marr put these blocks in place bit by bit by first of all using English as the hook to explain what he would do and develop through similar articles and themes in Gaelic the finished product. He was true to his own definition: 'What is the meaning of the phrase 'to learn a language'? It means to translate our own individuality into comprehensible sounds.'[16]

What a beautiful definition! Don't we hear birds do exactly that among themselves (if we listen closely enough) when we awake in the morning? This almost universal definition Erskine applied to Scotland. Gaelic was, is and would be Scotland's language. He worked for this over the next thirty years with a messianic zeal. As he put it, the language is, '...the badge, the outward and visible sign of our nationality'.[17] No language, no nation! While the periodical continued to examine questions of Scottish history it also started to utilise its network of writers to explore European questions such as 'Poland's struggle for existence'[18] and Austria-Hungary as a model for Unionism.[19] Erskine was moving into the political space that Scottish nationalists had kept well away from:

Alas! The English party system blocks the way. The question of autonomy for Scotland, instead of being a national question as the Norwegians, to their everlasting honour be it said, made the question of national emancipation for Norway, is dragged at the tail of English political factions.[20]

His conclusion was that the English party system and Westminster had 'almost destroyed' Scottish nationalism. The confirmation of such conclusions and the short skip and a jump to full national independence for Scotland was not proven by the Norwegian or Polish examples – helpful though they were. He only had to look across the North Channel.

The late Bob Purdie, a former Marxist turned Scottish nationalist writer and academic, wrote that the attempt to read Scottish nationalism through the prism of Ireland was 'cognitive dissonance'.[21] This may have a lot of truth underpinning it as Scotland and Ireland have not shared the same historical experiences. It has not stopped Ireland – her story and her rebels – being a powerful, living prism for many Scottish radicals through the ages. Ruaraidh Erskine was no different. Maybe incognisant resonances are more powerful.

Erskine discovered Ireland through her language and culture in Wales in 1899. There he met Patrick Pearse and Douglas Hyde. In the first volume of *Guth na Bliadhna* he started to explore the links between Ireland and Scotland. He was only continuing what he had started in *Am Bàrd*. What differed was that he was now espousing a Sinn Féin line:

> Our political salvation we expect neither from the east nor from the West, nor from the North, nor from the South; which is but another way of saying that we intend to mind not other people's business but our own… [22]

This was written in Winter 1904, a year before Arthur Griffith formed Sinn Féin in Dublin. This position of 'ourselves alone' was not Erskine's. My contention is that he was in contact with Irish Gaelic activists since that Pan-Celtic Congress and was aware of political developments including the direction in which Griffith was moving. It is not impossible to assume that he was over in Dublin to see the Gaelic League in action observing first hand that it was a more political organisation and certainly no Scottish Gaelic organisation came close to it.

Such forays led to a coup for his own magazine. In the Winter 1905 edition, Patrick Pearse submitted an article on "Education' in the West of Ireland'. This showed that Erskine, as he would demonstrate in years to come, had pulling power. Pearse's intention was to enlighten his Scottish Gaelic reader of the situation faced by native speaking children in schools in the Gaeltacht:

> Understand that they are being 'educated.' We have unique and wonderful 'educational' methods in the west of Ireland. One of them is to ignore the only language spoken by the pupils. Another is to pretend that there is no such place as Ireland. A third is to inculcate that the English Government is Almighty Providence, and that America is an El Dorado in which gold is to be picked up on the streets.[23]

Pearse developed this theme and it would have struck a real chord with his Scottish audience at a time when still 5% of the population spoke Gaelic. It also resonated with Erskine and he would develop his own arguments around creating a Gaelic 'Atmosphere' in schools.[24] Pearse himself would develop these themes into his own powerful critique of the English system of education in Ireland entitled 'The Murder Machine.' It is interesting that their paths should cross again in 1905. While there is much that is different in the two men there are some similarities. The main one being that both were about to embark on a serious process of radicalisation that would fuse their language and political activism together. This radicalisation would end in martyrdom for Pearse. A year before he led the Easter Rising in Dublin, Pearse gave the oration at the funeral of the old Fenian, Jeremiah O' Donovan Rossa and he summed up the political ethos of both men when he articulated his vision of Ireland: ' …not free merely but Gaelic as well; not Gaelic merely, but free as well'.[25]

For Erskine, this radicalisation and the 'Atmosphere' he envisioned would see Gaelic taught in all Scottish schools – Lowland and Highland. Gaelic would no longer be submissive. It would be assertive and truly national. Erskine's own radicalisation saw him take his position of 'no language, no nation' to a new level. By the end of 1905 he has no time for the national Mòd as it is subservient and all the key business is done in English. This was reinforced by his more radical approach to teaching Gaelic in schools. Interestingly he turns to economic matters, the 'bread and butter' matters that nobody bar the socialists were talking about:

> The grievance of Alba is primarily and fundamentally an economic one; and if we would make the national cause not only attractive but essential to the vast bulk of our countrymen, we must embrace all available means to improve their social condition. Two hundred years of distress and stagnation are not a bad capital to start a comprehensive national campaign.[26]

He had come a long way since his banquets with the great and the good in London. Now he was writing about improving the 'social condition' of the Scottish people. It is important to remember his old stomping grounds. His old newspaper in Northampton (where his father still lived) could not believe this transformation. He was a Lowlander with a Lowland father and an English mother. Why this fashion to Gaelicise his name? They could not understand, ' …wherein he is Highland, or why he should Gaelicise the good Scandinavian name of Roderick'.[27] Thanks to this journal we know that Erskine was trying to publish a peerage in Gaelic and that he was staying for the only time in his life in the west coast of Scotland in Argyll.[28]

While the journal developed Irish-Scottish links and the notion of a Gaelic Confederation, *Guth na Bliadhna* continued to encourage top quality writing in both languages. Cunninghame Graham wrote a couple of short stories and there was also an article from an R MacDonald on 'Parliament and the Gael' which linked the success of the nascent Labour Party to the demise of the status quo and labelling the English Parliament a 'feudal institution'.[29] From the tone and the subject matter of the article it is hard to draw any other conclusion than that this was the future first Labour Prime Minister himself.

By the end of 1906, Erskine was courting the Left and calling for, 'a united Scotland and a Gaelic State'.[30] Now it may be disingenuous to suggest that there was no nationalist organisation pushing such a line. *Guth na Bliadhna* became the campaigning group for national independence and the restoration of the Gaelic language and it would be Ruaraidh Erskine of Marr who would be the magnet for all such activists and writers.

The vision was there. To fuse a radical Scottish nationalism with the preservation of the national language. The means was there and only there. A magazine such as *Guth na Bliadhna* was a powerful vehicle and, as we have seen, attracted top quality writers. However, there was as yet no organisation to carry the cause forward. The cause belonged to a disparate group of writers and poets gathered around Erskine.

Erskine knew that the success of *Guth na Bliadhna* was key. He also knew that there were potential lessons to be learned from across the water. He again looked into the prism that was Ireland.

Sinn Féin were still a small organisation. The name literally means 'Ourselves'. It has been translated as 'Ourselves Alone' due to a shortening of an old Irish slogan: sinn féin, sinn féin amháin, or ourselves, ourselves alone. Erskine had been influenced by Arthur Griffith's book, *The Resurrection of Hungary* in 1904 which influenced the article in *Guth na Bliadhna*. Griffith argued that Hungary had progressed from being a subordinate part of the Austrian Empire to being separate and equal to Austria as part of a dual monarchy. While being no monarchist, he used this as a transitory argument for his own country to progress to.[31] In other words, the early Sinn Féin was not a republican organisation but they were separatist.

This would have been a big hook for Erskine. It allowed him to think about the nature of the Anglo-Scottish Union and forge a different position from other Scottish nationalist groupings. Erskine himself was no republican. He did however believe that nothing could be achieved for Scotland in Westminster and the position of 'ourselves alone' was a persuasive one. This was a defining time in Erskine's politics. He may have flirted with many ideas in his life but he remained from this point on a Scottish Sinn Féiner!

The logical next step was to go over and find out more. In 1907 he started to write for the *Sinn Féin* newspaper and contributed a series of articles on 'Ireland and Scotland.' This went hand in hand with cultivating a relationship with Griffith and it is not inconceivable that he visited Dublin to find out more about the political organisation and the links with the Gaelic League and the equally political Gaelic Athletic Association. That year Sinn Féin joined the political arena by unsuccessfully contesting the North Leitrim by election. If successful they would not have taken their seat in Westminster.

Erskine's articles are significant as they are part of a thread of support and solidarity with Ireland's long struggle for independence that dated back to his trip with Parnell and would jump forward to the Easter Rising and the War of Independence. Cognitive dissonance or not, he was a true friend of Ireland. These articles also allowed him to take the Scottish position to an Irish readership. The Scots, he wrote, have no 'national politics.' They have only the British parties of Liberal and Tory. This formed a narrative that informed culture and history and he drew a parallel between the two countries:

The history of Ireland in Scotland and of Scotland in Ireland remains to be written; I venture here to express hope that it will be undertaken by someone to whom the various threads of Gaelic politics are familiar. We have too much history written from the point of view of England in Ireland and England in Scotland.[32]

He brought this position back to his Scottish Gaelic readership. Iain Morair Mhàirr was commissioned to write a piece on 'Sinn Féin' and praised the fact that Gaelic was being learned and spoken in rural schools and abroad by emigrants. Erskine joined the debate and started to raise a Scottish Sinn Féin banner:

…agus nuair a tha sinn a' dèanamh nan nithe sin às còir dhuinn a dhèanamh a rèir a' Brosnachaidh so, na leigeamaid air di-chuimhne air choir air bith aona chuid Pàrliamaid Shasuinn, no iadsan a chaidh a thaghadh airson air cùisean fèin a chur am feabhas agus a thoirt air adhart an Westminster.[33]

While he is referring here to de-selecting those existing MPs, he states his position with more clarity later in the year: 'We regard the Sinn Féin standpoint, namely, that it is better to have nothing to do with Westminster as by far the wisest, most dignified and most consistent attitude for all Nationalists, Irish or Scottish, to adapt…'[34]

Ireland – with a majority of pro-Westminster Irish Party MPs – was not yet ready for this position, let alone Scotland who had neither such a Party nor elected representatives. But it did mark Erskine and his journal out as distinctive. He had been well and truly educated to the point of persuasion and he could see that culturally and politically Scotland was light years behind other nationalist movements. So, it followed that his offensive would be cultural and political. In the same edition of *Guth na Bliadhna*, Erskine remarked that there were only two Gaelic journals in Scotland and he believed that the bi-lingual nature of his own publication involved, 'unnecessary English padding.'[35] He was about to push the boundaries of Gaelic publication again and would spend 1908 seeking the funding and support to do so.

The fruits of his work over the next two years resulted in two new, all Gaelic publications. The first was a weekly newspaper -the first ever such newspaper in Scotland – called *Alba* which bore the masthead 'Alba airson nan Albannach' or 'Scotland for the Scots.' It came out every Saturday and ran for a year (from February 1908 to the following February) finding a new printer in Greenock to replace his Perth publisher along the way.

His primary interest in this undertaking was cultural. This was about the language and raising the banner of the Gael which affected the subject matter – land, crofting, fishing, Gaelic education, early Scottish history and Gaelic song. This wasn't totally new, of course, but the focus was purely on the Gàidhealtachd. There is little coverage in his paper on independence. From later 1908 to early 1909 there is a return to the subject of the English party system and a rejection of the two main parties as well as to the Irish Question. Erskine set out three aims in the first issue:

1. To establish the first all Gaelic journal and consolidate it across the country;
2. To give the land back and the tongue as part of the heritage of all the Scottish people;
3. A Gaelic Revival focussing on maintenance of the method and speech of the Gael while also taking them forward progressively.

Alba was a bold undertaking. The paper cited an impressive circulation: from Stornoway and Castlebay and Portree to Beauly and Dingwall up north and down to the central belt with an outlet in London too. Erskine's problem was the lack of contributors. His personal magnetism which attracted many to the 'Voice of the Year' was not so attractive in this newspaper. The vast bulk of the articles were written by the editor himself which made *Alba* a massive as well as bold undertaking for Erskine of Marr. This was not sustainable. While the letters column increased in late 1908, it was only a matter of time before the newspaper went under.

The editor was undaunted. It was a personal trait. His confidence and usage in the language had grown by contributing so much of its output. He also now had a new acronym: RAM which stood for Ruaraidh Arascainn is Mhàirr. As usual with Erskine, the Gaelic came before the English and this would inform how he would be known for the rest of his life. Alba was a sweeping, all embracing, heart and soul introduction to an all-Gaelic publication. It was too imaginative, too revolutionary. The question was what would the Gaels connect with? The answer lay in stories and song.

The answer was *An Sgeulaiche* or *The Storyteller.* This journal lasted just under two years and was devoted purely to fiction. It can be seen that Erskine was moving in a direction, as he set out to do, to progressively develop the language through creative writing. RAM himself wrote a piece called, 'Bruadar'(Dream). The story is about a car driver who is overtaken by fear on a trip to the mountains. His fear is irrational with every sound and noise raising an alarm within him. He sees a Chinese man in his car who then vanishes in front of him. As the short story unfolds, the fear seems to be of death. Thousands and thousands of little lights or orbs seem to light up the sky as the colour of death; lighting up outside as a little picture while he is travelling: ' …chaidh miltean an dèigh miltean de mheanbh-sholuis, is iad de chaochladh dath, air an lasadh a suas a staigh do na dealbhan siùbhlach so.'[36] It may sound morbid but it is a beautifully written story that shows Erskine as an anxious human being trying to understand his own soul.

It should be stressed that *Guth na Bliadhna* was still going strong alongside these new ventures which, again, shows his personal energy and dynamism devoted to the cause of the Gaelic tongue.

His commitment was expressed in a letter to the expatriate Charles Loch. Loch was a mining engineer who worked between Malaya and Australia for many years and whose interest was lexicography.[37] He learned Gaelic from Highland expatriates in Australia where he was resident when Erskine was writing to him in 1909. We can ascertain from his letter to Loch that the Erskines had moved address to Banchory, still in Aberdeenshire. Ruaraidh stated that he hoped that the new magazine would stimulate, 'a taste for learning literature'. The challenge and task for the language was to produce, 'more serious reading matter'.[38] The letter finishes almost as a begging letter stating that the new journal needs two or three subscribers who could furnish £100 each. Loch and Erskine were friends and corresponded over many years although many of the letters are lost. The finance must have been forthcoming as the journal lasted for almost two years.

Erskine entered the new decade with a growing reputation as a Gaelic publisher and editor. He would stay true to his vision while his country and Britain and Europe were about to change irrevocably.

Chapter Six

God Save Scotland!

Gaelic has a different sense of time, purpose and achievement: the ideal is to maintain an equilibrium. A saying from South Uist expresses it beautifully: 'Eat bread and weave grass, and then this year shall be as thou wast last year.' It's close to the philosopher Hannah Arendt's definition of wisdom as a loving concern for the continuity of the world.[1]

Madeleine Bunting expressed these sentiments in 2016 – extolling Gaelic as the secret language of revolution! She doesn't mention Erskine, not surprisingly, even though he had beaten her to it by 100 years. For Erskine, notions of balance were key to Gaelic culture while, admittedly, there wasn't always a balance in his politics.

The new decade saw a move into direct political and cultural activism using Gaelic as a truly revolutionary weapon of change. It began in London with fellow exiles and would continue through to a resurrected Highland Land League raising the battle cry of 'God Save Scotland!' in praising imitation of the Irish Fenian martyrs' cry before their execution in Manchester in 1867. The writing was still powerful and the supplementing activity was more powerful still. Erskine would be defined by it. Ireland would be the inspiration and London would be its second home.

London would also be its birthplace. In 1910 the Scottish National League (Comunn na h-Albannach) was formed in the imperial capital. Purdie has argued that this was the birth of modern Scottish nationalism.[2] It is hard to argue with this. What passed for Scottish nationalism at this time has been rightly called 'Unionist-nationalism.'[3] A call for Home Rule to make the running of Scotland and Britain smoother which was aligned to the Liberal Party and which never questioned the integrity of the United Kingdom. As we have seen there were voices that were edging closer to a more nationalist line. Erskine of Marr took the leap of nationalist faith first. He knew that a truly nationalist organisation needed vision and a basis in culture with a sprinkling of spirituality and soul. These things make you passionate. Home Rule makes you functional.

NO LANGUAGE! NO NATION!

In 1910, these things also needed ex-pats! Nationalists, Gaelic speakers and culture enthusiasts all based in London dreaming of a better Scotland. Erskine still had a foot firmly in the London camp. It was at this time that he formed an active partnership with William Gillies who, like his friend, adopted his native name of Liam Mac Gille Iosa. He was also born in the South of England, in Paddington, to be precise, in 1865. He had known John Murdoch and worked for his newspaper, *Highlander*, when he was 17. Although his family settled in Maxwelltown near Dumfries, exile had also given him a passion for Gaelic. Gillies had written a play in the early 1900s called *The Four Scourges of Gaeldom: Feudalism, Militarism, the Church and Whisky* and he had founded the Gaelic Society in London as well as a Gaelic choir in the first decade of the new century.[4] Gillies and Erskine were kindred spirits.

We will explore the link with their own new and improved Scots National League ten years later (in chapter eight). However, the 1910 version was short lived but was able to raise a separatist banner for Scottish nationalism. At its inaugural meeting its aims were clear:

> The Gaelic spirit must be revived within us. The fire and enthusiasm that should characterise the dweller among the hills must be welded with the sturdiness and perseverance of the peasant farmer of the Lowlands. For this union we must work. Our aim, our ideal should be a Scottish Scotland.[5]

The meeting finished with the singing of Thomas Davis's Irish anthem, *A Nation Once Again!* While it may seem incongruous to be extolling the Highland crofter and the Lowland peasant in London, the practice was no different to Russian emigrés extolling the idealised worker in St Petersburg.. Exile brings out passion. The language of Ireland mingled with the experience of exile to create a new kind of Scottish nationalism. It didn't create much of a stir in Scotland in 1910 but it sowed some seeds. It was the culmination of Murdoch's radical land and language agitation of the 1870s and 1880s; of Morrison Davison's challenging of the British State at the turn of the century and of Erskine's interaction with Pearse and Griffith over the water. Kindred spirits came together to think about new visions of Scotland – some of them in old clothing, and certainly in an old tongue; but they would develop into something radical and lasting that would change nationalism in Scotland… but not in 1910.

It is interesting to note that *Guth na Bliadhna* was not used as a vehicle to promulgate the new organisation. Erskine was wise enough to know that the demand was not yet there for it back in the old country. It is also worthy of note that he did use his journal to lay some foundations. Rather than publishing the manifesto of the Scots National League directly, he published it indirectly. He used a column in *Guth na Bliadhna* on Modh-Sgriobhaidh (Writing Style) by a pseudonymous contributor to review the manifesto from the point of view of its literary style. The article was in Gaelic but published the short manifesto in English. It clearly demonstrated the new radicalism in its rejection of both 'Imperial domination' and Scotland's part in empire building: 'The old Scottish 'empty boasts' are worthless and it is time for a new course… and this be your slogan, your high resolve and your victory signal: Scotland free, Scotland sovereign, Scotland a Nation once again!'[6]

This was supplemented by letters to the editor commenting on the new organisation and criticising An Comunn Gàidhealachd for their fawning letter to the new British monarch, George V, who had recently acceded after the death of Edward VII. It allowed a dialogue on this new, radical nationalism with the language at its heart amongst *Guth na Bliadhna*'s significant readership which stretched from Inverness to Dublin via London. Subtly, and critically bearing in mind the readership, Erskine used a piece on writing style in Gaelic to launch his new movement: Gaelic as the secret language of revolution!

Erskine knew that Scotland was not politically ready for its own Sinn Fhèin organisation. He used the lead up to the war to prepare the cultural landscape, to create a Scottish Scotland just like the Gaelic League were attempting to do for their own country across the water. From 1910–1912, Erskine used his journal to unleash a wave of literary creativity that had made *Guth na Bliadhna* such an important journal in Gaelic culture. At that time, it was all to play for. In the summer edition of 1911, one of his contributors reviewed the recently published census figures which showed that 6.1% of those resident in the country spoke Gaelic.[7] Poetry, prose and song would be key battle grounds to take the language away from the National Mòd whose idiom was English with Gaelic on parade for singing and recital. Instead, the aim was to breathe life into the language: 'We write it, we speak it and every other cultural thing of beauty flows from it'.

Erskine may not have won this battle but his language of revolution had significant victories. The cultural battle he fought was partly against An Comunn Gàidhealachd, as I have alluded to, and against what he saw as the 'Anglo-school.' The particular Anglo-Celtic school that he would critique may have been a construct of his own mind based on what he saw through the prism of Ireland. In Dublin, the Abbey Theatre had been founded in 1904 as a response to progressive movements in European theatre – especially France and Russia – and was assisted by the talent of dramatists such as J M Synge, W B Yeats and Lady Gregory.[8] The Gaelic League were critical of the predominance of English as the main idiom. In Scotland, Erskine took up the fight. In 1912 he derided the view that two idioms and geniuses could produce one new literature.[9]

It is fair to read into this comment that Erskine wasn't daft. With almost 94% of the population speaking English, the odds were stacked against a national, Gaelic theatre. This prompted our erstwhile Gaelic activist to take radical measures. In the same year that he advertised in the Autumn edition, he carried adverts for literary competitions for Season 1912/13 with a prize of one Guinea for the best Gaelic essay and, in addition, a silver presentation Cup and £10 cash prize for the best Gaelic play on the subject of MacBeth. 'Whaur's your Wullie Shakespeare noo?' As someone had famously shouted many, many years before! A new 'MacBeth' in Gaelic? The editor also encouraged entries in Irish Gaelic.

This was innovative stuff. It was backed up by radical organisations aiming to further the cause. Erskine set up two groups around this period:

1. The Scottish Gaelic Academy or Àrd-Chomhlairle na Gàidhlig.
2. The Scottish Society of Letters or Comunn Litreachas na h-Albain.[10]

Not a lot is known about the organisations. The Academy had only 21 members and met only twice a year with a remit to preserve the grammar and form of the language which was a challenge to the mainstream An Comunn Gàidhealachd. It does show, as well as through the competitions, that he was at the forefront of a new activism that was spearheading language revival.

A positive spin off was in the 'find' that was Donald Sinclair. Sinclair came from the heartland – a Barra boy from that beautiful island's capital, Castlebay. There is no evidence that he entered Erskine's competition but he was influenced enough to submit two plays in the language that were both serialised in *Guth na Bliadhna*. The second and more powerful piece, *Crois-Tàra (Fiery Cross)* was published over 1915 and is an account of the 1745 rebellion which questions the role of Alasdair MacMhaighstir Alasdair as a propagandist for Charlie. Alasdair was a poet who had taught the young Prince some Gaelic. To challenge the poet's role was radical and noteworthy and, again, raised the profile of Erskine's work as living, modern drama on Gaelic themes.[11]

Sinclair is only one example of how Erskine drew on Gaelic talent at that time. There were others in journalism and poetry too. It is significant that both men were nationalists who saw the importance of the language revival in their work. Around this time Erskine was developing the theme of a 'national atmosphere.' Marr loved his little phrases. They weren't always fully thought through and could be quite esoteric. He had been talking about an 'atmosphere' in education after Pearse's article back in 1906. What is different is that the 'national atmosphere' ties in with Bunting's view about balance in Gaelic culture. He was seeking continuity with a past and innovating to protect the future, to provide continuity.

In this regard he saw a distinction between Scotland and Ireland. Scotland had no such Anglo school as the Irish had. There was no Abbey Theatre. He believed that this meant that, 'the way is clear for Gaelic drama.' Scotland had no Synge or Lady Gregory and in a note of praise to Sinclair he continued: 'We're all Donalds here, in the sense that, if a National Theatre is really destined to arise in modern Scotland it will surely be throughout as Gaelic as the peats.'[12]

He called for a Gaelic play to be staged at the Mòd. Glasgow, as the previous industrial, whisky drinking den of iniquity, with its large Gaelic population could be the centre for training Gaelic speaking actors and this would ' …increase the vogue of the national speech; it would encourage our existing dramatists… it would raise the whole tone and level of Celtic entertainment.'[13] This was where the battle was lost in that this was unlikely to happen any time soon. The small victories of his activism and propaganda, however, laid some foundations.

In Autumn 1912, Erskine took stock of the progress of *Guth na Bliadhna* so far. He believed that it had become the rallying ground for those who uphold, 'National principles.'[14] With the rallying cry of No language! No nation! it had 'succinctly summarised the gospel of Nationalism'.[15] The editor was pleased that the journal set no limits on the progress of nationalism:

' 'You cannot set thought free for certain purposes only', says Lord

Haldane. The 'loyal' managers, crampers and restrainers within the Movement should remember this'.[16]

Over the next couple of years, his focus would be on the cultural side as he sought to lay certain foundations of a Scottish Scotland. This would need to be supplemented by a political campaign to bolster the political side of his nationalism. The 'crampers and restrainers' referred to were Home Rulers and they had been active around Liberal politics trying to secure Scotland's deal in a 'Home Rule all round' solution. Big meetings had been taking place in Edinburgh and in 1911 a Scottish Home Rule bill raised by Sir Henry Dalziel, MP for Kirkcaldy, had been passed in the Commons by 172 votes to 73 at first reading.[17] Erskine held no truck with such activity. Impending world war would grind Home Rule for all the Celtic countries to a halt. Impending world war would see Erskine launch a new political initiative that would be another defining literary intervention and another rallying ground for those of sound National principles.

It was new wine in an old bottle. *The Scottish Review* had been around since 1882 and ran until 1900 under the Editorship of Lord Bute. It was a thoroughly Presbyterian and Unionist journal so entrenched in its Unionism that it even saw the Liberal Party as separatist.[18] Erskine resurrected the name and the name only in 1914. It would be a very different journal. While Erskine crafted and moulded *Guth na Bliadhna* in his own fashion, the opposite was true with the *Scottish Review*. He was moulded and shaped by it in many ways as the political times and crises changed.

The new journal was launched with European crisis imminent and the 600th anniversary of Bruce's victory at the Battle of Bannockburn which was being commandeered by Unionist politicians and mocked by the Left. Erskine used both journals to claim the memory of the battle for the cause of modern-day independence. While being unequivocal on this battle, he struggled with the coming European conflagration. In the Autumn issue of both journals, he took two very different lines toward the same conflict.

In a Gaelic piece in *Guth na Bliadhna*, Erskine took issue with Joseph Chamberlain as the 'Missionary of Empire.' In the year of commemorating Freedom's Battle in Scotland, Chamberlain's message, he suggested, meant the chains of slavery for small nations. Erskine put across a different vision:

Thug sinn uile saothair mhòr air ar saoghal a chreidsinn gu'n deach là nan Stàidean beaga seachad; nach robh tuilleadh feum ri aotainn annta; agus gur i an t-Iompaireachd solus is slàinair a' chruinne gu h-iomlan.

Mhair na beachdan meallta so againn fad fin foinneach oidhche ar n-aineolais; ach, le briseadh an là, chunnaic sinn gu'n robh atharrach dreach air cùisean nach lèir duinn gu ceart roimh so.

Thuig sinn mu dheireadh nach deach là nan Stàidean beaga seachad, ach, an àite sin, gu'n robh tuagh na firinne air a leigeadh gu freumhan aosda craoibhe na h-Iompaireachd.[19]

This was a critique of the notion of the British Empire as the light of the world and civilisation itself. Small nations should stand firm against the big empires because they had a place in the new world. While, in the *Scottish Review* in the same month, he tied himself in knots on the subject of racialism and how the main races of Europe – Celt, Slav, Hun and Teuton – should find a balance out of the conflict.[20] He was all over the place; progressive anti-imperialist to confused, if inoffensive, racialist all in the same month.

The *Scottish Review* would be defined in other ways and a better tone was set with the first issue. 'A Scottish Artisan' (probably Erskine if the writing style is anything to go by) reviewed a Fabian pamphlet and used this as an opportunity to review the state of the British political parties in Scotland. After the usual line regarding the Tories and Liberals, the most intriguing comments are reserved for the Labour party and he is prescient: 'Is it not notorious that the 'orders' and 'instructions' of the English bosses of these organisations run as freely in many parts of industrial Scotland as does the King's writ throughout the length and breadth of the Kingdom?'

Socialists in Scotland, he continues, dream about a Scottish working-class platform as often as they dream of a socialist expedition to the Sahara Desert! The point, which would inform Scottish nationalist politics for many years to come, was that there was still no political party to represent Scotland's interests. Erskine's new journal would be a unique nationalist voice and counterpoint to British, Westminsterist politics. A new line would evolve that would be leftist yet independent; nationalist yet internationalist too. The driving force would not be Ruaraidh Erskine of Marr but an Aberdonian trade unionist called William Diack. It was Diack who provided insight, direction and some cogency which inspired debate and contribution. Erskine reaped the benefit and was drawn in to the debate and learned fast. After war was declared, Diack's piece on Scotland and the War, written from a pacifist and Scottish nationalist point of view argued that all countries would be worse off for the war through increased privation and disease. Scottish nationalists could not be unsympathetic to Belgium's plight although Scottish Home Rule had still, 'to be fought and won'. Scotland was once again being dragged into the 'foreign adventures of the predominant partner.'[22] This was lucid and provided a much-needed nationalist response to war that was lacking in Erskine's own analysis. Diack would develop this and develop his thoughts on land redistribution looking to the end of the war and its implications with depth and heart.

With such a distinct left-leaning, nationalist line the *Review* would draw in other notable contributors. Jimmy Maxton of the Independent Labour Party (ILP) contributed on the branch status of the Scottish ILP compared to the English party.[23] A young, unknown writer from Edinburgh called Lewis Spence, who would play an important part in developing nationalist politics, and the Welsh Nationalist MP, Edward T John, are some other examples. The journal was highly readable in a better typeset than some of its contemporaries and as it evolved so too did Erskine's thinking. He was about to move into a phase of revolutionary nationalist activity that would see his personal star rise.

This was the result of the hard work put in through his cultural and then political activity. The latter was not just through the *Scottish Review* but also in direct connection with the Highland Land League: a resurrected organisation that had a past in the land agitations of the 1880s and a future to play in moulding a left nationalist response to the unfolding of the war.

1916 was such a pivotal year in so many ways for the course of the war, for the families back home across Europe counting the fallen, for Ireland and for Erskine himself. He was strongly influenced by the events in Dublin on that momentous Easter Week (more later.) Erskine liked the interventions of the American President, Woodrow Wilson (more soon.) He also helped to steer the direction of the Highland Land League that year.

This was the second incarnation of the League. Its rationale still lay in Highland grievances over land. It couldn't have been put any better than by John Murdoch himself in 1875:

> The people of England lay no claim now to any property in the soil. There is no tradition, no song, no sgeulachd, among them to keep the sense of this right alive in their minds…In the Highlands however, we retain some of the lore belonging to it. One of the most important items handed down from sire to son in this

language is that the people were the real owners of the soil, and that the chief was simply the captain in the strife of battle.[24]

Murdoch, the Gaelic radical, merged the political with the cultural. Like a baton it was passed on to the next organisation which was the first incarnation of the League which itself was a product of the Highland Land Law Reform Association (HLLRA) The League was responsible for fielding six 'Crofting' candidates in the 1886 election. While they were closely allied with the Liberal Party they had their own independent stance on land and on Home Rule. A sole example will suffice: G B Clark was elected as the MP for Caithness that year. He stood on a platform of land nationalisation that sat consistently with his membership of the International Working Men's Association that had been founded by Karl Marx.[25] Clark was embroidered on that forgotten, hidden part of the tapestry of Scottish radicalism: London! He had been president of the London branch of the HLLRA. To be fair, not all were as left-leaning.

The second Highland Land League was formed in 1909 and looked very much to the left. In its formation it proclaimed that, 'official Liberalism has been the deadly enemy of the Highland proletariat'.[26] The proletarian language is more than indicative. Crofters and workers were to be united in a common cause and a link with the young Labour Party would last throughout its existence until its demise sometime in the early 1920s. One of its early leaders was Tom Johnston, then editor of the Independent Labour Party's influential *Forward* newspaper.

A significant meeting was held in the John Street schoolroom, London, on 12th April 1917. The AGM of the League was held and a report was published on its activities in 1916. This AGM adopted new objects and aims. Scottish autonomy should be a 'foremost plank' of policy.[27] The Gaelic language would become central to the League's activities in addition to the old chestnuts of fighting elections on crofters' grievances and the return of the land to the people, 'for their use and enjoyment.' A motion was passed that, 'Land Leaguers and Gaels generally should combine to make a radical alteration in the Highland representation at the first opportunity.'[28]

Autonomy for a country can be vague. What is noteworthy is that the Highland Land League weren't committed to Home Rule but to Scottish autonomy but they thought they knew what they meant. They were a hop, skip and a jump away from supporting Scottish independence – which would come a year or so later. Hopping, skipping and jumping with them were Erskine and Gillies who were elected to the League's Committee as Vice-President and Council member respectively. The strong Labour connection was upheld by the election of the Reverent J D Barr who would become one of the Red Clydeside MPs of 1922.

There is undoubtedly a large element of tactical politics in these two cultural nationalists becoming involved in this left-leaning organisation. Yet they themselves were influenced by the times and is it any accident that new aims and objects were adopted that fitted the political trajectory of the *Scottish Review* at that time. Erskine's and Gillies's stamp is all over this Highland Land League document.

From this time on League meetings were highly culturally politicised affairs. Ending with the rallying cry of 'God Save Scotland!', it was also known for Gaelic songs and hymns to be interspersed with the Internationale and workers' songs. They saw no contradiction.[29] Erskine never took to the term or concept of internationalism. Yet he was no narrow nationalist. Many of his interventions were internationalist in character because he could see the big picture in what was going on.

Over 1915 and 1916, he had been developing some themes of faith with little prayers and supplications in *Guth na Bliadhna*. In an article titled 'A' Chriosdachd agus an Cogadh' (Christians and the War) in the Summer 1916 edition, Erskine was calling on the power of God and the Trinity to act as a force for good to bring the war to an end. Indeed, what other force was there but 'the force called God'.[30]

His faith was part of him but he did not just look to God. He also looked across the Atlantic Ocean to the United States. Woodrow Wilson had not yet entered the War. In his neutrality he was talking the language of peace. Scottish salvation could also come through this route. In Autumn 1915 in a Gaelic editorial, 'Ceartas!' (Justice!) Erskine hooked into the fact that American efforts for peace gave an opportunity to the Celts especially if there was going to be a peace congress in the Hague. It was not the English way, he pointed out, to look out for Celtic interests.[31] A year later he came back to the theme just as President Wilson himself had developed his thoughts into 'the League to Enforce Peace.' Erskine then explored the concept of national self-determination arguing that every people has the right to choose sovereignty as well as the fact that the world has the right to be free from disturbance or aggression. He was certainly impressed by Wilson's words and sentiments:

Bhùidhich iad, cuideachd, air gach ni a b' ionmhiunn na chèile leo nach ghabhadh iad gu bràth cur an cleachdadh, air cho miannaich air an cron a cheartachadh, agus linn na miorbhuilean a ghreasad air aghaidh, sa dh'fhaodadh iad uile a bhith.[32]

This would become his enduring campaign over the next couple of years; his 'National Protest.' We must leave it for the moment in the Winter of 1917. The *Scottish Review* was now subtitled, 'A Quarterly Journal Devoted to the Cause of the Independence of Scotland'. Erskine articulated his thoughts in a seminal piece, 'Ireland and Scotland at the Peace Congress'. Rooting his argument in the coming end of the War as well as in the historical fact of Scotland as a perpetual nation, this influential piece tied the causes of Scotland and Ireland together. Although he acknowledged a key difference. Both countries wanted to 'protest their sovereignty' while the Irish, 'design to ask Christendom to give effect to Irish sovereignty, in name of that country and people'.[33] This political realism tied both countries' radicals together and that would forge a stronger relationship as we shall see. It was also a statement of Scottish intent that no other nationalist or left grouping was making at that point. Erskine was a force for change and others would come with him.

As always, he was ably assisted by the *Review*'s chief theoretician of Scottish democracy, William Diack. He wasn't talking in any abstract language of history or nationality. In the same issue he was talking an anti-war language that raised its horrors while being sensitive to its Scottish participants:

Our young men from the straths and glens have done their work nobly and well. Their task is finished, and the time has come for them to return from the Hell into which the old men have sent them. Sooner or later the questions at issue must be settled by negotiation. Why not now? In these coming negotiations Scotland, as a nation, must be represented.[34]

The horror of the trenches would persist for another year.

The Derry Journal favourably reviewed 'Ireland and Scotland at the Peace Congress' and praised the *Review* and 'its accomplished editor.'[35] Not only does this demonstrate that he was read in Ireland nor even of his wider reach in the world of ideas and politics; it also demonstrates just how his star was rising.

He had made some political capital during the Dundee by-election in July 1917, obtaining some publicity by claiming to be standing as a National Democrat against Churchill who would go on to win it for the Liberals. He issued a statement stating that the 'Whigs' are:

> ...poisoning the political life of Scotland and fast reducing it to the province that Fletcher of Saltoun (a sound Republican) prophesied... It is a pity that the democratic forces in Scotland are not as a whole more alive to the fact that a Scots Parliament means a parliament in which democracy will be supreme.[36]

Democracy? Republicanism? The Honourable Erskine of Marr had come a long way. He had no intentions of standing. His worst nightmare would have been to have won the election and to have been Westminster bound as an MP – joining his elder brother, Montagu, who was in the House of Lords. His saviour was his statement that he would not stand if the Prohibitionist candidate, Edwyn Scrimgeour stood. The feelers were being put out to the Left. He sought 'cordial relations' with the socialists and the ILP as long as they were 'sound on the autonomy question '.

The publicity did him no harm at all. In 1918 Erskine was the subject of a portrait in the *Celtic Annual*. This was good recognition for his services to the culture of the Gael and his tireless activity in politics and publishing. The profiler is anonymous. There is a photograph of Erskine with a very aristocratic moustache and air about his appearance. His contribution to 'Gaelic letters and Scottish nationalism' are acknowledged and it is justly stated that in these matters he is a, 'force to be recognised' and he 'wields a graceful, vigorous and convincing pen'.[37] Erskine claimed to hold the honours bestowed by James VIII or the Old Pretender. This may have been true, but he was prone to some grandiose claims!

Ruaraidh was 49 at the time of this profile. He had spent the last ten or so years building a cultural and political network. His two periodicals were successful and had reach and impact. He had almost single-handedly radicalised Scottish nationalism and Gaelic activism. Yet there was one defeat. Erskine used his *Guth na Bliadhna* to publish an open letter in critique of the 1918 Scottish Education Act. This letter had seven signatories including H C MacNeil, Liam Gillies and Donald Sinclair.

This Act was a landmark piece of legislation in the setting up of Catholic schools in Scotland and this right is still vigorously defended by the Catholic community. While most of the signatories to Erskine's letter were themselves Catholic, there is no mention of this advance for faith schools in the text. Instead it is seen as an English Act and an English imposition on Celtic education. They make the point that the Gaels are being bullied into accepting an Act that gives no safeguards to the language and, further, the signatories feel that the English Parliament have taken advantage of the War to push through this legislation while so many Gaels are fighting at the Front. Frustration is the primary emotion that comes through in their letter. They are frustrated that the status of Gaelic has gone down again as a European language; frustrated at the Gaels themselves who seem to have a sense of the inevitable. At one point they call on the Gaels to come into the age of reason ('A' Ghaidheala, an tig sibh gu bràth gu aois reusoin?').[38] The letter finishes with a call to return the Act home to England where it belongs. They have no problem with education or knowledge or even a scrap of paper until they want those things themselves and can bring success and fullness to their own house.

Arguably, the 1872 Act did more to harm the language as it made no provision for non-English education and led to acts of corporal punishment for children who used the language. Ironically, Erskine would have been three years of age at that time and possibly being introduced to the language by his nanny. The 1918 Act allowed for some provision where there were Gaelic speakers. While the mainstream debate centred upon Catholic schooling, Erskine's letter raises the banner of Gaelic education and, as such, the letter is a real contribution in the language to the cause of Gaelic education. The teaching of the language and, indeed, teaching in the language was a cause worth fighting for. The future victories in achieving Gaelic medium education were a long way off in the future. Still, the signatories raised the banner when it was not fashionable to do so. Erskine had a habit of doing just that.

Chapter Seven

Citizen Marr

...if you are as anxious as I am that you should be a Scottish force in the establishment of Justice, Peace and Democracy on Earth.' – John MacLean, 1919.[1]

The date was Wednesday 21st July 1920; a nice summer's day in Glasgow. Erskine had travelled from London for an interview. It was not your usual interview for a job or with the press. It was his own word to describe how he had, 'fixed up an appointment with John McLean (*sic*)'.[2] MacLean was a Marxist and the foremost revolutionary socialist in the British Isles at that time. He had been imprisoned three times for his stance against the War. Until 1918 he had always been an orthodox British socialist with a moderate support for Home Rule but never particularly nationalist in outlook. His approach to his own national identity, however, had been seeping into his Marxist politics for a while. And here he was having a cup of tea and a chat with the foremost cultural nationalist in Scotland in his living room in Pollokshaws.

It is intriguing to think of what they spoke about. We will never know for certain. Erskine had promised to give Art O'Brien, who will come into our story soon, 'a general idea how things go at the interview.'[3] This may have happened verbally but certainly not in writing. There were, however, outputs. From these outputs we can ascertain that the two learned men spoke about Scottish history, the prospects for Scottish independence, Celtic communism, Ireland and MacLean's dispute with the leaders of the new British communist organisation that was to become the Communist Party of Great Britain.

How do we know? Within a month, MacLean had written, published and was distributing a leaflet: *All Hail, the Scottish Workers Republic!* This was an immensely important leaflet as it committed MacLean to the cause of national independence and it would send shockwaves throughout the Left. Erskine's influence is clearly there as MacLean was starting to give serious consideration to the Clearances, the Jacobite rebellions of 1715 and 1745 and was talking about 'the communism of the clans'.[4] This was a major turning point for the Glasgow Marxist in his political journey and this 'interview' played a large part in it.[5] Also, in August, MacLean was praising *Guth na Bliadhna* in his own *Vanguard* newspaper for its commitment to the cause of independence.[6]

There were outputs from Erskine too. He committed to a series of ground-breaking articles on Celtic communism for the *Vanguard*. He was also able to get MacLean's support for the Scots National League and its work. It is also safe to assume that Erskine must have listened to MacLean's woes about the shenanigans of the British communists and Marr would soon join the debate in the ILP's *Forward* newspaper.

It was a period where MacLean and Erskine would become very close. It was not the first contact that they had with each other and it would not be the last. Perhaps it is an allegory for a period of extreme flirtation that Erskine would undergo with the Left. MacLean was one of a number of political seductions that Ruaraidh would undertake at a time when the Left were debating the national question and their support for Scottish self-determination was strong. Maybe Andrew Marr was right when he said that the Scottish Left were, and still are, tolerant of eccentric aristocrats![7] Jimmy Maxton, Tom Johnston and Roland Muirhead were other examples of his associations with socialists in Scotland.

One thing we do know for certain is that he did not take old copies of *The Whirlwind* to give to John. MacLean would have probably thrown him out onto Auldhouse Road! Thankfully that didn't happen.

Nothing happens in a vacuum. Erskine did not waken up one morning ready to explore links with the Scottish Left. Diack and the development of the *Scottish Review* were hugely influential and the journal was becoming a vehicle for left nationalism. Likewise, I don't think anyone would have woke up one morning expecting to see Citoyen Marr defending La Révolution!

'Praise to the Bolsheviks! Honour to the Revolutionaries!' he exclaimed in *Guth na Bliadhna*. The October Revolution in Russia, 'bids fair to inscribe in large and indelible letters on the pages of the great book of Universal National Rights certain priceless principles', which have been, 'preached but to be abnegated by the pulpiteers…'[8] In fairness, there was a consistency in what Citizen Ruaraidh was saying. The priority wasn't workers' control of the means of production or a socialist internationalism. Rather, it was the Bolsheviks' insistence on self-determination for all nations and peoples and no annexations. Hadn't he also urged a closer cooperation between nationalists and socialists who were sound on the national question in Dundee in 1917?

In the same piece, he developed the three principles of the Celtic movement; the principles that would become his Celtic gospel:

1. National self-determination;
2. Land for the people;
3. Priority to native language and culture.

This was the position of the Highland Land League. He also claimed to have the support of the Miners' leader, Robert Smillie, which in effect he did.[9] The short version of the story is that the two movements – Celtic and Labour – were aligned as they would be for a few years yet and this alignment unleashed some fantastic, creative, if doomed, activity.

Aristocracy, monarchy and capitalism have 'had their day.' As the young Soviet Republic came under external attack and civil war, Erskine jumped to their defence: 'Until the people reign – until the proletariat is everywhere in undisputed power – it were folly to expect enduring peace, drastic retrenchment or honest and searching reform.'[10]

There was a 'but' in that the Socialist experiment may fail as it was untried, yet it could not possibly 'sin' against humanity any worse than the other political systems that came before it. Neither Erskine nor his Marxist friend had the benefit of hindsight. Erskine, though, was no socialist. He was genuine in his flirtation – being swept along on a wave of revolutionary and radical enthusiasm that a better world could arise out of the carnage of the last four years. He genuinely wanted that better world and for Scotland to be part of it and part of the re-building process. The young aristocratic editor of *The Whirlwind* was virulently hostile to socialism. The middle-aged editor of the *Scottish Review* was giving it critical support. The Earl of Marr had come a long way.

Unlike most of the Left, he still had faith in President Woodrow Wilson in his attempts to re-build Europe. His plan with massive reserves of energy to back it up was to get Scottish representation at the Peace Congress that would end the war. His plan was labelled the National Protest. He launched it in the Review in Autumn 1917. He wanted a 'Grand National Committee' to lead the Protest. Organised labour was to him: 'A PROTEST, in the name and on behalf of National Scotland, is to be entered at the International Congress to be held after the War.'[11]

His 'Protest' would do two things: firstly, protest against the exclusion of Scotland – which has an 'indefensible right to send her own representatives'; secondly, to protest against the 'pretended right of England' to represent Scotland. Erskine set about building a political and historical case to underpin the 'Protest' while also building his National Committee and reaching out to the Left.

The initial signs of support were good. The Scottish Iron Moulders Union carried a back-page advert in the Winter edition of the *Review* supporting the campaign. In the Summer of 1918, the STUC passed a motion at their national conference in Ayr calling for a restored Scottish Parliament and Scottish representation at the Peace conference.[12] Marr was delighted, although he qualified his support by calling on the 'Labour Parliament' to put deeds to the fine words.

Erskine had a message for the British government and Lloyd George. He knew that the Irish claim was making Lloyd George uncomfortable. Scotland will also be there, 'to whisper into their ears home truths and sharp unpleasantries touching 'National Self-Determination', 'small nations' and other 'win the war' shibboleths of high degree.'[13] He was exposing the hypocrisy in the language of the western leaders as these shibboleths only applied to the defeated states especially in the carve up of the old Austro-Hungarian empire.

Being a man of history, Erskine gave a historical context to Scotland's claim. After the 'scrap of paper' in 1707, a radical tradition of revolt had arisen with the radical risings of the 1790s and the Chartists of 1848. Force and fraud have not sunk our 'sovereign rights… we demand admission to your Congress'.[14] Scotland's claim had political and historical justification and it was another first for Ruaraidh Erskine of Marr – the first to articulate a radical tradition of protest against the Union in Scotland that would be taken up and developed by his left nationalist friends and comrades in short space of time.

This was not protest without any responsibility. There was a document: the National Memorial. This was to be the rallying cry, the manifesto if you care, of the great 'Protest'. In the winter of 1918, Erskine proclaimed that it had been written, translated into French and was being prepared in Gaelic.[15] This would become, by the Spring 1919 edition of the *Review*, the 'Petition Nationale de l'Ecosse'. Here he was mirroring developments in Ireland as the newly elected Sinn Féin MPs had prepared their Democratic Programme in French (English and Irish too) in order to obtain international ratification for the independent Parliament, or Dáil, that they had set up in Dublin in

January 1919 in defiance of the might of the British Empire. By this time there was a peace conference convening in Paris.

In December of 1918 there had been the general election that saw Ireland vote for a republican party. Erskine had also been busy in that election and claimed that his petition was signed by 43 prospective candidates including the Liberal, J M Hogge, and the Labour candidates such as Maxton, Neil MacLean, Manny Shinwell and David Kirkwood as well as John MacLean who was standing as a Labour candidate due to his affiliation as a British Socialist Party member. In other words, Red Clydeside was behind him.

This was the first contact between the Earl and the Marxist. It is a fascinating digression to look at this story. MacLean may have signed the petition but he did not join, at this stage, the National Committee which Marr was setting up. MacLean told the Irish socialist, Cathal O'Shannon, that his 'blood revolts' against thanking President Wilson for what he has done for the cause of self-determination of nations. The Bolsheviks were truer friends of Scottish Home Rule and, indeed, only the socialist republic could deliver Home Rule. O' Shannon continues:

> Maclean then goes on to express his joy at learning of your revolt against your class and your family and continues, I am not acquainted with the extent of your new beliefs, but as one who would like to see you become a 'chief' in thought and action on behalf of humanity, I may be forgiven if I urge you to read Marx's Capital, and his other writings, Engels' Socialism: Utopian and Scientific.[16]

O' Shannon ends positively with a rhetorical question, 'Does John want the descendent of the Jacobite Duke of Marr to become the Citoyen Egalité of the Social Revolution?'

Two things stand out. Primarily, the Irish knew Erskine of Marr very well. He was a friend of Ireland and her cause and this would have facilitated and shaped MacLean's response as the Glasgow socialist was himself starting to forge links with the Irish cause. Also, Citoyen Marr rose to the challenge. He even added Engels's *The Origin of the Family, Private Property and the State* to his repertoire of left-wing literature as he looked at Celtic communism. A close political friendship was formed and if you go through the various books on MacLean and articles on Erskine, it is almost as if the two were inseparable at this period and a large part of this is due to the empathy shown by the Citizen Earl as he helped a fellow traveller explore his feelings of national identity on his own political journey.

Fundamentally, the petition made it easy for the Left to support it. It was basically an appeal for Scottish representation but, as Erskine explained: 'The purpose of the Memorial is to draw general attention to the unsinkable rights of the Scottish Republic.'[17]

The Memorial invited and obtained substantial support. The Committee almost doubled in size over the course of 1919 to 15 members including 4 MPs, 2 trade union leaders with Robert Smillie being an ever-present, 2 newspaper editors, and featuring the future Scottish Secretary, Tom Johnston, Jimmy Maxton and John MacLean.[18] Erskine believed the task of the Committee to be one of 'baiting' the new League of Nations and of being a European focal point for the cause of independence. The Committee itself would be purely symbolic in many ways. They didn't do much other than sign some letters and the individuals did add kudos to the enterprise.

Symbolic also because by the winter of 1919 the chances of Scotland being entertained at Paris or Versailles were nil. A United Kingdom which had won the war was never going to see its unity and autonomy undermined by Celtic demands for self-determination. Erskine did receive a written acknowledgement of the receipt of the National Memorial by the French President, Poincaré but that was all. He was also receiving reports from his eyes and ears in France, Francis Stuart, to his home in Hove, Sussex. Erskine wrote to Art O'Brien, the Irish Republic's representative in London, that Stuart was pessimistic about France, ' …and says the one idea of the imperialists is not to antagonise England. The Govt again won't look at our Memorial.'[19]

O'Brien and the Irish were generally supportive of the Scottish case. Stuart met the Irish delegation in Paris (Sean T O' Kelly and Gavan Duffy). These two republican heavyweights were cordial and Stuart wrote back to Erskine that the Irish cause was 'in good hands' and wishes it 'every success from my heart' but regrets that the cause of Scotland, 'does not appear to be such a good one.'[20] Erskine heard it from his man in the know. His Great Protest was dead in the water by May 1919. Realistically, the Irish case was dependent upon American support as the nascent Republic was in open rebellion with London.

The imperialists were sticking together. President Wilson had elevated the principle of self-determination and the floodgates had opened with lots of requests from many nationalities. If he was idealistic and genuine in wanting to re-draw the map of the world on democratic lines motivated by the principle of self-determining peoples then that principle soon evaporated among the imperial and political interests of the victors. As Wilson himself commented: 'It was not within the privilege of the conference of peace to act upon the right of self-determination of any peoples except those which had been included in the territories of the defeated empires.'[21]

Wilson could hide behind this piece of realpolitik and proffer that this state of affairs was forced upon him. However, a diary entry from one of the American delegation, Hunter Miller, shows that he was personally antipathetic to the Irish demand as he had been incensed by the approach of an Irish delegation in America prior to him leaving for Europe. He had made no promises regarding Irish independence and had instead, 'wanted to tell them (the Irish) to go to hell'. It puts fresh light on the Scots' decision to piggy-back the Irish delegation to the peace conference. It made practical sense but even that was a non-starter. Perhaps John MacLean was right about Woodrow Wilson all along.

Erskine still kept up the pressure into 1920. He had a Committee of influence and wanted to use it. The focus turned to the Irish case as the situation developed into full scale war in Ireland. A memo from the 9th February reads:

> The Scottish National Committee fraternally salutes the representatives of the Irish Republic, and prepares with them for the dawn of that not far distant day when English control of Ireland and Scotland will cease to be.
> Robert Smillie, President (Nat. Committee)
> R. Erskine of Marr, Convenor.[23]

By the middle of 1920, in a flurry of letters, Erskine's ideas got grander and grander. The Irish and the Scots could fit out a ship to go from foreign port to foreign port distributing leaflets in French and Spanish advertising the national claims of the two countries. It was typical of Erskine; not to give up without a fight and then to give up with a riposte. On this occasion, bemoaning the French and their 'bourgeois mind'.[24] Of course, that ship would never sail.

It would be easy to see the obvious failure in the whole enterprise although it had one remarkable and lasting legacy – the notion of the Scottish Democracy in action. Jump forward seventy years and there is a Scottish Constitutional Convention promoting Scotland's Claim of Right consisting primarily of left of centre politicians, Church and trade union leaders and renegade nationalists with some community activists. This Claim of Right was the demand of the Scottish Democracy for a Scottish Parliament. Jump forward 15 years even and similar groupings were forming Popular Fronts against fascism.

The Honourable Erskine of Marr blazed a trail in coalescing the Scottish Democracy in a campaign for national self-determination when there was a real demand on the Scottish Left in particular for this cause. The great and the good of the Left – the male component at any rate – are all there. Marr can't claim all the credit but he facilitated it through the *Scottish Review*.

The brain of the operation was the Aberdonian, Diack. His vision was to realise the 'essential unity of National and Labour ideals'.[25] These ideas had been swirling around Diack's mind since the start of the War, and in 1917 Diack came to a conclusion that would have inspired Canon Kenyon Wright seventy years later: ' ...the ideals and aspirations of Scottish Nationalism and Scottish Labour are in complete harmony... the 'Scottish democracy' will [work for] the re-organisation of European society on a democratic basis and the overthrow of militarism.'[26]

The thread that ran through Diack's thesis was that there is no contradiction between nationalism and internationalism. He was guilty – if that is the word – of looking through that tempting prism of Celtic colour and light that is Ireland. James Connolly was a major influence; it was Diack who adapted to a different political situation in Scotland and gave the *Review* and Erskine a real political magnetism to a Left looking for a better Scotland and world at the end of the War. Erskine added his stamp. The national Democracy should stand for the Scottish Cooperative Commonwealth and the Review unfurled its flag:

> The flag of the Scottish Cooperative Commonwealth is boldly nailed to the mast; and the arrangement for linking up the Cooperative and Labour movements represents a big step forward in industrial and political organisation. It is the unification of the two great democratic forces in the national life of Scotland.[27]

There is an eloquence in this argument that none on the Left, including MacLean, articulated quite so powerfully. Yet they fell under its sway. Members of mainstream, British socialist organisations such as the ILP or the BSP were talking the language of independence. Johnston's *Forward* was calling for a Scottish State. The Highland Land League were in the Labour Party arguing for independence. Maxton would use the language of the Scottish socialist commonwealth for many years. The two MacLeans – Neil and John – would come out for independence in their own unique fashions. You cannot separate this period in the history of the Scottish left from the influence of Erskine and Diack and yet, with the exception of the late James D Young, they are almost never mentioned in official labour histories.

The National Committee, for me, has to be seen in this light as the first real manifestation of a Scottish democracy whose time had not yet come. It had a presence, pulling power and a manifesto, the Memorial, to rally around. The magnet was Citoyen Erskine; radicalised and radicaliser, influenced and influencer drawing disparate groups notwithstanding his own cadre of Gaelic nationalists to the flag. Had it not been for an about-turn by the Scottish Labour Party, this national democracy could and should have helped to deliver Home Rule in the 1920s. Alas, that banner would be taken on by others.

Erskine's flirtation with the Left would have one other by-product; a historical curiosity that has given his reputation some clout with the modern Left. I refer to his notion of 'Celtic communism'. While it is true that Celtic communism is usually associated with the two foremost Celtic Marxists – Connolly and MacLean – in part as explanation as to why they could balance nationalist notions of independence from Britain with their socialist internationalism; it is truer to say that the theoretician of a Celtic communism was Erskine. John MacLean facilitated this by commissioning the articles for his *Vanguard* newspaper in late 1920. I have no doubt that these articles were an output of their meeting back in July in MacLean's house.

Erskine's contention was that the ancient Celtic polity was derived from the Eastern tradition; a tradition of contraries which delivered a balance of power. This view he believes to be in line with where the Celts came from. It wasn't about tartan and kilts and bagpipes but rather, '…in an extremely ingenious, and according to my way of thinking highly philosophic form of polity. There can be no question, too, but that its true end was democracy… '[28] Erskine sees the Picts as the inheritors of this system and the demise of this Celtic, egalitarian society began with the rise of feudalism and its notion of the Àrd Righ/High King.

The influence was Lewis Morgan and Frederick Engels. The concept was Erskine of Marr's and he would develop it in the *Vanguard*. MacLean was so impressed that he wanted his working-class readership to get familiar with the ideas. So much so that when he was given a supplement in *The Socialist* newspaper in 1922 after his release from a fifth stint in prison, he printed some remaining material from Erskine. MacLean really believed that the roots of the Scottish communist consciousness lay, in part, in this Celtic communist past.

Like Connolly, the Glasgow Marxist never used the term in his own writings. Connolly saw a communal past in the ancient Gaelic society of Ireland but never articulated this as communist; communal, yes, but not communist. Indeed, Connolly was critical of those romantics who hailed Celtic native characteristics which he saw as, 'the birth marks of slavery':

> One of these slave birth marks is a belief in the capitalist system of society; the Irishman frees himself from such a mark of slavery when he realises that the capitalist system is the most foreign thing in Ireland.[29]

There is a tacit recognition that the ancient Gaelic society was indigenous to Ireland but no real development of the argument as, for example, Engels developed it through his analysis of the Gens in Celtic society. Erskine was arguably more Marxian in his method and argument than Connolly and MacLean combined when he reviewed the destruction of that society and the foreign imposition of feudalism.

Unlike the two Marxists who had little to say about this aspect of Marxian study, Erskine praised Engels's analysis and stated that, despite the negative efforts of historians, 'the human race was cradled in communism and lived in this communist stage for hundreds of thousands of years'.[30] To a readership mostly uninitiated in Scottish history, he linked this back to Scotland: 'A Celtic clan consisted of a body of people anything from one hundred to many thousands strong all bearing the same name being descended from a common ancestor and occupying a common territory.'[31]

His examples were the famous Campbells of Argyll, the Stewarts in Appin and the MacLeans in Mull.[32] Erskine would have been aware that his Marxist friend was of Mull stock. These articles were specially commissioned by MacLean and he was still keen to get this argument across two years after the first articles appeared in the *Vanguard* – a left-wing paper that was mostly ultra-leftist and syndicalist in outlook. Erskine concluded his series by explaining that Culloden and the Highland Clearances were a necessary part of the development of the British State. Primitive communism had to give way to other stages of historical development but these developments would ensure that, 'the world communism of the future will arise'.[33] It is safe to assume that this would have been well received by the readers. What is unknown is when these articles were actually written. Were they unprinted articles from two years before at the height of his love affair with the Left or freshly written at MacLean's request?

We can only guess. The Gaelic sources in *Guth na Bliadhna* indicate that, from the Spring of 1921, he was starting to question the Marxist experiment in Russia. Bolshevik policies were 'extremely improper' and had left sub-divisions in the country. The north of the country had given placid support to Lenin's state of emergency. They benefitted while the rest of the country got debt and 'evil intention'. As a result, town and country had been divided. To be fair, Erskine knew that Soviet Russia was up against it. He praised the Russians in seeking to inspire each country and build a fortress. In allusion to the workers, it was a fortress of the ants – 'mar a dhùn an t-seangain' – but the socialist experiment was unravelling.[34]

To question the Bolsheviks' intention was prescient. His message was for the Scottish Gael; a guidance that he expects to be to their agreement, ' …a chumail do ghnàth an cuimhne' or 'keep the traditions of the past'. The Lowlanders have lost their Celtic culture so it is incumbent on the Gaels to put back the tradition gained from their ancestors. This was consistent with his three principles of the Celtic movement articulated back in 1918 – his Celtic gospel. Marx and his class politics were dividing town from country to the betterment of the urban dwellers. As Erskine put it: 'Is marbh Karl Marx, ach air mhaireann tha an soisgeul Ceilteach.'[35]

This analysis of where he saw things going wrong in Russia would seem to indicate that his fling with the Left was coming to an end. It would also suggest that if he did see any future for communism it was on Celtic and not Marxian lines. It is worth emphasising that Erskine was consistent. He never at any point in this period said that he was a socialist, let alone a communist. The aim was to work with the Left to advance the common cause of national self-determination at a time when the Scottish Left were exploring this option after four years of imperialist carnage. In doing so, he made some real achievements. To paraphrase Erskine himself: 'All praise to William Diack! All honour to the *Scottish Review*!' Thanks to both, Scottish nationalism became radicalised and taken in a left of centre direction that would infuse his other main activities over 1919 through to 1922.

The *Review* went out of business in the Spring of 1920. In the last issue, Diack had a piece on the miners' struggle and he heaped praise on Smillie and his campaign to nationalise the mines. His use of data to contradict the privateers' abuse of their ownership of the mines was striking. In arguing for nationalisation, he summed up by paraphrasing Fintan Lalor, a pioneer Irish socialist. The guiding principle for Scottish nationalists should be: '…that the entire ownership of Scotland, moral and material, up to the sun and down to the centre, is vested in the people of Scotland.'[36]

It was a fitting, eloquent way to sign off the *Review* and its political input to Scottish nationalism that is not always remembered or adhered to today. Erskine, for his part, would have agreed with every word. He tried to use Diack's piece to get financial support for the *Review* from the wider (British) trade union movement. He wrote as editor of the *Review* to the head of the union's Mines Commission to enquire if they would be interested in obtaining extra copies through subscription in order to propel Diack's article to an English audience. If anything proves the validity of a separate Scottish socialism then it would be in the reply which curtly stated that they would not be interested as there would be little interest south of the border.[37] It was a last throw of the dice for the *Review* which financially could not survive.

Erskine would stay friendly with MacLean up to his untimely death on 30th November 1923. This involved defending MacLean in his opposition to the Communist Party of Great Britain and his determination to set up a separate Scottish party. 'If that Party is truly anti-imperial why does it adopt an imperial title?'[38] This was so typical of Erskine; to cut to the chase. Scottish communists should take the lead from MacLean, and not the party in London, because he was, ' …a Nationalist as well as a Communist.' MacLean was in HMP Barlinnie when these words were written – the last of five stints in prison. They were worthy recognition from Erskine at a time when his friend needed it.

The friendship and political collaboration were at the heart of both of their stories in this period of their lives. The Earl and the Marxist mutually influencing each other.

Chapter Eight

Doing his bit for Ireland!

Mise Éire:
Sine mé ná an Chailleach Bhéarra
Mór mo ghlóir:
Mé a rug Cú Chulainn cróga.
Mór mo náir:
Mo chlann féin a dhíol a máthair.
Mór mo phian:
Bithnaimhde do mo shíorchiapadh.
Mór mo bhrón:
D'éag an dream inar chuireas dóchas.
Mise Éire:
Sine mé ná an Chailleach Bhéarra

I am Ireland:
I am older than the old woman of Beare.
Great my glory:
I who bore Cuchulainn, the brave.
Great my shame:
My own children who sold their mother.
Great my pain:
My irreconcilable enemy who harrasses me continually
Great my sorrow
That crowd, in whom I placed my trust, died.
I am Ireland:
I am lonelier than the old woman of Beare.

P H Pearse[1]

A striking, famous image of Ireland. Written in Irish and translated into English which probably explains why its real power and imagery lie in its Gaelic form. Such imagery was endemic in Irish Ireland. For all Erskine's fine efforts there was nothing comparable in Scotland. Indeed, Scotland's Gaelic nationalists could only look on with envy and a real sense of admiration. Still, they looked; with more intensity as things unravelled in the early years of the twentieth century.

Ireland was a prism. Its light reflected and distorted, at different times, as all prisms tend to do. Its light held the gaze of many an unsuspecting Scottish radical. John Murdoch was inspired by the Irish land agitation. Erskine, Gillies and their band of Gaelic nationalists looked to the Gaelic League and Sinn Féin for their inspiration. John MacLean, too, was mesmerised by its light and the Irish cause played a major part in his thinking and doing in Scotland after the War. Even if this was 'cognitive dissonance', it was powerful. Scotland was compared with; moulded to; excited by and at times disappointed in her Celtic neighbour across the water. Compton MacKenzie, Hugh MacDiarmid, Wendy Wood and Oliver Brown kept the prism alive right up until the 1940s.

Of course, the prism of Ireland did not just attract the radicals. Arguably, Gladstone in the later nineteenth century and the reactionary co-editor of *The Whirlwind*, Herbert Vivian, in the early twentieth century were drawn to Ireland and her politics.

There is no single explanation. All had their reasons and all saw different things through the prism. The old woman's bravery or her shame and pain may have struck different chords with different observers. Yet they looked.

Pearse, who wrote the poem, also read a declaration from the steps of the General Post Office in Dublin in April 1916. He proclaimed the Irish Republic as his socialist friend, James Connolly looked on. He would lead a small force against the might of Britain in wartime. He would feel glory and pain and shame and he would die; executed by a British court-martial. Not only the Scots but the whole world was watching – reflecting, distorting – on the aftermath of the Easter Rising.

In the midst of wartime censorship, Erskine jumped to the defence of the rebels. It was another defining moment and the beginning of how he did his own personal bit for Ireland.

We know that this was certainly not his first intervention in the cause of Ireland. He had toured with Parnell, met Pearse in Wales at a pan-Celtic Congress and learned old fashioned Sinn Féin politics from Griffith in Dublin with its emphasis on autonomy, national self-reliance and a monarchical model based on the Austro-Hungarian empire. He had written for the *Sinn Féin Daily*. Erskine had drawn in Irish writers to his publications and had become well known in Irish

Gaelic nationalist circles in the process.

His response to the Rising would be extremely important. Home Rulers in Scotland would join with their Irish counterparts in condemnation of the rebellion. Erskine was no Home Ruler and his response to Easter Week would propound his radicalised, separatist nationalism in Scotland. His response was published in English in the Review as 'Who Fears to Speak of Easter Week.' This would reach a wider audience. You will note the lack of any question mark in the title. Grammatically poor, perhaps, but politically strong as there is no room for doubt or interpretation. Erskine's was a critical support and it should be mentioned that, in wartime, his piece was written with the censor in mind.

His tone was sombre and realistic at the start of the piece. The Rising was doomed to failure. In making the point that Ireland could be 'no match' for England he elaborates by stating that the Rising was: ' …the forlornest of forlorn chances. Nothing short of a miracle from Heaven could have caused it to prosper.'[2]

From a practical point of view, it is hard to argue. Had all of Ireland arisen then that may have been a different matter which brings in an interesting contextual point. As Erskine had cultivated a relationship with the Gaelic League over the past few years, he had got close with Eoin MacNeill. MacNeill had contributed to the Summer edition of the *Review* with an article on Hebridean history. They were both learned men with a common interest in ancient Gaelic culture and history and all things Celtic. For the Ulster-born Professor, the term Celtic was, 'indicative more of language, not of race.'[3] MacNeill was also, in 1916, the head of the Irish Volunteers, the main militarised body in Ireland. For those who know their history of the Easter Rising, MacNeill was also the man who nearly called it all off by sending out a countermanding order for the Volunteers to step down on Easter Sunday; the day before the Rising. He did not believe that it was militarily the right thing to do and was kept out of the secretive loop of the secretive Irish Republican Brotherhood (IRB) who had been preparing the rebellion. Many blame MacNeill for the lack of any real provincial support to Dublin that would have strengthened the rebels' position. Be that as it may, if Erskine was close to MacNeill then it is fair to assume in the absence of hard evidence that he may have taken MacNeill's version of it.

For all that, Erskine was generally supportive and he could see the significance of the blow struck to the Empire's heart. Arthur Griffith and the formation of Sinn Féin was a contributory cause although Griffith is acknowledged as a pacifist. Another cause was England.

By raising the cry at the start of the war for 'St George for Belgium and the Little States', then it was only right that others would take the Prime Minister, Asquith, and his government at face value:

> In the circumstances in which that country was then placed, what other effect on Ireland could his cry of 'Long live the Small States!' produce therein than that which it actually had during Easter Week.[4]

Erskine did set a pattern that he would stick to over the next six years or so: Celtic unity. He was tentatively thinking of a Celtic Confederacy after the War was over. In a positive finale, he did not confuse the issue at hand by dwelling on this because this was about Irish freedom, ' …nothing short of the full possession' of liberty will, 'content them or lay aside their resistance to the levelling and de-nationalising tendencies of English rule and civilisation. This is the true spring of the recent Irish Rising.' He concluded that this should be, 'plainly discovered and as fearlessly announced'.[5] This would set the tone for a fearless announcement of Irish demands over the next, few turbulent years in that country's history and while Erskine was not the only Scottish friend of Ireland in this period, few gave as much of themselves in the cause. 'Who Fears to Speak of Easter Week' was not a manifesto or rallying cry but it was an important marker.

In private, he was saying the same thing to his friend, the collector and Gaelic enthusiast Charles Loch, who was resident in Australia at that time. In June, Erskine gave him an update of the 'Sinn Féin Rising' informing him that it should never have been undertaken: 'They made the same mistakes as the Jacobites of 1715 & 1745 did. Still it was a brave attempt and honourable to those who engaged in it, though I can't say much for their intelligence.'[6]

Erskine of Marr was never a diplomat in word or deed. This letter is valuable for more than just an insight into his view on the politics of Ireland. He reveals that he is a Godparent to Loch's son, Stuart, 'the heir'. By December, his Australian friend had sent him a photograph and Ruaraidh was delighted! He had no children with Dona Maria and he valued the relationship with young Stuart. For a child to have a Godparent, 'is half the battle of life already won'.[7] It is easy to wrap a political figure like Erskine in political cotton wool or gauze, depending upon your viewpoint. Common humanity too often gets lost in the politics.

The aftermath of the Rising in Ireland unleashed different political forces that radicalised Griffith's party into a separatist, republican organisation and galvanised international opinion against the British government for its callous executions. As we have seen, Erskine saw the political opportunities for Scotland as 1917 evolved. Ireland, and unity with Irish aspirations, was central to his strategy.

The events in Dublin in 1916 certainly nudged him in this direction. The brightest light from the prism shone after the general election of December 1918. Ireland had come around, albeit in exceptional circumstances, to Griffith's vision of 1904; namely, that Irish political interests could not be served in England. Sinn Féin stood on an abstentionist platform as did William Scrimgeour in Dundee. One wanted to abstain from alcohol; the others wanted to abstain from Westminster. The Old Party – the Irish Party – paid a heavy price. They were left with 6 seats out of 105. Sinn Féin won 73 seats and swept the board.

The Irish Party's leader since 1900, John Redmond, did not live to see it. He passed away on 6th March 1918. Erskine carried a short obituary in the *Scottish Review*. It must be said that the obituary was blunt and insensitive. Redmond was not seen as a 'great man'. A good debater, yes, but 'not superlative'. Without mentioning his replacement, John Dillon, by name, Erskine states that Redmond's 'room has been easily filled by a corresponding figure'.[8]

I can't help but sense some bluster in Erskine's words. He didn't print many obituaries and Redmond's death did affect him as he knew him personally. In the 1930s, with the passage of time, Erskine was more candid and revealing of the personal relationship. Erskine first met Redmond during Parnell's last political campaign and does recall him as a great orator. Whenever Redmond visited Scotland his reception was always 'generous and sincere'.[9] No dates are given to the recollections of visits to the House of Commons and the discussions on the Irish language and political tactics. His allegiance to the legacy of O'Connell and Parnell combined with his jealousy of Sinn Féin had given him a 'mental blindness'. Erskine, as a traditional 1905 vintage Sinn Féiner, could see the flaws in parliamentarism as expressed through Westminster. Redmond's failure was not to see the failure of this policy: ' …seeing yet he disbelieved, and, disbelieving yet he turned his back on it.'[10]

With the passage of time, it is a better, more sober and human reflection on Redmond's contribution to the forward march of Ireland. It also helps to put the obituary into perspective. Redmond's death would be closely followed by the political death of his party. On the other hand, Erskine's political zeal would spring to life when the 73 newly elected Sinn Féin MPs refused to take their seat in the Imperial Parliament and, better still, stayed at home to form their own republican parliament in Dublin. The new Dáil was an inspiration. We have seen how the Irish Democratic Programme inspired the Scottish National Petition. The *Review* threw its weight behind support of the nascent Republic. H C MacNeacail, a long-time associate of Erskine's, wrote that no nation had suffered more than Ireland. Invoking the spirit of 1916, he quoted Pearse citing him as, 'one of the noblest Nationalists of his generation '.[11] All Scottish Nationalists offered the new Irish Republic, 'the best of good wishes'.[12] This was a statement of intent and solidarity from Erskine's group of Scottish nationalists that would set the tone of their response.

The editor himself kept up the pressure. The Dáil's stand and demand for recognition had given President Wilson two acid tests for his peace discussions: Ireland, of course, and Alsace-Lorraine on the Franco-German border:

> With regard to Ireland, a Republican government based on the suffrage of the people already exists in that country., which being so, England should be invited under pain of being excluded from the League in the event of her refusal to conform her conduct to its principles, to evacuate Ireland, and to leave that country to its own devices.[13]

This succinct statement of solidarity and principle would form the basis of the support given as Ireland spiralled into revolution as Britain flagrantly ignored the democratic will of its own general election.

The Scottish Review passed the baton to the journal of the Scottish Home Rule Association: *Liberty*. As the title suggests, this journal existed to promulgate Home Rule. It was edited by John MacArthur whose sympathy for a more separatist nationalism allowed the journal to be taken over by Erskine's band of radical nationalists. By April 1920 the heading had changed to *Liberty: the Scottish National Journal* with the indicative masthead: 'Enlightened nationalism is the basis of true internationalism'.

The journal lived up to its word and its support for the Irish revolutionary war against the full force of the British State as it raged over 1920 into 1921 was a true litmus test of its internationalism.

An Irish activist from Greenock, Alexander McGill, set the scene with his simply stated, 'The Case for Ireland'. McGill had written for Erskine before and was broadly sympathetic to the Scots case for independence. In this article, espousing the Irish claim to freedom, he fired a warning shot to those Scottish nationalists being attracted by the glow of Ireland's prism: 'The main difference between the Scots and Irish case is that while Scotland became reconciled to the conditions of union, Ireland never did.'[14]

While this may seem an obvious point to many, it floated over the heads of his fellow contributors. Over the next six months the paper carried articles on the struggles in India, Mexico and Egypt. Ireland, of course, was closer to their hearts.

Erskine began the active assault by speaking at a demonstration in London's Trafalgar Square against the imprisonment of Archbishop Mannix. While he was the Catholic Archbishop of Melbourne, he was born in Cork. He was visiting Ireland from America and had been arrested by British troops while trying to disembark at Cork harbour and then transferred to London. Sinn Féin had organised a big demonstration in Trafalgar Square to protest against the treatment of the Archbishop. It is testament to Erskine's status in Irish political circles that he was invited to speak. He made the most of the opportunity in front of 20000 people.

There were initial scuffles as some tried to prevent the filming of the event. Erskine told the crowd that the Scots would have a party as strong as the Irish soon and he predicted in grandiloquent fashion the rising of the Scottish Gael. This new Scottish party, ' ...would burst asunder the fetters of the English government and Scotland would have its rights'. PJ Kelly, Art O'Brien and Cathal O'Shannon also spoke.[15] As with the demand for representation at Paris, so too in London; the Irish republicans were giving Scotland a platform and Erskine was the voice and leader of this radical, separatist Scottish nationalism.

Gillies also was on the attack criticising Scottish soldiers and calling for 'direct action' to defend 'our kith and kin'.[16] By October subscriptions and sales must have been good as the paper became a weekly publication. This was hailed, famously, with its most powerful front page. A photo of Balbriggan, in ruins, after a raid by the infamous Black and Tans, 'NO, YOU'RE WRONG! This is not a scene in occupied Belgium'.[17] It was a scene that most Scots would have been ignorant of. It was as a direct negative to the majority view that the IRA were the terrorists. In this exposition of British terror and outrage in Ireland, Liberty rallied to the cause; they had a cause célebre in that of Terence MacSwiney.

MacSwiney was a playwright and author who had been elected as one of the abstentionist MPs for a Cork seat in December 1918.

During the War of Independence, he became that city's Lord Mayor. He was arrested in August 1920 on charges of sedition and transferred to Brixton prison. He was not treated as a political prisoner and, in objection, he went on hunger strike. After 74 long, cruel days he died in October.

Erskine and Gillies were active in solidarity activities in London at this time. Gillies joined in prayer and rosary groups outside the prison walls while MacSwiney was inside.[18] The Catholic Erskine must have joined these too. They were both among the many visitors to MacSwiney in prison including Churchmen and politicians. Gillies was especially moved. As he related in his obituary in *Liberty*: 'When I grasped his hand a few days before he was taken, I knew I was in the presence of a Gael and a Christian and felt humble for the meanness of our strivings in Scotland. We shall do better yet; God grant or we perish and that miserably.'[19]

In the same issue of the paper, the editor reported that a deputation of Scottish nationalists were invited to the requiem mass in Southwark cathedral and had a place of honour immediately after the Irish deputation as the funeral cortege, led by uniformed IRA men, wound its way through the streets of London to Euston station. Thousands lined the streets. It was a momentous occasion for the Scots to witness. Seumas MacGaraidh, from Arbroath, wrote that MacSwiney's martyrdom was 'fifty times' more awful than that of William Wallace. The 'Wallaces of Ireland' are going to their graves every day for high ideals.[20] Erskine continued the onslaught by indicting Lloyd George. World opinion was turning against Britain after MacSwiney's death. In trying to influence Scottish opinion, Erskine stated that Lloyd George did not have terror in Ireland by the throat, as he claimed, but rather he held liberty by the throat. Erskine asked his readers for practical ways to help Ireland: ' …for in a multitude of voices there are found, on occasions, the wisdom that justifieth counsel and the guile that saveth nations and causes.'[21] Erskine was always one for ideas to move things on. His weren't always the most practical but he did listen. His 'multitude of voices' would not be heard in a war situation yet he was right to pose the question. The juxtaposition of war and peace was prevalent in his writings. The new world to emerge would be a 'trial of relative strength' between these two opposing forces. Imperialism and war should not be allowed to have their own way which meant that the forces for peace, 'must wear a sword in self-defence, as well as carry an olive branch'.[22] Superficially read, such thoughts can, of course, justify Ireland's war of self-defence against the might of Britain. At a deeper level Erskine was thinking about this new world that was going to emerge from the ruins of a world war. He put it another way in a lovely, descriptive sentence at the end of 1920: ' …there can be no true New World for us to inhabit unless our hearts are made the first scene of the vital change on which mankind deserves to enter.'[23]

The public activity of Erskine and *Liberty* would have been contribution enough. However, Erskine did his bit for Ireland privately too and this comes out most clearly in his correspondence with Art O'Brien. O'Brien (O'Briain in Irish) was born in London in 1872 of Irish parents. He joined that city's branch of the Gaelic League in 1899 which drew him into Irish nationalism. It was the Easter Rising which made him a political activist and he organised a campaign in London to commute Roger Casement's death sentence. His contribution was recognised back in Dublin and after the formation of the Dáil, O'Brien became its envoy to Britain and he formed the Sinn Féin cover organisation, the Irish Self Determination League of Great Britain.[24]

Relationships are the most striking thing about the correspondence. We have seen that Erskine was well known in Irish radical political circles and how, through 1919, his idea of a 'Celtic Entente' was winning admirers in Ireland. So, he was known and, fair to say respected, at a superficial level. Depth came through London. Darragh Gannon has argued very persuasively that it was exile that bound Erskine, Gillies and O'Brien together.[25] Exile gave a common bond of culture, language and nationality. O'Brien used his position as President of the Gaelic League in London to give the Scots a platform. This was formalised when the branch agreed to admit, 'Nationals of the sister Gaelic nation of Scotland' to full membership.[26] This, Gannon argues, gave the London branch a real 'pan-Celtic feel.'

Reading the correspondence, you cannot miss the personal bond. There is no doubting that O'Brien and Gillies were closer but that should not detract from the relationship struck between Erskine and O'Brien. At times, professional and business-like; always cordial and respectful and human. This stretched to moments of insensitivity. For example, O'Brien was not happy that his clerk had to wait at Erskine's door 'for some time' before he got a reply. This was a security concern as it could attract attention. In fact, O'Brien's courtesy in asking Erskine to facilitate that the clerk could wait inside masked the true security risk that could have put O'Brien's entire London operation in peril.[27]

At no time in the correspondence is there a hint of a falling out or disagreement. Erskine raised objections to the use of the term 'Britain' by President Valera (as he called him). O'Brien replied that he was on-side with Erskine and it was a pity, 'that the old mis-use of the word has crept in again'. He assured Erskine that he would forward the Scot's letter to the President himself.[28] There were semi-regular meet ups and very regular contact on the key political points which extended to Dona Maria who was sent a copy of the Spanish edition of the Dáil's Address to the Foreign Nations to which Mrs Erskine replied with thanks and a need to meet up with Art for lunch.[29]

It was the cultivation of this relationship that gave a special credence to the Scottish nationalists' solidarity work. They were writing and working and praying and organising from the inside. The O'Brien link as Celts in exile allowed Gillies to be there beside Terence MacSwiney and gave Erskine the platform in Trafalgar Square as well as in being able to address big pro-Irish rallies in the Albert Hall. Scottish nationalism had a public platform standing side by side with Irish republicans in the imperial capital city in support of the latter's struggle.

Sometimes, Erskine's motives were not always altruistic. Support for Ireland was paramount; could Scotland's cause be advanced at the same time? Publicly, the party line didn't change. It was still the 'Gaels divided by the sea.' The papers have a typed Objects and Organisation for 'An Comunn Comh-Gaidhealach.' The 'Objects' are the handiwork of Messrs Gillies and Erskine: 'To work for the complete independence, political, intellectual, economic and social of the Gaelic Race by the establishment of independent Gaelic Republics in the two sister nations of Scotland and Ireland.'[30]

Privately, something else was happening. The Scots were seeking support for a project of their own. What was it? Stephen Coyle and Máirtín Ó Cáthain in separate works point to the existence of a Scottish paramilitary organisation called Fianna na h-Alba.[31] Both these historians have given an intriguing insight into the Scots developing intentions to support Ireland and themselves and the organisation in some form probably did exist. However, neither Erskine nor Gillies name it directly in the papers.

Piecing together the evidence, something was definitely in the air. The first mention comes in July 1920 when Erskine surreptitiously states that he is waiting on 'word from Stirling.' A week later, Erskine was writing to O'Brien telling him that Gillies will update him so that he can 'push things through' when he visits Dublin: 'I think our plans are riper than your friend thinks but on the other hand, our organisation on the new lines, which G will explain, is only just begun. It will take time to render it efficient…'[32]

Taking a step forward, we shall see that the Scots were also building a new political organisation in the Scots National League and, of course, it is conceivable that Erskine may have been referring to this. Yet why use guarded language? And why justify the plans as being 'riper' in reference to a purely political organisation? British State censors would not have been too interested in the Scots' political organisation. There is nothing of this nature until December when O'Brien wrote that the Acting President, Arthur Griffith, had been in touch with the view that Marr's 'projections' were 'much too rosy.' Griffith would like Erskine to visit Dublin to discuss these but it was not practical at that time as O'Brien had to cancel a visit to Dublin and Griffith himself had just been arrested.[33]

So far, we have projections and plans and ripeness but nothing concrete. These would be too circumstantial if only read from the Scottish side of things as we should remember the Irish forbearance and patience of the many Scottish requests for support ranging from financial (for *Liberty*) and political (for a pan-Celtic grouping) at a time when there was a revolutionary war raging.

More light is shed from the internal Irish correspondence. This tells us that the Republican leadership were discussing 'Scottish business' and 'Scotch affairs' from July 1919. Indeed, O'Brien had written to Michael Collins himself stating that he was, 'anxious to keep on good terms with Erskine of Marr.' He also asked Collins to 'broach the matter with Griffiths' so that he could give Erskine an update.[34] This was followed up by an 'interview' with Erskine who had told O'Brien that he was disappointed that there was no news with the comment from O'Brien that, 'He seems to have his plans pretty well laid'.[35]

The Irish, for their part, genuinely saw the Scots as useful and this has to be seen in context. Support for some form of self-determination was strong after the December 1918 election; among the Left, the Scottish Democracy and Erskine's two publications. Also, there was a campaign for Scottish representation at Paris which could only assist Ireland's claim. Finally, there was a base of support for Ireland's freedom in Scotland from some of the same sources as cited above with the addition of the Irish emigrant community and John MacLean.

The Irish line toward Erskine was therefore one of guarded encouragement. In August 1920 O'Brien decided to accept Erskine's request for Irish representation on his National Committee.[36] Collins was receiving regular updates and literature from Scotland.[37] His responses to O'Brien are the strongest evidence that, in addition to requests for financial support, both Erskine and Gillies had made requests for military support to incite disaffection in Scotland. On St Patricks Day in 1921, Collins started a series of memos to O'Brien as to why the Irish Republic could not provide military assistance to the Scottish nationalists: they just weren't ready. Even when the Irish Republican Brotherhood was at its weakest, in 1904, it was still stronger than the Scots' current organisation.[38]

There was genuine regret that another front could not be opened up across the water. 'Isn't it a pity,' wrote Collins, 'that their end of it was not more advanced at this juncture.' With a genuine empathy for the conflation of social and national questions in Scotland, Collins added that the Coal Strike across the water may lead to a, 'reviving of the spirit of nationality in the Scots generally', especially if armed conflicts ensue.[39] It was a 'no' to military assistance for any Scottish armed rising and the Scots received very generous financial support – as recognition for their support for Ireland - for the Liberty newspaper; £250 in July 1921 and £270 in October of the same year.

Consideration was given to the personalities involved. De Valera seemed to prefer Erskine whom he knew and was 'a bit doubtful' about the 'Gaelic Leaguer in the kilt'; which was probably an apt description of Gillies as he cut about London.[40] Collins leaned towards Mac Gille Iosa.[41] Art O'Brien was always in the middle batting for Erskine and Gillies when it was appropriate, stalling when it was also appropriate and in Dublin's interests but always providing a picture for the Republican leadership to enable them to make an informed judgement. It was O'Brien who provided his informed opinion to Collins in late March which led to Collins' decision.

Being closer to Gillies he broached the subject with him of his initial doubts about Erskine. This is not surprising. Erskine's brother was in the House of Lords, he was still aristocratic in culture and outlook and was not security conscious.[42] We learn that Gillies, 'cautiously agreed' with O'Brien.[43] Again, this is hardly surprising as Gillies, the Scottish republican, was forging political links with a known Jacobite sympathiser. We should not forget that these initial barriers were real nor that the trust built was real too. O'Brien did not let his trust cloud his judgement and stated that he believed that Erskine was 'mistaken' in his calculations.

The evidence points to an intention, a desire, on the behalf of the Scottish nationalists to emulate their Irish brethren. Was it more than this? It is hard to say without more hard evidence from the Scottish side. From the Irish side we know that something was afoot.

A planned Scottish insurrection exactly one hundred years after the last one in 1820? C Desmond Greaves has written in a biography of Liam Mellows, the socialist Quartermaster General of the IRA:

> And a Scottish Nationalist Volunteer Force, Fianna na h Alba, was said to be contemplating military action for the liberation of Scotland. Mellows wondered how serious a threat to Irish supplies its arms and requirements were likely to be.[44]

No source is given in Greaves's book for this quotation. It is true that Mellows's thoughts are in line with the rest of the Irish leadership. The first part of the quote does leave the door open to the existence of on the ground, paramilitary style organisation in Scotland. This could have overlapped with John MacLean's efforts to get a Scottish Citizen Army off the ground. We know that MacLean met with the Irish Republican Brotherhood in Risk Street in the Calton in Glasgow's east end in January 1919 discussing the prospects of revolutionary activity in Scotland and that MacLean's associates ran guns over to Ireland during the War of Independence. He also discussed a Scottish Defence Force with Constance Markiewicz.[45] We know that Erskine and MacLean were close during this period. We just don't know if any such Nationalist Volunteer force existed. We can only go with the evidence that there was an intention, a desire and, to be fair, practical solidarity with fellow Irish nationalists that earned Erskine, Gillies and MacLean the respect of their Irish peers.

In this desire, they were mistaken. Scotland was not Ireland. The prism, we should remember, can distort as well as it can reflect. The Scots were drawn in and carried away on a tide of revolutionary excitement that the actual Irish war dissipated in some while others, like Erskine and Gillies, continued to hold on to that excitement, that belief that something was going to change for the better. Even in August 1921, when the Irish had their minds on concluding the war, Erskine returned from a 'tour of Scotland' and met O'Brien in London. He did not want to exaggerate, but the Scots were 'well on the way' to getting their people organised.[46] O'Brien politely informed him and Dublin by memo that nothing had changed. This would not have done Marr's credibility any good but he had the good sense to see that financial support could still be forthcoming.

He was drawn wholeheartedly into the prism of Ireland. It is tempting to see Erskine as some kind of 'Scottish Pearse.' As Patrick Witt put it: 'He imagined playing Pearse's role in a Scottish context.'[47]

It is a seductive argument in an excellent essay. The personal connection with Pearse notwithstanding, both men had the same desire to transform their countries into separatist, Gaelic nations. Both men forged links with the leading Marxian socialists in their respective countries. Both men had inspired and transformed the language movement and taken it in an overtly political direction. Ó Cáthain contributed to the analogy in his description of Collins' decision on the potential of Scottish armed support: 'Counsels of restraint, however, met these 1916 groupies rather than weaponry.'[48]

It is easy to fall in line with this argument. After all, were not Erskine's group trying to precipitate some kind of doomed intervention in Scotland that would provoke a popular nationalist response similar to what happened in Ireland post-1916? Weren't Erskine's group romantically drawn to the prism of Ireland?

There was a significant difference between the two Gaelic nationalists. The thing about the Honourable Ruaraidh Erskine of Marr is that he was both realist and idealist at the same time. His support for the Rising of 1916 was qualified. We have seen how privately and publicly he was critical of the leaders' tactics and foolhardiness and did not even mention Pearse by name, even though they had personally met and Erskine had sought his contribution to *Guth na Bliadhna*. In his heart of hearts, he knew what the political realities of life were in Scotland and sought to develop his Celtic gospel within its confines. The same dichotomy between realism and idealism was played out in his love: hate relationship with Jacobitism.

Options could be kept open. For example, at the same time as he was lobbying the Irish for Scotland's cause, the same Erskine was lobbying the Labour Party for Ireland's cause and was looking for a way out of the impasse of war. He believed that a confederation of countries should replace the Empire and wanted to sound out the Labour leader, Nathaniel Clynes, on his proposal. He also wrote to O'Brien and De Valera. De Valera told Collins that Erskine had, 'an idea with reference to the changing of the British Empire into a cooperative group. There is not much in it... certainly nothing constructive to attract attention'.[49] Clynes and O'Brien were more amenable to the proposals. Erskine met the Labour leader in May 1921 and reported back to O'Brien. Clynes wanted an agreement that was 'amenable to both parties' and that this was a 'duty' of the Labour Party as much as it was in their interests.[50]

This shows another dimension to Erskine's character – that of the statesman and peacemaker. He believed he was acting in Ireland's interests but it was certainly not Pearsite in character! It did tie in more with that of another Irish leader; Arthur Griffith. If Erskine's group were '1916 groupies' then they certainly adapted to the situation before them just as the participants and survivors of 1916 had to do as well. These groupies were talking the language of pragmatism especially in response to the on-going Treaty negotiations taking place in London between the Irish delegation led by Collins and the British government led by Lloyd George.

Solidarity activity certainly continued but to a lesser extent. Erskine addressed a meeting of 10000 present from Irish Ireland societies in the Albert Hall in London in late 1921 along with speakers from Egypt and India. Though heartened, Marr found this 'a sobering experience' as it really put into perspective the Scots lack of endeavour.[51] The terms of the Treaty were being debated in Ireland. With regard to any Irish treaty, the Scottish nationalists were taking a political line under the guise of not taking a line. MacNeacail wrote that it was not for the Scots to give advice to the Irish negotiators. His belief was that the Republic would not die and the Treaty would not kill it as it offered Ireland 'way beyond' what has previously been offered.[52] This was followed up by Gillies in the same issue of the Standard. The Treaty would help Scotland's national movement by killing the notion of Home Rule. His qualification:

> We Scots nationalists have also to confess our shame at the way Scotland as a whole stood idly by whilst Irish men and Irish women and Irish children too, were maintaining an unequal war for freedom, not only of the Gael, but for the oppressed in every land.[53]

The prism of Ireland was now reflecting a different Scotland back to the nationalist enthusiasts.

Erskine joined in this pragmatic acceptance of the Treaty and a partitioned Irish Free State in a letter to the old Irish Fenian leader in America, John Devoy. Ireland, he explained to Devoy, has to go through, 'political evolution': from Free State to Republic. In characteristically over the top language he criticised the Republicans in the debate as, 'in the vast majority of cases honest; but their intelligence, vision and knowledge of political history are small'.[54] The language is similar to that of his letter to Charles Loch after the Easter Rising. It was such language that undid all his attempts to play the statesman. He did hope that Ireland and Scotland could resume their old ties once some kind of order was returned to Ireland. On a positive note he informed Devoy that the Scots National League was growing in branches.

The Scots response was in many ways the response of a nationalist grouping anywhere: how does the situation somewhere else affect my country? It is understandable at this level and understandable for a group of nationalists who had at times expressed their separatism through the notion of a Scottish Free State. They could not conceive of their Free State minus, say, Edinburgh and the Borders who could hypothetically be called Southern Scotland and partitioned from the rest of the country. The lack of any dialogue on the partition of Ireland is a glowing omission but should not detract from the Scots' overall contribution to the support of fellow nationalists.

Erskine was no 'Scottish Pearse'. Witt summarised very powerfully the true influence at work which amidst the seeming contradictions give Erskine a consistency in his politics:

Acknowledging a lack of widespread separatism, he vowed to tutor Scots on the disagreeable nature of union. His carefully formed argument, asserting the fallacy of any notion of a shared Brittanic nationality, and his declaration that Scottish negotiators had betrayed the interests of the Scottish people, borrowed from the rationale articulated by Arthur Griffith.[55]

If anything, he was a 'Scottish Griffith.' It maybe doesn't have the same poetic ring to it. Yet it ties in far more neatly. He was until he died an old-style Scottish Sinn Féiner of the 1904 Dual Monarchy, Griffith vintage. He could relate to the pragmatic Griffith who did not fight in 1916 but participated passionately in the struggle afterward; the pragmatist who negotiated the Free State Treaty and passionately sought to build that Free State assisted by, among others, his old compadré, Professor Eoin MacNeill. That mix of passion and pragmatism sits with Erskine of Marr.

That said, his support for the Irish republican struggle was not opportunist. As he said in later years, Ireland was his inspiration; his prism if you care as it was for his friend MacLean. His pragmatism allowed him to build a Scottish Democracy in politics and contribute indirectly to a new Ireland in practice. The last piece of the jigsaw in this turbulent post war period was one of passion not pragmatism; namely, the building of a separatist nationalist organisation that both Griffith and Pearse would have been proud of.

To end this chapter, three Postscripts on Ireland.

Firstly, Ruaraidh's older brother, the 6th Baron Erskine on Ireland didn't make many speeches in the House of Lords. However, on 23rd November 1922 he made a contribution in response to the King's speech on the subject of Ireland. It is an interesting insight into the Unionist position that birth and position should have given Stuart Erskine too. Montagu believed:

> ...that this country was honestly and earnestly striving to banish any grievance that the Irish people had against it, and was only waiting for the reciprocating hand-grip of friendship to see a lasting and enduring peace. Ireland, however, would not have it so.[56]

This is pretty predictable. Not so predictable is his criticism of the English people and their 'callous indifference'. If they had spoken up, he suggests, they may have, 'stopped an unhappy chapter in our history that must now be written'.

Secondly, the extent of anti-Irish racism in Scotland is often underestimated. In 1923 the Church of Scotland published its infamous, *The Menace of the Irish Race to the Scottish Nation.* Erskine stood up for the Irish community in Scotland by denouncing the Kirk's report as being motivated by 'bigotry and spite'. He called for Scots-Irish unity against common oppression. The Irishman in Scotland, he said, is, 'my country's ally and friend.'

Thirdly, recognition by Ireland allowed Erskine and Hugh MacDiarmid to attend the Irish version of the Olympic Games on 1st August 1924. Sport and a Celtic past were used as a propaganda tool for the regime that was emerging victorious from a bitter civil war.[57] The Celtic Queen, Tailté gave her name to the Games and led off the opening ceremony. In truth, Erskine's attendance was a fitting recognition of his contribution by the Free State and he was there as a guest of the Dáil.[58] He would have enjoyed the Celtic flavour as a newly independent country celebrated and the Scottish shinty team played the Irish hurling team.[59]

De Valera, Yeats, St John Gogarty and AE (or George Russell) all added to a star-studded line up that was enhanced by the future Tarzan actor, Johnny Weismuller who swam for the United States of America in the pond at Dublin Zoo.

However, some of the 12000 republicans who had been imprisoned during the years of civil war could not be there as they were still in prison.

Erskine's father: William Macnaghten Erskine, 5th Baron Erskine of Restormel Castle.

Above:

Morrison Davidson, a Socialist and Scottish Nationalist pioneer who pushed the boundaries of the Home Rule movement.

First edition of the *Whirlwind*, 'A Lively and Eccentric Newspaper.'

Left:

The co-editor of *The Whirlwind* and fellow Jacobite, Herbert Vivian

Above:

Before and after: the lively and eccentric young journalist changes image in *The Whirlwind*. Gone is the long, wavy hair and youthful look; in comes the dapper, man of 1890s Society.

Right

Stewart lineage: The first edition of the *Whirlwind* carried this genealogical table on page 2, Volume 1, number 2 (5/7/1890).

Erskine was looking forward to the claimant's birthday on 12th July: 'Mary, wife of Prince Louis of Bavaria who, but for the exclusion of Roman Catholics, would be Queen of England, born 1849.' (p. 29) Scottish readers may note the use of the English numerals for the Stewart kings.

THE following genealogical table is too little known in this country:—

JAMES I

CHARLES THE MARTYR — Elizabeth = Frederick, King of Bohemia (From this marriage the present occupant of the English throne is descended.)

CHARLES II — JAMES II — Henrietta = Philip, Duke of Orleans

JAMES III — Anne = Victor Amadeus II, King of Sardinia

CHARLES III — HENRY IX — Charles Emmanuel III, King of Sardinia

Victor Amadeus III

CHARLES IV — VICTOR EMANUEL I = Mary Theresa of Austria (King of Sardinia) (King of Sardinia)

MARY = Francis IV, Duke of Modena

FRANCIS (Duke of Modena) — Ferdinand

MARY = Louis of Bavaria (whom God preserve)

Left:

This print of Saint Columba's sojourn from Derry to Scotland captures the landing and emphasises the significance of Iona. It was also notable as the only print or graphic reproduced in 21 years of *Guth na Bliadhna*, appearing in Volume 2, number 2, 1905.

The title page of *Guth na Bliadhna* with its distinctive anthropomorphic figurehead

Below:

Celtic celebrity: photograph of Erskine from his profile in the *Celtic Review* of 1918-19. He would have been approaching his 50th birthday.

Guth Na Bliadhna.

LEABHAR XVII   AN SAMHRADH 1920   AIREAMH 2

CLEARING THE LAND

REPUBLICAN VICTORY

Above:

'The Complete Nationalist': William Gillies, also known as Liam Mac Gillie Iosa, co-founder of the Scots National League in both its incarnations and leading light of the *Liberty* group of radical Scottish nationalists.

Art O'Brien, or Art O'Briain, was the Irish republicans' man in London, heading up the Irish Self-Determination League of Great Britain. He was a fellow Celticist and political comrade of the London branch of the Scots National League. He was a backer of the Scots' own plans for a revolutionary organisation.

The prism of Ireland: Sinn Féin's historic general election victory of December 1918 is visually celebrated as a new political beginning for Ireland. Scottish nationalists, such as Erskine and Gillies looked on in awe.

The frontispiece of a limited-edition Gaelic play in pamphlet form, written by Erskine which was entitled, *Fo Chromadh an Taighe*. This was designed by Stewart Carmichael and appeared in the *Scottish Nation* of 4th December 1923.

The anarchist/ communist Journal *Liberty*.

Some Scotland's Day Speakers

R. Cunninghame Graham, MP

Mrs Marjory Kennedy-Fraser

The Hon. Ruaraidh Erskine of Marr

Scotland's Day: Scots National League and the Scottish Home Rule Association had been working closely in organising big demonstrations for Home Rule throughout the twenties primarily at Stirling and Elderslie. Speakers from the Independent Labour Party, including Tom Johnston, David Kirkwood and Neil Maclean, were regular attenders. This front-page advert from *Scottish Home Rule* pitches the ever-dapper Erskine with the equally dapper Cunninghame Graham and the popular Scottish singer, Marjory Kennedy-Fraser.

Left:

Scottish Democrat: William Diack was a key contributor to the *Scottish Review* taking the journal in a left-wing direction. A proud Aberdonian, tireless socialist and trade unionist activist and writer he forged links that helped build the notion of a Scottish Democracy which Erskine tapped into.

Promoting the Party 2: Roland Muirhead's election leaflet from West Renfrewshire in 1931. After years of being at the helm of the Scottish Home Rule Association and suffering the disappointment of failed Home Rule bills in the Westminster Parliament, Muirhead felt liberated at being able to support a Nationalist Party. His experience would soon lead to his own radicalisation; a radicalisation he would share in print with Erskine in the twilight of both their years.

Think First of Scotland !

R. E. MUIRHEAD

Vote Nationalist !

Above:

Lewis Spence was a former editor of the *Scotsman.* He was a member of the Scots National League before breaking away to form the Scottish National Movement. His own group contributed to the formation of the new National Party of Scotland in 1929 and he would become their first parliamentary candidate in the Midlothian by-election in 1929.

The big guns went out on a speaking tour across the country promoting the new nationalist Party. This advert is for the big rallies in the two main cities in late 1928. The first National Party candidate:

Separatist: a painting of Wendy Wood by David Foggie in 1932. This beautiful painting is another side of her which, as she conceded in her autobiography, *Yours Sincerely, for Scotland,* there were many. She is best known for her strident separatism and taking on the mantle of the Scots National League into the thirties and through to the late sixties with her Scottish Patriots. Not so well known is that she presented the popular children's programme, *Jackanory* on BBC.

John MacLean M. A.

The Marxist friend: John MacLean was of Highland descent and indeed called himself a Gael, though he was not a Gaelic speaker. Both MacLean and Erskine struck up a political friendship and MacLean was very supportive of his aristocratic friend's shift to the Left in the early 1920s.

The last known photograph: Erskine was interviewed by Derick Thomson for *Gairm* in 1956 aged 87. His Gaelic was rusty but the passion had never left him. Ireland, he said, was his inspiration. Scotland still came across as his heart.

Chapter Nine

The Scots National League

A dedicated nationalist organisation was central to the activities described in the previous two chapters. While there is no doubting the influence of Erskine's two publications, they were just that: publications. Erskine and Gillies came to see the advantages of organising a nationalist body and there was only one place to start and that was in the home of the exiles. The Scots National League (SNL) was born in London, formed and developed in London while, of course, dreaming of the homeland.

The League was re-formed in 1920. I will argue that it was primarily the same organisation that was formed in London in 1909 at Gillies' instigation. Many of the same faces were still there in 1920. The same core principles were enshrined. Critically, however, it remained a developing organisation; radical yet continually radicalising and increasingly, after the hiatus of War, providing a focus for Celtic solidarity and support for the struggle being waged in Ireland. These themes have interested those historians of Scottish nationalism who have delved into the League post 1920 especially in its role as a precursor to a National Party of Scotland. They were there from 1909.

The League initially went by its Gaelic name – Comunn nan Albannach. From its inception in 1909 it had a plan. There were cultural and political strands and these came together in a syllabus.[1] This syllabus informs us that the League had a base, a headquarters in Reform Hall, 4 Furnival Street, London. We also know the League's initial four objectives:

1. Recognition of Gaelic as the national language.
2. Home Rule (to at least the same extent as the self-governing Colonies).
3. Study and development of Scottish national literature, music, art and history.
4. Cultivating 'mutual friendship and assistance' with Wales and Ireland.

While it was still a Home Rule organisation, its scope and remit took it beyond the other nationalist organisations at that time.

Erskine did not hold any office initially. He was still officially based in Aberdeenshire. Gillies was the president and H C MacNeil was the Press Secretary. The two men who would keep the organisation going over the next few years were Kenneth MacKenzie and James Kennedy who were both office bearers. It was not an all-male affair and there appears to be a bit of gender balance on the Committee which had strengthened by 1912.

The syllabus itself opened on 6th October 1909 with a talk by Gillies on 'History and its Lessons.' A very strong line up followed that included the future Irish republican envoy to the Paris talks, Gavan Duffy; MacNeil on the 'Highland–Lowland Bogey' (with illustrations too!); Hugh Paterson gave a lecture in Gaelic on 'Sinn Féin a-mhàin.' The playwright Donald Campbell gave a futuristic talk on 'Scotland in 2001' which he had also delivered in Belfast. Erskine's slot was there but not yet firmed up. There were also 'inter debates' lined up with the pro-Liberal, Young Scots Society and the Gaelic Society of London. The syllabus was fresh and combative and appealing to an exile community.

With 'Home Rule all round' in the air, the League were looking forward to the 'Election to the Scots Parliament session of 1912' and had a meeting on 8th December 1909 to discuss proposed candidates. Again, the list tells us so much about the make-up of this nascent nationalist body:

Separatist – Dòmhnull Caimbeul (Campbell).
Humanitarian and anti-Suffragette – F. Baile Mead
Honourable Trade Protectionist – Seumas Ceannadaidh (Kennedy).
Crofter Candidate – Ragnall MacAonghais.
Provost – Liam Mac Gille Iosa.[2]

Even at this early stage the League fancied itself as a Scottish Sinn Féin. It is also slightly amusing that such a reactionary stance on the issue of female suffrage is given a humanitarian twist! I have been unable to fathom the identity of F Baile Meadhon.

This political line was galvanised in 1910 by the publication of the League's manifesto. This was in two parts. The first part was in Gaelic – 'Brosnachadh do na Gàidheal', or 'Rallying the Gael'. The aim of the first part was to shed light on the state of Scotland at this time and the appeal was to all Scots and Gaels, men and women to rally for the Home Rule Bill not just for its own sake but for truth and justice too;

a theme that is continued in the second part which is in English. 'A Manifesto to the Scottish People' which, as we have seen, Erskine had promoted in Gaelic in *Guth na Bliadhna*. Scotland's social ills are listed from urban overcrowding, infant mortality, housing and the 'demon drink'. 'But we are powerless'.[3]

Slogans are cleverly woven into the document in bold. Although Home Rule is the aim, pro-Imperial Home Rulers are put in their place. There is no national pride to be taken in providing Scottish Prime Ministers of England, Archbishops of Canterbury, famous soldiers or even royal gardeners. There is no place for unionist nationalism: 'A country which cannot pass into law measures approved by its own representatives is not a free and unconquered country'.[4]

This is in complete contrast to the majority Home Rule movement who prided themselves on Scotland's contribution to Empire. For the London exiles, Scotland was not, is not British. Erskine and Gillies' stamp is all over the document.

Of course, this is not a party-political manifesto. It is simple and to the point. 'Look away from Vienna' was the call from Ferenc Deák to the Hungarian people. So too the League looked to Scotland to solve her own ills. Language would be at the heart as it was in Hungary, Ireland, Norway and Greece. The national language would be reintroduced in schools, universities, chambers of commerce and 'centres of law'. This would create a Scottish Scotland. Self-government would be self-generating with an emphasis on agitation at home and 'national self-reliance.' It was a nod to Griffith's elevation of Sinn Féin as principle and tactic applied to Scotland: 'Any further appeal for land reform to a parliament composed largely of landlords and sporting people is mere folly.'[5]

This anti-parliamentarianism, or to be more precise, anti-Westminsterism was a constant feature of the politics of the Scots National League and this is why I believe that the same organisation with the same name was re-vamped in 1920. The cause was Home Rule and a Scots parliament but the language was separatist. The manifesto finishes by stating that implementation of the Manifesto will see Scotland become 'A Nation Once Again'. That is the beating heart of the document. Home Rule was as far as they could go at that time and they paid lip service to it.

Gillies took more of a back seat from the organisation but we know that it continued until the War; certainly to 1913. The League proclaimed that it was hosting the 'First Bi-lingual Concert' at New Year 1912 and a programme for this event survives in the National Library in Edinburgh. This concert was held in Baker Street, in the

Portman Rooms on 6th January 1912. This concert was not out to replace the annual all Gaelic concert. Its programme was pretty staid with pipers, sword dancers from Lochaber and songs finishing with the communal singing of Burns's *Auld Lang Syne* and the Gaelic standard, *Togaibh I, Togaibh I, cànain ar dùthcha.*

The point lies not in the rather conservative entertainment. Rather, it is that in 1912 there was a self-perpetuating organisation in London running weekly Gaelic classes and a Gaelic choir and a syllabus of talks planned on topics such as Fletcher of Saltoun, bi-lingual education and 'Gaelic & Nationality'. MacKenzie and Kennedy were the driving forces and the politics were just as sharp. Their object was, 'Scotland free, Scotland sovereign, Scotland a nation once again'. Gaelic as a political weapon was stressed in the programme's introduction: 'The Gaelic Movement is the resumption of the struggle against uniformity of language under the British Crown'.[6]

This radical nationalist organisation was limited geographically to the political exiles of London. Exile would also resurrect it in 1920 but only partly. It was new wine in a preserved, nice old bottle. It just may have tasted and looked the same as the old wine! War had created a hiatus for the League and, as we have seen, Erskine was pivotal in formulating a nationalist response. He had stimulated a Scottish democracy, raised this in support of Scottish representation at the Paris peace conference and helped build a Highland Land League to run in tandem with the rising support for Scottish self-determination within the Labour movement. The time would be right to resurrect the League. As we have also seen, in London, Art O'Brien was building the Gaelic League as a political front for Irish republican activity which proved a welcoming home for exiled Scottish nationalists.

It was thoroughly fitting that the Scots National League should be resurrected and resurrected at home. It was also fitting that one eye to the past should give the impetus to building their progressive movement. That eye was turned to a commemoration of the declaration of Scottish independence at Arbroath exactly 600 years before. Scottish history had always been a key cultural dynamic in the educational activities of the nationalist radicals. The 600th anniversary of Bernard de Linton's famous letter to the Pope proclaiming Scotland's freedom was a tailor-made opportunity to bring the League home. There had been a safe, conventional commemoration earlier in the year by the town council led by the Lord Provost. The SNL's local branch organised a 'monster meeting' at Brothock Bridge in September to protest against this 'sham'.[7] No numbers are cited and the location was chosen as they did not get permission to be near the famous Abbey itself.

Erskine had to give his apologies. He was due to speak but took ill and was confined to home. His activity and powers of persuasion had pulled off the coup of having the leading Marxist in the British Isles chair the meeting. According to the reporter in *Liberty*, MacLean made some 'caustic comments' about the fact that Scottish freedom was being celebrated but they did not have the freedom to be in Arbroath itself. MacLean probably thought that it was Glasgow humour. He was very complimentary toward *Liberty* and its editor, John MacArthur, who was teaching 'true Scots history' and not the 'false and perverted variety taught in the school books'.[8]

This was a nice introduction for MacArthur who gave apologies for Erskine's absence and spoke on the theme of how 'the work of 1320 was undone in 1707' and moved a unanimous motion for the restoration of Scottish independence and was followed by Alex Ross from the local branch who 'entertained' the crowd with 'tit bits from the history of the area and its local land grabbers'.[9] Not surprisingly, the meeting was hailed as a success.

Success or otherwise, the League had come home – reaching out to fellow travellers like MacLean and giving a stimulus to further expansion in Scotland itself. Indeed, the same report announced that there were branch secretaries in place and they were called on to take advantage of speakers and prepare the ground for the next Spring. The League would soon open an office in Edinburgh.

It is fair to say that this was not the re-launch of the League as preparatory work had been done to make this happen. Erskine was hailed as president of the League at the Arbroath meeting. After this mass meeting, the London branch met to elect Angus MacDonald of the Highland Land League as its president. There is little requirement to spell out the left leaning credentials of the Scots National League. The Clydeside Labour MP, Neil MacLean, joined along with his namesake from Pollokshaws. Bob Smillie was also in there and the Irish socialist leader, Cathal O'Shannon spoke at the official launch of the London Branch on 26th February 1921.[10] O'Shannon emphasised his Ulster Scots credentials and Erskine chaired the meeting under the heading, The Blue Banner of Scotland is raised again! Erskine reiterated the continuity back to the 'largely and influentially signed protest' as leading to an awakening of national feeling. He was right. Thanks to his dynamism – though not solely his – the League was a bridge between past efforts to build a nationalist organisation in London and future efforts to build a credible nationalist party in Scotland. The continuity was there in the speakers – Calder, Hector Munro, MacArthur and Sinclair. As MacArthur put it, they were taking a stand with the 'Scottish democracy of 1707'.

What he also could have said is that this was because they *were* the Scottish democracy of 1920. Burns' anthem, *Scots Wha Hae*, was being adopted as the national anthem with all its revolutionary connotations and connections. The glue that held the League together was the periodical, *Liberty*.

This newspaper started life as *Liberty: the Scottish Home Rule Journal* and to have read the publication from January to March 1920, it would have felt in many ways like reading Tom Johnston's *Forward*. To explain this is to pay tribute to the fact that *Forward* and the Independent Labour Party in general were aware of Scottish working-class history. The conclusions drawn, however, were British conclusions. Political change through an all British Labour Party would give Scotland home rule and – in that logic - was the demand of Scottish radical protest. Liberty, in its early days, did not deviate too much from this. This was the influence of the SHRA. Prominent home rulers, including the soon to be Labour MP, the Reverent J Stuart Barr wrote on 'Famous Scots' and took Fletcher of Saltoun, Bruce and Wallace in a libertarian, socialist direction. A good example of this was his assertion that Wallace, 'paved the way for a democratic principle in government'.[11] This, of course, made patriotic heroes such as Wallace safe for reformers and home rulers.

Erskine, Gillies and their group had other ideas. They had MacArthur's ear and their sweet words of nationalism must have had an influence. In April 1920 the masthead changed. *Liberty: the Scottish National Journal* put a different slant on things. The strap line, as we have observed was even more powerful in its juxtaposition of nationalism and internationalism.

Erskine's group began a systematic takeover of the journal that was quite remarkable; a takeover that facilitated the changes that would see it surpass the radicalism of the *Scottish Review* and probably beat it for passion also. *Liberty* became an avowedly nationalist journal which lived up to its internationalist and left-wing pretensions. There were still the old ingredients: Scottish history, the national language, Ireland and the demand for independence. Added in to the mix were some new ones as well.

Republicanism ran through the journal; a Scottish republicanism. There just seemed to be an assumption among many of the writers that an independent Scotland would be a republic. I can't point to a single article entitled, 'The Case for a Scottish Republic' because it is not there. What you will find are many phrases such as 'the Scottish Republic of the future', 'when Scotland becomes a republic… ' and such like. Mac Gille Iosa, MacGaraidh and MacNeacail were in the vanguard in arguing for a republic. Erskine, though no republican at heart, was swept along in the moment as he had every right to be. MacNeacail summarised it succinctly for the *Liberty* group in January 1921 when he argued that the Scottish republic must be, 'imbued with Celtic culture'.[12]

This republicanism fed into the other new ingredient; namely, their presentation of Scottish history. The late Jim Young defined this as a 'left nationalist historiography'.[13] Before *Liberty,* Scottish nationalists were comfortable with pre-Union history: the story of Wallace and Bruce, the Reformation and the Covenanters. This new breed of nationalist wanted to explore the hidden history of a radical, working class nationalism in the response to the emerging British State after 1707. Not only did this lead to a fresh look at Charlie and the '45; it also led to an exploration of radical unrest in the country in the 1790s, the United Scotsmen, the radical rising in Scotland in 1820 and Chartism. William Gillies was at the heart of this with some pioneering articles that challenged the old assumptions of the British left that Scottish radical responses were part of a wider British response and in matter of fact whose identity was subsumed in the general British response so much so that Scots knew more about Peterloo and the Tolpuddle Martyrs than they did about the events in the west of Scotland in 1820.

One of Gillies' articles clearly stands out. 'How the Republic went down' looked at the happenings towards the end of 1793 and the hysterical reaction of the British State to demands for reform. Leaders such as Thomas Muir were on the hulks in chains and spies were crawling all over the movement. Gillies takes up the story:

Such was the position, when on a dark December night, the Council of the Republic met for the last time until we Scots get busy again and call it into existence once more. Picture the scene, then, as the Sheriff and his train of officials, with the servile and ignorant fencibles in the background approach the meeting of those who in those dark days stood for what LIBERTY now upholds – the freedom of Scotland. Up the close they go with a rush. The wynd and adjacent street are well guarded and English law and order bursts in upon the Cabinet maker's workshop where the Council is assembled… The Scottish Republic is dead! Long live the Scottish Republic that is to be!'[14]

The narrative is striking. Be it good history or bad, the point is that Gillies is adopting a republican line on Scottish history which set out the first tentative steps to exploring what can be called the Scottish radical tradition – as distinct from that tradition south of the border. There has been much written and debated about the existence of this tradition which is tribute to Gillies' argument. It also had an influence, in time, in England. When the Marxist historian, Edward Thompson, wrote his seminal study of the English working class in the 1960's he emphasised that Scottish Jacobin activity was 'more intense and more heroic. But the Scottish story', he added, 'is significantly different'.[15]

In short, the Scots National League activists, minimal in number in the extreme, were hugely influential in forging a radical, at times revolutionary, cultural nationalism. While this cultural nationalism was Celtic with the Gaelic language at its heart, it was certainly not ethnic. The SNL group were republicans and internationalists too. Erskine played his part in this. From late 1920 he started to muse on the bigger issues facing Scotland and the world. In a lovely and descriptive article on the new world that could emerge, Erskine wrote: '…there can be no true New world for us to inhabit, unless our hearts are made the first scene of the vital change on which mankind desires to enter.'[16]

A month later Marr was arguing that peace and harmony between Scotland and England were essential and commerce and prosperity would follow.[17] Marr, in common with the rest of the group, saw a distinction between England and English imperialism. He wrote a series of articles on 'The British Superstition' which was critical of the Bannockburn 'borestone patriots' and those who confuse England with Britain. This was important to maintain a Scottish distinctiveness. However, after working so hard to establish a National Committee and to engage with politically minded Scots on Ireland, it was right that his sights were more global. The response of the victorious powers at Versailles to their own national minorities exposed their imperialism and it was this ideology that was holding back the world. In reply to the South Lanarkshire Unionist MP, Captain Walter Elliott, who had dismissed Scottish nationalism as a form of regionalism and who seemed to be taking an international higher ground, Erskine of Marr came out with a fine piece of internationalism:

But until national frontiers shall be entirely obliterated, race abolished, nationality prohibited, national culture proscribed and lastly, but by no means least, some common language evolved which shall take the place of the existing national tongues, the fool is not the man who wishes to restore her independence to Scotland but such as captain Walter Elliott, Imperialist and Capitalist MP.[18]

The SNL were engaged in an ideological offensive for Scotland but they did not lose sight of the big picture. Internationalism did not lie in the creation of an international monolith; a world state. Internationalism was in diversity and culture and until a genuine breaking down of the barriers among common humanity occurred, a difference of equals with genuine self-determination for all peoples would pave the way to a new world. While Erskine would become disillusioned with the Bolsheviks' notion of instant internationalism by spreading revolution, I don't believe that he lost his own sense of the world and its commonality.

Liberty can also boast, if that is the right word, to be the only nationalist/republican journal to give its support to a football team: Glasgow Rangers! It is quite remarkable to see the journal which promoted solidarity with the Irish revolution carrying a full team picture of the league championship winning Rangers team for season 1919-20.[19] The reason was the editor, John MacArthur, who was a big Rangers fan and who sold the paper outside Ibrox Park at Rangers' home games. His support for his team spilled over into immaturity, as it does with most football fans, when Rangers were knocked out of the Cup by a smaller team early in the next season which led to an editorial calling for the expulsion of smaller teams from the competition! It is doubtful if this was a party line within the Scots National League.

Socialists had long held to a motto: 'Educate! Agitate! Organise!' There could be no doubting the League's propagandist qualities as a small group on the fringe of politics with big messages and lots of activity on Ireland, the language and even attempts to set up some extracurricular, revolutionary body. Organisation would be a different matter. Erskine, for his part, was certainly no organiser. He was the joint President and figurehead; joint president with Neil MacLean, MP.[20] The chairman, Hugh Paterson, was a Gaelic actor and long-time collaborator with Marr. Gillies was the heartbeat of the organisation. They could count on Hugh MacDiarmid, then resident in Montrose, John MacLean and Robert Smillie as members. The great and the good can only get you so far and indeed the left-wing fellow travellers were intermittent activists albeit useful members to have.

As we have seen, premises were acquired in the capital city. Branches grew up in all the main cities and the big Arbroath rally had been a spark for recruitment. The playwright, Donald Sinclair, had formed a branch in Manchester. League activities made the press on both sides of the border. No less than the *Liverpool Evening Express* reported on a fall out between Erskine and Neil MacLean as they did not see 'eye to eye' on points of policy leading to MacLean's resignation as joint president.[21] Various newspapers were reporting on Erskine's speeches to various branches. Erskine played a pivotal role in enhancing recruitment. Always eloquent, listenable and had a real pulling power.

His mood though could vary. He delivered a quite melancholic president's address to the London Branch in January 1922. While empires had crumbled and the Peace Conference had concluded, neither Ireland nor Scotland were in a good place. Ireland was 'seething discontent' within the British empire and Scotland's 'tragic census figures pointed to a 'depopulated countryside and a decaying national language'.[22] He had no uplifting response to these things. Yet, the same President delivered an 'impassioned speech' (according to the *Daily Record*) later in the year arguing that anyone who accepted anything less than independence was a 'slave and truckler to England'.[23] This was on the occasion of the League's national convention in Edinburgh on the anniversary of the battle of Bannockburn. It was in this same speech he relayed his acquaintance with Charles Stewart Parnell.

This was a year of focus on growth. As president, Erskine took it upon himself to take the lead. He wrote a promotional article in the *New Witness* arguing that the League was open to all men and women who believe in independence and who want the nation's institutions to be democratic and 'distinctively Scottish'. In what would become a classic nationalist position, political issues of left and right such as the monarchy, the Commonwealth and Anglo-Scottish relations (Erskine's examples) will be decided post-independence.[24] If we substitute the word 'independence' for 'home rule' then it would probably be fair to say that Muirhead and the Scottish Home Rule Association had a similar position. The difference, and it was a major one, lay in the fact that Muirhead's body would move and shake with the main British political parties to achieve their objective of a Scottish Parliament. The SNL would have no truck with the 'imperialist' parties and only the Scottish people could obtain the real prize that would not be won through the parliamentary gift of the House of Commons.

This fundamentalist position asserted itself as the General Election November 1922 approached. Erskine addressed the London Branch of the League in October. 'The feeble beans of a General Election were not going to pierce the dense clouds of popular apathy', he proclaimed. This political apathy was the League's opportunity. He believed that hearts and minds in Scotland were turning away from Westminster.[25] The Scots National League got actively inactive over this election campaign. Activists took to the streets handing out an election leaflet that was signed by Erskine and MacArthur. The League had no intention of fielding candidates and advised Scottish voters:

1. Abstain from voting.
2. Hold a national convention.
3. The Sovereign Scottish People take control of the public affairs of the country. These are the League's alternatives. Fellow countrymen and countrywomen choose them in place of Westminster and further impoverishment and National extinction. God Save Scotland!'[26]

An election manifesto was also published. Pounds, shillings and pence were placed on Scotland's subjection. £119,753,000 was taken out of Scotland in 1921 and England kept £96,657,000 for imperial purposes. This was greater than the national revenue of Japan and was the result of 'the pretended Union of 1707'. The message was to abstain from voting and form a national convention that could go to the League of Nations with Scotland's cause where, 'Scotland's indefeasible right to national independence shall be re-affirmed and re-established'.[27]

There is a nationalist logic to this position. The problem lay in the fact that there were no candidates; no faces to articulate this position for the voters in Scotland. Sinn Féin had declared in the 1918 election that they would not go to Westminster but put up candidates that would, and did, form an alternative national parliament on home soil. And, of course, the Irish situation was radically different in 1918. The other drawback for the League's intervention was the growth of class politics in the central belt of the country. The Labour Party were gaining ground and this election would see Clydeside, and Fife too, go red on the political map. These newly elected MPs gave hope to Scotland's working-class heartlands that they could deliver social change. Abstention from voting was never on the cards. Still, some publicity accrued and the banner of radical nationalism was raised in Scotland! The *Dundee Courier* naughtily called Erskine, 'the staunchest

Little Scotlander alive'.[28]

And yet over 1923 and 1924 the League and the SHRA came a little bit closer together. The *Standard* had folded at the end of 1922 and the following year was one of consolidation for the League. They could not operate in isolation. The Clydeside group of Labour MPs were preparing a home rule bill with Muirhead's support. With home rule on the agenda, again, the fundamentalists in the League had to engage and the vehicle was MacDiarmid's short-lived paper, *The Scottish Nation*. It was through this journal that Lewis Spence rose to prominence. Spence was five years the junior of Erskine and hailed from Monifeith in Angus and who had a career in journalism including a spell as editor of the *Scotsman*. His line was that the League was cross party and therefore had 'no politics'.[29]

Spence did, however, throw down the gauntlet to the SHRA as they got too cosy with the 'Westminster club':

> The Home Rulers are all too aware that they stand before a locked door. They may knock as long as they please, but it will never be opened to them. From that door the Scots National League turns away. It seeks to build a house of its own; on the portals of which it will have no need to knock. And it asks the Home Rulers and all who truly love their native land to help in the building of that house.[30]

Erskine of Marr was a bit more conciliatory. He became a borestone patriot for the evening and was the principal speaker at the annual rally in 1923. He took on the claim that the Scots were apathetic on the question of home rule. These claims were unfounded and he understood that the SHRA had been told this too. He called for the Scottish people to be given a 'respectable opportunity' to prove that it was not true.[31] He did not articulate what this opportunity should be but it does sound suspiciously like a referendum.

This was a big rally which was also addressed by David Kirkwood, MP. The socialist parliamentarians were regular attenders at nationalist rallies. Maxton addressed the Wallace day rally at Elderslie in August and a total of ten MPs marched in a massive rally of 30000 in Glasgow organised by the SHRA.[32] These MPs were genuine in their commitment and it is to Erskine's credit that he did not come across as the political sectarian.

His own speech came on the back of the League's second annual convention in their 'commodious HQ' in George Street, Edinburgh. Erskine was in the chair and hailed by Spence as, 'our noble and popular president'.[33] He was at the height of his popularity within the League and he was still their undisputed leader. It was Erskine who summed up the mood of nationalism at this time with a real spirituality and passion. Scotland's soul was at stake. It was not dead but was under a 'dark cloud.'. For there to be a re-awakening among working class Scots then nationalism must precede internationalism. Marr argued that he could see this with the 'more nationally minded' Scottish Labour MPs who were showing 'disgust and contempt' for the English House of Commons and this was hand in hand with a growing awareness that there can be no social or economic progress while there is Union: 'I apprehend that it will not be long before the clouds that presently obscure the soul of our people are rolled away, and the sun of Scotland, a nation, rises high once again in the firmament of the comity of free peoples.'[34]

Erskine used the year to write a one-act Gaelic play entitled *Fo Chromadh An Taighe*. MacDiarmid used his paper to heavily advertise its publication as a limited-edition pamphlet although little is known about its premiere or if it toured. We do know that his activism on the language did not falter. *Guth na Bliadhna* was still going strong as it would do until 1925 and his focus for the language was on the youth of the Gaidhealtachd and on education. His unwavering commitment to the language had saw the resurrection of *Alba* for a short period in 1921 and to some creative Gaelic writing in *An Ròsarnach*.

While Erskine was distracted things were changing within the League. Lewis Spence was not the only new name to appear. In 1924, Tom Gibson joined. Gibson came from Dennistoun in the east end of Glasgow and had previously been a member of the Young Scots and the SHRA. Richard Finlay relates the circumstances of his conversion and linking up with the League.[35] Gibson had been unhappy with Muirhead's links with and personal leaning to the Labour Party. The old bilateral approach between Labour and Liberals in their support for Home Rule seemed to have gone. The final straw was when there was a collection for Agnes MacLean, John's widow who was in real financial penury, on the premises of the Association in Glasgow. Gibson left in disgust and joined the League because they were uncompromising in their nationalism. Obviously, Gibson was unaware that MacLean had also been a member of the League and that the London branch had sent a nice obituary letter to Agnes after he died in November 1923.[36]

Finlay is right to focus on Gibson as a key figure in transforming the League. Much as he liked the League's fundamentalism, he could see that they were disorganised. The League had grown but would never go anywhere with no programme or organisation. As a 'tireless and in many ways ruthless operator'. Gibson set about restructuring the League and its Celtic idealism was definitely in his sights as a barrier to progress among the people. Naturally the Celtic idealists themselves would have to go and this would radically alter the relationship between Erskine and Gillies with the League. Two things stand out. First of all, Gibson engaged combatively with Muirhead on the SHRA's position on the Reverent Barr's Home Rule Bill as it was debated in Parliament in 1924. The correspondence itself is not of importance but the wedge it would drive between Erskine and Gibson is highly significant. Muirhead's old head succinctly summarised the need for unity: '…Scots men and women have been too sticking about points of agreement and differences with regard to policy, and that is one of the chief reasons that Scotland is still without self-government.' [37]

The inference, as Erskine had himself argued in terms of the League's stance, was to debate and discuss after the Bill had been enacted. The younger head of Gibson disagreed and took the harder line. His Glasgow Area branch of the League passed a motion of no confidence in Erskine after he spoke at the SHRA's Wallace day event at Robroyston in Glasgow. The League's President was accused of collaborating with Muirhead's's group who were clearly in bed with the 'Westminster club.' Although this motion did not have any immediate impact on Erskine's position within the League, it was certainly a serious blow to his political credibility and it set in chain, a series of events that would lead to the 'move upstairs' when Gillies and Erskine were made honorary presidents in 1926.[38]

Secondly, Gibson was instrumental in passing a five-point programme for the League at their convention in January 1925. Prior to his involvement there was no inclination to formulate a programme. The League, in its post 1920 incarnation, held to an amalgam of ideas that were separatist, Celtic and republican. The closest that they had come to articulating a line came in the Manifesto of October 1922. This position was strengthened at the SNL's half-yearly conference in Edinburgh in June.[39] The League agreed that they should use the existing political machinery to put up candidates who would remain on Scottish soil to 'resume the powers of government in Scotland.'

This had Gibson's stamp all over it. While Gibson agreed with an abstentionist line in terms of Scottish MPs withdrawing from Westminster, he did not agree that voters should abstain from voting.

Therefore, the League's position had to change meaning that the Scottish electorate should have a Nationalist candidate to vote for. The 5 points agreed by the League supplemented by the motion passed in June brought in a touch of pragmatism. Just a touch. Independence is not mentioned. The 'inalienable right' to be recognised as a 'distinct nation' with the Scots people having the 'sole right' to choose the scheme of self-government. The League, in a sideswipe at the SHRA, repudiates any scheme submitted to the English Parliament for Home Rule. The last three points focussed on relationships with England, with the Commonwealth and with the wider family of nations of the world. Again, it was for Scotland to decide the nature of these relationships.[40] In truth, they are rather dull and are a portent for the direction that the League would gravitate to: namely, the formation of a political party of nationalism.

It is this author's belief that no incarnation of these political parties – neither the National Party of Scotland as formed in 1928 nor the modern SNP – can match the Scots National League for its radicalism, its passion and its internationalist nationalism in the League's heyday. It was the logical extension of Erskine's Scottish democracy applied to a world in flux after the War. It would be easy to focus on the Celticism and the cultural nationalism but they were channelled in positive directions in support of the Irish cause and language revival. The demise of the League would see the more reactionary side of the cultural movement as it went into retreat.

The Irish labour leader, Jim Larkin, published an obituary to John MacLean and from the perspective in Dublin of the anonymous author in December 1923, he saw 'Erskine of Marr's Scots National League' as a 'Gaelic proletarian movement'.[41] While it is important not to get carried away by hyperbole or exaggeration, the point is that Erskine's group, like MacLean's group of Scottish republicans, were a counterpoint to a British perspective on revolution or radicalism. They were distinctive and radical and Scottish and more progressive nationalists than what came later.

The League's story would continue for another couple of years but a massive change was coming due to this gravitation towards a Party. Ruaraidh Erskine of Marr would soon find himself at a crossroads that was not all of his own choosing.

Chapter Ten

Drifting Away

Sometime in 1925, Erskine discovered a science. He called it Bordology or 'table-lore' and he claimed to, 'have discovered an infallible means of determining human characteristics'.[1] It almost lures you in until you discover it is, in Marr's own words, 'simple': just sit opposite a person and look at what they eat and drink. Simple. He elaborated on this argument with plenty of words and no substance to such a degree that the best that can be said is that he had his tongue very much in his cheek.

The significance lies not in this little, insignificant, forgettable pamphlet; rather, in the fact that it was written as a London society article, originally appearing in the *Evening Standard* at a time when there was a battle to be fought within the Scots National League. It feels like a retreat away from politics. In some ways it was exactly that, albeit a very partial retreat. It was certainly the early signs of a disengagement. It was the start of his slow drift away.

In isolation it could be dismissed as a bit of fun. However, in 1925 Erskine was back on the society circuit speaking at clan Erskine events with his big brother. At a dinner in South Shields, the local newspaper commended his talk on clan Erskine in particular and the clans in general.[2] He too was gravitating back to his own roots but not fully because he was still the honorary president of the League. Indeed, perhaps this was the reason: the lack of any active role within the League. Boredom was the result of a move upstairs and he sought to fill his own personal intellectual void.

It should be remembered that it was only partial. He was still in the nationalist fold. Hugh MacDiarmid, in his real persona of C M Grieve, paid him a fine tribute in the *Scottish Educational Journal* on a personal and political level praising his contribution to Gaelic arts and literature and to Scottish nationalism. Grieve identifies *Guth na Bliadhna* and the *Scottish Review* specifically hailing Erskine as, 'one of the most remarkable personalities in modern Scottish history' with 'a great charm and fineness of character'.[3] For all of Erskine's eccentricity, I believe that Grieve was absolutely right. It was more than a nice tribute and really summed up Erskine's contribution over the last twenty years. The feedback was genuinely given and would hail a collaboration in the not too distant future; genuine also because the two men disagreed on the Doric or Scots language. Erskine saw Scots as a distraction from the 'first principles in politics and art and literature'[4] which lay in Gaelic.

Erskine certainly used the headspace which the pending move upstairs in the League had given him by developing some ideas in Grieve's journal. The letters pages redounded with a debate between Erskine and the scholar, Donald A MacKenzie on the Gaelic language. Language activism, said Erskine, had opened the schools to Gaelic.[5] MacKenzie called Erskine a 'dilettante'.[6]

These letters and articles took Erskine into new territory. For example, he pondered de-centralisation: '...the day of the single national parliament is over...(the future of mankind rests on) regionalistic councils as a means to tackle and solve the many complex social questions by which modern society is everywhere faced.'[7] Erskine was still part of the Scottish democracy and William Diack would have been proud.

1925 also saw the demise of *Guth na Bliadhna.* The journal had been struggling financially for some time but had managed to keep going, incredibly, since 1904 which puts Donald MacKenzie's jibe into perspective. For the last three years it had been a solely Gaelic journal and its demise would leave a hole in the field of Gaelic journalism and literature. Erskine himself would try to fill that hole with other ventures but nothing like the same impact.

It is fair to say that 1925 was a watershed for both the League and for Erskine himself. The League was certainly setting out on a journey of political activism, in the style if not the output of the main British parties and this political activism was in marked contrast to the political-cultural activity that the League had been accustomed to. Gibson was of the opinion that talks and lectures had their place but would not win the hearts and minds of the Scottish people. The five points were the starting point for Gibson in this process with the end point being the creation of a Party at some point in the not too distant future. This probably – more than probably - would not have happened under the leadership of Erskine and Gillies.

These things are always a transition. The talks and lectures did not stop. In many ways, they kept Erskine and Gillies busy while Gibson and Gillies' son, Eoin, set about modernising the League. Art O'Brien was invited over to deliver a lecture in Edinburgh on 'The Political and Cultural Relations of Scotland and Ireland'. The theme was not new: the two countries should still be 'shoulder to shoulder' against a common, 'merciless' enemy. Gaelic laws and customs may help to shape the world as the world needed new ideas.[8]

Ireland was still important to the League and Gibson was shrewd enough to see the benefit of maintaining links with the Irish community in Scotland and also astute enough to see the uses of Erskine in reaching out to that community. A series of letters between Erskine and Gibson throughout early 1926 show that there was a meeting of minds of both men on the subject. Gibson was looking for Erskine's help in building the League in the west of Scotland. Erskine had helped to get a couple of speakers – Gibson and Malcolm MacColl – to a Republican event in the St. Mungo's halls in February. MacColl had made an impression with his talk on James Connolly and Nationalism.

This resulted in an invitation from Sinn Féin's Scottish Committee to MacColl to speak at the tenth anniversary Easter Week concert in St Mary's Halls, Glasgow chaired and addressed by Father O'Flanagan, the left-leaning Republican priest who had travelled over from Ireland for the event. Gibson and Erskine also received tickets for the event although Erskine could not attend. Erskine did write to say that he had read the report of the event in the Daily Record and was glad the League was represented at the, 'recent Sinn Féin, or rather Republican meeting'.[9] Again, echoing the old arguments used by O'Brien in his lecture he went on to suggest that the League should have a representative in Dublin. Gibson, in a cordial reply, said that the Reverend Father, 'made an appeal to the audience to support us in every way they could'.[10] Certainly, the Reverend Father invoked the memory of William Wallace as inspiration for his Scots-Irish audience:

> I suppose that the greatest man in the history of Scotland is not Andrew Carnegie but William Wallace. Yet from the point of view of temporal success I suppose Andrew Carnegie was the most successful of Scotsmen, but the name of Carnegie will never thrill the blood of Scotland as does the name of Wallace. William Wallace from the practical view of the practical men of his time was just another foolish man like Robert Emmet or Padraig Pearse…It is not by such rules that the world of future generations will judge the actions of men.[11]

Gibson concluded his report on the commemoration by asking

Erskine for support specifically in Paisley, Clydebank and Airdrie.

Nominally, this correspondence suggests that the political relationship between the two men was fine and had not been hampered by the vote of no confidence alluded to above. Certainly, there is no hint of any personal animosity at all in any of their correspondence. Yet the political cracks were emerging. Erskine was passionate in his belief in building as many branches as possible and in increasing the League's membership throughout Scotland. He saw this as his prime role and offered his services to Gibson to do this.[12] This was an organic, evolutionary approach to League expansion while Gibson's was more revolutionary. He wanted the Scots National League to field candidates at elections and had used a committee meeting to push this through. Erskine did not say that he was against fighting elections as a principle but believed that organic growth of the League would see this become 'practical politics' as opposed to the ideas that emerge from an 'academic strata'.[13] He objected to a strata/committee railroading this through. It should have been discussed at the conference.

If this was his first throw of the dice against the direction of the League, his second throw was revealed in his letter to Gibson quoted above. His insistence on the distinction between a Sinn Féin and a Republican meeting is the most revealing about where his political head was still at – in the past. He must have been the only person in the whole of the British Isles who could still see such a distinction. Sinn Féin were an avowedly Republican organisation and had been since 1917. Marr still saw the 1904 incarnation of Griffiths and this still dictated his politics. Debates about republics and monarchies could wait until after independence. Ourselves alone meant just that and non-participation in the Imperial parliament was an absolute point of principle to him. This non-republican, old style Scottish Sinn Féiner was laying down a marker. He stood at this marker and watched as the League moved on and he was left behind.

The League developed a new newspaper, the *Scots Independent* as a monthly 'organ of Scots Nationality.' Erskine, again out of step, didn't care much for the name. He saw it as a 'mouthful' preferring instead 'The Scot' or the 'True Scot'.[14] To be fair, Erskine was practicing what he preached as he was based still in Aboyne and building the Aberdeen branch putting his hopes on a young Mr. Baird as a potential rising star.[15] He also ensured that, for all his reservations, he was doing his bit to promote the new paper and had 50 copies despatched at his own expense to the London branch.[16] When back in London in October he wrote to Gibson wishing the *Scots Independent* well and suggesting a concerted campaign in a different town to raise the profile of the paper.[17]

For all of his positive and well-meant words, he was on a process of drifting away. He was now the honorary president and was well into the process of looking backward. Most of his energy was directed to working on a book on MacBeth and he was battling with his health at this time through the recurring problem of his chest.

The *Scots Independent* originally bore a strong resemblance to *Liberty/The Standard*. By flicking through the issues, it soon becomes apparent that Erskine was not so regular a contributor. The few pieces that he did contribute were mostly of a historical nature; to combat England's use of 'historical perversion'.[18] One opportunity to be contemporary was spurned. In a piece on 'The League and Its Journal',[19] Erskine called on all activists to find new ways to propagate the League's work but did not specify any of his own. It was a half-hearted piece that lacked his usual eloquence and would have inspired no one. His heart did not seem in it any more.

Yet the League was still on-side with his abstentionist message at this stage. Roland Muirhead attempted to form a National Convention to bring the disparate nationalist groups together in late 1926. Muirhead was already thinking about a National Party. This Convention convened in Glasgow on 30th October with Dr James H Steel in the chair. Elections were a sticking point for the League and, as Muirhead had predicted back in 1924, 'sticking' would get in the way of unity. The League had published their own 'ultra' proposals of endorsing a programme of national independence and of giving Scottish MPs a mandate to withdraw from Westminster.[20] As this was not accepted as a basis for united work across the groups then the League refused to participate in the Convention. Murray Pittock has argued that this was the first instance of a fundamentalist/gradualist split within Scottish nationalism.[21]

Further, it led to the first split within the League. Lewis Spence had been involved in setting up the Convention and, when it refused to participate, Spence left in early 1927 to form his own group – the Scottish National Movement. However, I suspect that Richard Finlay is right to suggest that personality and fall outs may have played their part[22] and there is evidence of Erskine having to deal with a complaint from Spence about a fellow League member prior to Spence's departure.[23]

We do not know Erskine's take on this act of 'Ourselves Alone' by the SNL. For all that it would be a pretty safe assumption to say that he would have concurred there is still the point, that contradictory part of Erskine's nature, that he respected Muirhead and believed in the organic growth of Scottish nationalism. This explains his gladness that the League would be cooperating with the SHRA at the 1927 Bannockburn event so long as there is 'no dilution' of the League's position.[24] On Easter Monday, he had written to Gibson again in the hope that Muirhead would come over to the League, 'when his Bill is knocked on the head as it will be…' and that he will bring people with him. 'Doubtless, Bannockburn will be a sign that he has changed his breeks a la Newman.'[25]This reference to the famous Anglican bishop who converted to Catholicism did not come to fruition. Muirhead held firm with his beloved Scottish Home Rule Association.

The letters at this time show that Erskine of Marr was not in the best of places. He confided to Gibson that he was only working 'half time' as he 'was not out of the woods yet'.[26] He also exposed a little bit of personal frailty in advertising his dislike of public speaking: 'shouting in the air', as he called it.[27] A real frustration is detectable. There is some unsavoury name calling, including an attack on Spence and a political outburst against the Clydeside Labour MPs: 'As froth-blowers the Clydeside politicians might be immense but as nationalists they are contemptible. The less we have to do with them the better.'[28]

This put him back in line with Gibson's position regarding cooperation with the Westminster parties to obtain home rule. His intemperate language suggests something deeper; a disquiet at the overall direction that the movement was taking and of his lessening influence on its direction perhaps. In the same year the *Scots Independent* itself became independent and the name of the League disappeared from its masthead. Things were moving and the paper itself became more like a Party newssheet although it would be unfair to suggest that there were no incisive political articles.

For his part, Tom Gibson was ever the political operator. His goal was still to bring about a National Party just as much as Muirhead and the Scottish Home Rulers. We will never know for definite, but probably at Dona Maria's insistence, the couple moved again; this time to Tenby in South Wales. His last piece of activism for the Scots National League that he had helped to form was to set up a Borders branch, in Galashiels, in May (technically, he still ceremonially chaired the League's last Conference in the summer of 1928). This would give him time to focus on his writing and would take him out of any direct loop in the formative discussions to form a National Party. He did try to influence from afar but in the main Erskine did what he tended to do in these situations: he looked to the past. Only, the past wasn't a foreign country to him. It was his own country under its old name – Pictland.

Chapter Eleven

Myself Alone

It seems strange on so many levels that Erskine would choose to launch a new journal, from his base in South Wales, that was so retro at a time when the nationalist movement was buzzing about the possible formation of a new party. Yet that is exactly what he did. Erskine edited the *Pictish Review*, founded in November 1927. It was short lived and folded in June 1928. His partner in crime was Chris Grieve and it was the poet who contributed most of the articles.

As a title itself, the magazine would have puzzled some nationalists and alienated others at a time of great momentum and energy. For Erskine, the Picts were a metaphor for the Celtic identity of Scotland and it was a pertinent metaphor in his world because his research on MacBeth was leading him into Pictish themes about Scottish identity. It was a retreat into 'Celticism' and it came at a price. It diverted time and energy away from the real issues facing the nationalist movement; emphasised a cultural nationalism that was seen as irrelevant at that point in time and, most importantly, began a process of self-imposed isolation from the movement.

Grieve had his agenda too and it was this that gave the *Pictish Review* its main contribution; namely, the notion of the 'Scottish Idea.' Grieve had been influenced by the Russian version of this developed by Dostoevsky.[1] The magazine was focussed on channelling Scottish national feeling and re-establishing national values. The theme was therefore Scottish national unity: specifically, the unity of Pict and Scot (for Erskine) and of Lowland and Highland (for Grieve). To their credit, both men wanted to imbue something deeper, even spiritual, into the nationalist movement. That movement wasn't ready for it and didn't understand it.

Thematically, the Scottish Idea would stay with both Erskine and Grieve/MacDiarmid. Linguistically, it gave life again to Erskine's Gaelic activism and helped the Langholm born Grieve appreciate that language's significance to Scotland. Grieve, for his part, was also exploring the Scots dialect – Lallans – as a distinctive linguistic form and contribution to national life although this would flower more in his independent poetry.

Again, the prism of Ireland is also instructive. Erskine's old compadré, Patrick Pearse, had developed a series of writings bearing fruit in the notion of the 'Separatist Idea.' For Pearse, separatism was a truth, a spiritual and material truth, that had been handed down by past rebels and martyrs. As he put it: 'Now, the truth as to what a nation's nationality is, what a nation's freedom, is not to be found in the statute-book of the nation's enemy. It is to be found in the books of the nation's fathers.'[2]

It is fair to say that Erskine's idea would have had more in common with Pearse than with the Russian school of writers who Grieve identified with.

Apart from the Scottish Idea, this *Review* was a retreat for Erskine. Not so for Grieve who could experiment and bring out themes that he could develop in his poetry which led to his articulating a specific Gaelic Idea and the *Review* called for the creation of a Gaelic Commonwealth. The poetry of Hugh MacDiarmid would flourish and contribute to another cultural renaissance. Erskine of Marr, however, had nowhere to go other than hope that fellow nationalists could see this way backward as a way forward. All the old themes were there including a few sideswipes, for old times sake, at Calvinism and John Knox. There was a return to some Catholic spirituality and a chance again to write some Gaelic articles and this duty was shared between Erskine and Aonghas MacEanruig. Marr's passion for the language is still strong. He looks to the Welsh example so that Scotland can learn from a 'scientific application' of the language in areas and to children who have had English as the first language for a long time. If English speaking children in Cardiff can be taught Welsh to enable them to retain the language then, with the scientific application, 'the seed of a living language can be made to flourish and grow practically anywhere'.[3]

Erskine's Achilles heel, as it is of many cultural nationalists, is the question of racialism. Racialism is racialism no matter what way we may wish to sugar coat it. Erskine's was his view of Celticism with his long-held belief that the Celt and the Teuton were different. He never argued for any Celtic superiority but saw a different set of Celtic values; his Celtic gospel that led him to reject the modern ideologies and seek a Gaelic, Celtic past that could be brought back to life. These Celtic principles, as he termed them, were, 'not an omnibus as it were, but a private vehicle for Celts'.[4] Instead of any Liberal/ Tory/ Socialist divisions, he saw a Celtic unity which, of course, did not exist. His ire was directed at any form of internationalism – especially socialist internationalism which he saw as sophistry as there could never be, 'an anti-nationalist world state'.[5]

Such views led the late historian, Jim Young, to argue that Erskine flirted with fascism after his flirtation with the Left; just as MacDiarmid had done in his *Scottish Nation*. In fact, Young argued that after John MacLean's death, Erskine, 'was soon to support Italian fascism'.[6] This view is erroneous. Marr addressed the question in an editorial in April 1928. He was writing from a conservative viewpoint certainly, yet states that fascism in Italy was out of touch with the Church and the Crown. Scots would resist, 'an armed attempt to impose fascism in Scotland'[7] Marr was certainly looking with interest at the direction that fascism would take but did not commit in any way to the fascist ideology of blood and soil. That is to his credit at a time when it would have been easy to do so. He had ample time over the next few years to commit to this but did not. He believed that his Celtic gospel was different; spiritual and anti-feudal not populist.

My view is that Erskine had the emotional intelligence to handle these difficult, problematic ideas. If he was a racialist in the pure sense of the term, then he was very much in a minority among fellow racialists. The cultural nationalists of the *Liberty* magazine also had this emotional intelligence and balanced notions of Celtic culture with internationalism, democracy and republicanism. Erskine had been their de facto leader. In retreat, he abandoned some of the positive aspects and clung on to an ideal that only he could hold. If there had been a mass movement behind him then his ideas could easily have spiralled out of control. That has to be acknowledged. Thankfully this didn't happen and Marr had time to regather his thoughts for the coming struggles ahead and fascism did not form any part of those thoughts.

There was, thankfully, a duality to Erskine of Marr at this time. While posterity tells us that his star may have been on the wane within nationalist circles, it didn't necessarily appear so at the time. From a distance he wanted to contribute to the formation of the new nationalist party. This contribution ran in tandem with his activity in the *Pictish Review*. In a letter in January, to Gibson, he sets out his thoughts on the organisation of the new National Party: areas should replace branches and those areas would have two cadres – speakers and canvassers.[8] Later that month, Ruaraidh praised Gibson for his efforts in moving the League forward in pursuance of a National Party of Scotland. Gibson had given the League the 'definite, immediate objective' that it had been wanting up until that point.[9]

A breach would come. The draft programme of the new Party committed it to self-government for Scotland. This probably had Muirhead's stamp all over it. Indeed, in 1927 he had published a one-page leaflet in Gaelic arguing for home rule/self-government as the term is the same in Gaelic.[10] A move away from the old, tired term of home rule and substituting this for self-government had its merits in terms of arguing for a stronger form of self-determination. Erskine was not impressed. He disliked the term and stood by complete national independence with the diplomatic caveat, 'within the British Isles.' He was profoundly opposed to any 'wedding with Westminster'.[11] Gibson's reply, a week later, brought Erskine back in line for the time being and is worth quoting as the reply of a political manager that would not be out of place with the late twentieth century notion of 'spin doctors'. Those who advocated independence had not brought many Scots with them. The new Party had to start afresh: 'A husbandman has always first to prepare the ground, then he plants the seeds , then he clears weeds that will retard or spoil the crop and then but only then does he get the crop; but we have quite a few people who think we can get the crop without doing the other things.'[12]

It took Erskine a month to ponder before he wrote back saying that he would support the Party in any way that he could and would come forward when the Party was launched.[13] He fell back in line and maybe saw the bigger picture as painted by Gibson but was his heart in it? It had, after all, taken a month to reply and he cited his work with the *Pictish Review* as taking up his time. He would come forward when it was launched and not before. Erskine was not instrumental in setting up the National Party of Scotland. It was not his Party and it would not become his home although he was true to his word. When the Party was launched at a rally in Kings Park, Stirling on 23rd June 1928, Erskine was one of the heavyweights and old timers who 'shouted in the air' to herald the first political party of Scottish nationalism.

The traditional Bannockburn Day rally was as good a place as any to launch the new party. A leaflet survives advertising Cunningham Graham as the headline speaker followed by Marr and then Compton MacKenzie with C M Grieve and Lewis Spence. There was a symmetry of sorts and the main organisations that formed the Party were represented. The old socialist home ruler – Cunninghame Graham - who had served his time in the Independent Labour Party addressing rallies with Eleanor Marx and Keir Hardie, as well as the Home Rule association, was also Chair of the rally. Then there were two English born, Scottish separatists – messrs Erskine and MacKenzie– who also happened to be from a spiritual Catholic tradition balanced perfectly by two younger radical nationalists. MacKenzie, as it happened didn't attend and his place was taken by a young rising star from the Glasgow University Nationalist Association; John McCormick.

Erskine was certainly true to his word to Gibson that he would support the Party once it was up and running. The hard work had been done and the new National Party of Scotland (NPS) was an amalgam of the Scots National League, the SHRA, Spence's Scottish National Movement and the Glasgow University Scottish Nationalist Association. Over the next few months, the same speakers would tour the country rallying support for the Party including two mass rallies in October in the two big cities of Glasgow and Edinburgh.

Doubtless to say, Marr was there on principle. Nationalism had a new vehicle and a chance to grow. So, for the first time perhaps, the old – soon to be 60 years old – aristocratic maverick was toeing the Party line. He must have felt as if he was at a crossroads. The leaflet for the Stirling event stated that it was for a Scottish Parliament. Erskine had spent the best part of the last 20 years arguing for full independence and here he was speaking for home rule or self-government to put a positive spin on it.

What did he say? It is fair to say that he would have been nervous. Sure, he had spoken eight years earlier to a big rally in Trafalgar Square for Ireland's freedom but most of his talks were indoor lectures and he had confided to Gibson of his dislike of outdoor speaking. It is worth pointing out that he had sent his apologies twice to the Bannockburn rally – in 1925 and 1927. I don't think that this was political, although he did receive criticism from Gibson within the League. Linking back to the apologies that he gave to the big commemoration in Arbroath then there seems to be a pattern and that could have been, in fairness, a combination of poor health and lack of confidence.

But he was there at the big launch resplendent in his kilt. As he put his bonnet on the table, he began. He was reminded of an unfortunate incident in Scotland's history and went on to compare the Duke of Albany's regency in the time of James V to Stanley Baldwin's premiership today with an unveiled criticism of career politicians and their promises with Lloyd George being thrown into the mix as his promises meant nothing as he cannot deliver.

Praise was duly given to the chair's opening remarks and his emphasis on sentiment in politics and history while stressing that there is a point beyond sentiment. The point?

> Scotsmen in or Scotmen out, Bruce here or Bruce there, the hills here or the hills away, the first thing is that we have got to get hold of the Government of our own country. If we do not, if we neglect to exercise the power which we have at the polling booths, then indeed we deserve to be branded with the taunt that we are labouring under an inferiority complex.

For all of his eccentric reputation, he was not missing the opportunity by getting lost in the mists of Scottish history. Amidst a near revolutionary call for getting hold of power, this was foursquare about Scotland's future and the cause that he had devoted so much of his life to...

'There was considerable danger,' he went on, 'that the Highlanders would neglect their native language, that they would allow their native civilisation to depart from them for a mess of pottage from Westminster but now , thank God, the youth of the Highlands are rising to their responsibilities; they are learning, they are loving their Gaelic language as they have not done for years and years, and with God's help the old language will soon be supreme in its old sphere as it used to be in the days of Saint Columba.'

This was the Honourable Ruaraidh Erskine of Marr in full flight reminding the National Movement not to forget its first principles and the language was still key to Scotland's sense of self. However, just as he was warming up and taking the crowd with him the old itinerant, bundle of energy signed off. 'I must not detain you any longer,' he said and lifted his bonnet to loud applause.[14]

His speech was short and to the point. It was a speech, modern Scottish nationalists should remember, that helped launch the Party. He set out his stall: forget Bannockburn, forget the hills and glens. We need to get the reins of government in Scotland, no doubt with a nod to Ireland, and we cannot forget who we are. No language, no nation. The mixture of support and warning would be prescient as to the months ahead in terms of his own journey within the National Party.

For all that, there was unity in the camp. Muirhead and Gibson behind the scenes, had what they wanted; a Party. Would the Honorable Earl of Marr be the one to change his breeks a la Cardinal Newman and settle for the long held SHRA line of self-government? This would have meant playing the game and becoming a party loyalist. The early signals were ambiguous. For example, in October of that year Erskine cancelled his subscription of 50 copies of the *Scots*

Independent. This may have been purely financial or it may have shown some unhappiness with the direction of the paper. Alternatively, he was doing the circuit promoting the Party. In July, Muirhead asked if he would be the NPS's candidate for Aberdeen North.[15] This was politely declined as he had let the house in Aboyne out for rent for the last two months. He did helpfully suggest that West Aberdeen may be a better seat to fight.[16]However, it was unlikely that he had any real intention of standing for Westminster.

Most of 1929 was spent in the new Party and Erskine was duly elected onto the Party's National Council (with Aberdeen South as his branch although he was still in Tenby.) Early factionalism had worried him and he used this as an excuse to put the question of elections on the back burner: 'I do not see how the Party can, all at sixes and sevens as it is, possibly contemplate a general election without first doing what it can to sort its own house in order.'[17]

Erskine did have a point. The Scottish Home Rule Association had not brought all its members with it and some of its socialist supporters in the Labour Party could not join this new Party for all of Muirhead's propagandising through their journal, Scottish Home Rule. Also, the month before Lewis Spence had been the first parliamentary Nationalist candidate in North Midlothian and had polled 842 votes out of 18,854 cast. Scotland was not ready for this new Party although he was consoled by Muirhead who reminded him that the great Keir Hardie himself had only polled 617 votes in Mid-Lanark back in 1888 for the Scottish Labour Party.[18]

First principles are always important and the first principles for Erskine as for many in the movement was the reversal of the 1707 Act of Union. He stayed out of electoralist debates for the time being and wrote a commissioned article for the *Current History* magazine based in New York on the case for Scottish (and Welsh) home rule. This is a fascinating piece of writing as he explains the case to his American audience and the case is the Party line. The old Marr is still there as he begins with a bit of a cook's tour of primarily Scottish history but goes to enlarge on the theme of an 'English ascendancy' within the British Isles and this is no more prevalent than in journalism. Issues are viewed from an English viewpoint and journalists in Scotland and Wales, 'creatures of English ascendancy interests'.[19] While the press and politicians stand by, English is encroaching on 'Celtic idioms': 'Unless the advance of English is arrested, it must soon drive the other languages from their last mountainous strongholds into the sea'.[20]

The Party loyalist argues strongly that 'self-government' can arrest this decline as it can give prestige to the indigenous languages. The key point is that Erskine accepted and argued for the Party compromise of self-government because it was defined as an independent Scotland within the British group of nations and this could unite home ruler and independence supporter; Erskine, of course, stresses the political independence that both countries could accrue. Nationalist parties are hailed as a big step forward in both countries with the Welsh party hailed as being an improvement due to its abstentionist line in relation to political activity at Westminster. Neither Party was ready yet to learn from the Irish experience of self-government as they are 'too fast in the net' of the Ascendancy.[21]

Despite Marr's point in relation to the Welsh Sinn Féin line, there was nothing in his article to indicate any disquiet with the new Party. He was an executive member using his reputation to raise its profile in the United States. This article was supplemented by a pamphlet that he worked on over 1929 for a native audience entitled, 'That Which Today Stands Roofless'. This is primarily a history of the coming about of the Union of 1707 with the motif of the national palace of Scotland, or in other words, our national constitution of government standing roofless as the 'building' was robbed and invaded by two bands of thieves in 1706 who took the riches and left it little more than a ruin.

Restoring this 'palace' to its old glory is the job of the National Party and he is still pushing the Party line of Scotland being, 'a sovereign member of the British group of self-ruling nations'.[22] Read between the lines and his disquiet is growing and he uses the pamphlet as a warning to his fellow nationalists on the path that they should travel. The 'Scottish surrender at Westminster' established 'a fatal precedent' as few Scottish politicians escape the seducing influence of, 'the best club in London if not the world'.[23]

The Clydeside Reds down at Westminster were proof if proof were needed. One by one they were abandoning their old, long standing commitment to Home Rule for Scotland and were seduced by the taste and feeling of the first British Labour government formed by Ramsay MacDonald in 1924. This did not happen overnight but gradually careerists were made out of some and loyal Unionist backbenchers out of others. Home Rule became a secondary concern until it was removed as policy altogether in the 1930s in favour of British working-class unity. MacDonald's cherished unity of the causes of labour and Scottish nationality back in the 1880's were torn asunder in the 1930s.

Tom Johnston is a case in point. The editor of the influential

Forward newspaper, which had always been pro-Home Rule had still been speaking at nationalist Wallace Day rallies in Elderslie as late as 1925 and still attending SHRA events for another year or two later. By the time of the formation of the NPS he had told Muirhead that socialism came first and Home Rule second and that the priority was a British socialism. Johnston was on a career trajectory that would see him become Secretary of State for Scotland in Churchill's wartime government.

Not all were seduced. Jimmy Maxton came to see that there would be no political advance to socialism gained in the palace of Westminster and he came to adopt the MacLean line of a Scottish road to socialism; the Scottish Socialist Commonwealth as he styled it. He soon became isolated and his breakaway group of Independent Labour Party MPs became isolated with Maxton himself becoming more disillusioned.

Erskine was interested in these developments and wrote to Gibson asking if an olive branch could be extended: 'Cannot Maxton and his group be got in?'[24] He well remembered the letters that he had from Maxton supporting Home Rule as well as his piece in the Scottish Review, no doubt, many years before. He could see a fall out coming with Ramsay MacDonald over his view of world peace and the world situation. No such olive branch was forthcoming. The National Party would have no truck with the British parties.

Erskine's disillusionment was growing. He was feeling as isolated within the National Party of Scotland as Maxton was feeling within the British Labour Party.

The published National Council of the NPS in 1930 did not have their member for Aberdeen South. He was not deselected; he just did not stand for re-election. His place was taken by a younger woman who would go to play an influential part in fringe nationalism; Wendy Wood.

For Erskine, something had to give. He could compromise on self-government and its definition but not on Ourselves Alone. The Party could fight elections but should never, ever take their seats. This issue was about the heart and soul of the new Party and it was a throwback to one of the unique selling points of the Scots National League. It became accentuated because, as a League and not a Party, it was easy to pontificate from the side lines. As a Party, they sought to engage the Scottish electorate and that meant fighting elections. What do you do if, when, you actually win a seat? You have to do what the Labourites had done don't you?

Back in 1927, from those very side lines, the Reverend Malcolm MacColl had challenged the Clydeside MPs in the pages of the Scots Independent. He was replying to Tom Johnston and called on all Scots Labour MPs to learn the lessons of 'the failed 90 years in Westminster of Irish Repealers and Home Rulers.'.[25] The challenge? Will they become a Scots party? This would force their English comrades to come good on self-determination for Scotland. While this was, of course, League orthodoxy, it was a real challenge for the left Scottish Members of Parliament and as we have seen there was weeping and gnashing of teeth among them.

The challenge came home in the discussions to form the National Party. These discussions took place through Muirhead's National Convention. We know that the League did not participate in the first Convention but there were two more and the Tom Gibson inspired SNL did take part in the second Convention. The main groups were together and starting to talk about what the Party should look like. For the purposes of this narrative, I will jump ahead to the third Convention held in Glasgow in December 1927. The headline in the SHRA's journal sums it concisely and accurately: 'Third Scottish National Convention: A Rousing Meeting Stands Adjourned – Free interchange of opinion!'[26]

Ex-Provost Cochrane, from Prestwick, was the convenor. He raised the motion that passing into law of a Bill for self-government depends upon the creation of a National Party of Scotland. The SHRA's own Alexander MacDonald moved the motion. With heady optimism in the room, Mr MacDonald could and should have expected an easy majority. Unfortunately, Chris Grieve aka Hugh MacDiarmid threw a verbal grenade into the room.

Erskine was not at any of the conventions and it is testament to the old philosophy of Ourselves Alone that he did not have to be for the issue to surface:

'Mr. Grieve: does the Scottish National Party Group mean a Scottish Parliamentary Party or a Scottish Sinn Féin Party?

'I cannot answer that question.'

Lewis Spence then joined the fray:

'Mr. Spence, what exactly does a 'Scottish National Party' mean? Does it mean a Party in Westminster or a Party in Scotland?'[27]

It would be fair to say that the chair and the mover of the motion were reeling. They did not expect this ambush. After some prevarication, Grieve insisted that the question be answered immediately. MacDonald, as mover of the motion, gave a long-winded reply. To be fair, he didn't definitively say, 'a parliamentary party', but that was the gist of his answer. In order to make Home Rule an issue again:

'We can only do that by creating a Party that will be called the Scottish National Party, which shall put up candidates at elections for this one question and this alone.'[28]

Further diversionary tactics ensued as the Labour Party members of the SHRA raised their division of loyalties. After all, they had a Party already which was committed to socialism. Would the new National Party commit to a socialist Scotland? This caused much debate and would eventually lead to a parting of the ways between the Clydesiders and the Home Rulers. The session was heading to an adjournment when the proverbial pooches, Grieve and Spence, came back with their bone. Grieve reiterated the point by asking what their candidates would do when they got elected. Spence's final intervention was intemperate but he did sum up the Sinn Féin position: 'I say most distinctly that if we send a party of professional politicians to Westminster, we at once damn our cause.'[29]

Looking into the prism of Ireland, he saw the County Councils as the keepers of the flame of self-government as they had done across the water, not the Parliamentary Party.

The third Convention adjourned and when it re-convened on 10th January 1928 a compromise was on the table. Grieve was absent. A delegate by the name of Balderstone moved the motion that was accepted that the Party would 'not necessarily' be a Parliamentary Party but would look to stand for town councils, parish councils and other local bodies and this would 'afford a bigger field for propaganda'.[30] The groups could unite around this as well as the definition of self-government that I have alluded to. The door was open for the National Party of Scotland.

All could work around the compromise for the good of the Party and unity. This vision of the Party – as Parliamentary or Sinn Féin – came to mean less and less to the earlier protagonists. Grieve, as MacDiarmid the poet, was examining questions of socialism and language. Spence was one of the early opportunists who went full circle and was the first Parliamentary candidate. He would have taken his seat if elected but the good people of North Midlothian spared his blushes. It didn't go away for one man and that was Erskine. We have seen his growing disquiet as the Party developed through 1929.

Nothing happens in a vacuum. This early victory for the forces of gradualism over fundamentalism help to explain Erskine's actions and they are rooted in disillusionment. Marr chose the *Modern Scot* which was edited by an old fellow traveller, J H Whyte and hailed to be an 'Organ of the Scottish Renaissance.' In so many ways it was apt that a cultural journal was the political space used for his political break with nationalism and to raise his last hurrah for cultural nationalism.

His position is rooted in the old League position that any belief in fighting for national freedom on the floor of the House of Commons should have died with John Redmond. He surveyed NPS members who show a similar belief in, 'destroying the English ascendancy in Scotland by sending members to the English parliament. It is a childlike sort of faith to hold'.[31] He does consider the majority viewpoint and accedes Spence's newly held view that the Scottish electorate would not understand why their MPs would abstain from taking their seats in Westminster as they are 'too obfuscated' by English party politics.

Erskine sees this challenge as a political battle that the nationalist party must fight: 'There was once a madman who proposed to extinguish a fire by adding fuel to the flames; but I do not know that anyone paid any serious attention to him.'[32]

Erskine also pushed back any romantic notions of Nationalist MPs turning Westminster upside down by using an anecdote from Spence's election campaign. A heckler asked him what he would do if he got elected. Spence's reply was that he would bring in a short bill dissolving the Union: 'Well,' replied Marr, 'the bill might be short, but shorter by far for sure would be the shrift accorded it by the English Commons. And what would happen then?'[33]

It was a fair question. The Clydesiders couldn't answer it nor could the evolving, growing Scottish National Party. Harry Hanham, as one of the earliest historians of Scottish nationalism, sees this article as significant while stressing his own view that this was a 'melancholy note' to part with, 'one of the most consistent and able nationalists Scotland has ever produced'.[34] It is a fitting tribute, a fair critique and yet, not the full story. Hanham believed that he withdrew from politics and withdrew immediately into a French exile which was not the case. Erskine certainly withdrew from the Party but hung around for a while yet trying to win those in the wider movement over to a Scottish Sinn Féin. It was not to be.

The inescapable point is that he went from a position of Ourselves Alone to a position of Myself Alone (bho Sinn Féin gu Mi Fhin.) He had taken a stand of pure principle and paid the price for it; political isolation. Very few Scots nationalists as I write will even have heard of Erskine of Marr because of this, his, decision to withdraw from the Party.

His sense of frustration was articulated at the end of his 'melancholy note.' He decried Scotland as a 'decadent nation', no more than 'imitators and copyists of England'.[35]

This sense of frustration and disillusionment would eat him up for a couple of years until he bounced back with a fresh venture.[36]

Chapter Twelve

Hardback Writer

Was Erskine obstinate? Too puritanical on an issue that even his sympathisers had moved away from? Was he incapable of seeing the big picture? These are pertinent questions but it should be remembered that Erskine of Marr was not by temperament a loner. He had always sought to build bridges, engage people in ideas and discussion and involve a wider group of like-minded individuals in whatever issue or cause he was fighting. I would argue that he was trying to do the same with the debate on parliamentary participation at Westminster.

There is an interesting digression that, I feel, proves this point. Aboyne, and Aberdeenshire in general, held a special place in the Erskines' heart. Over the course of 1929, Erskine contributed to the debate on the feasibility and desirability of a National Park for Scotland.[1] Many big names such as Ramsay MacDonald, George Lansbury, Tom Johnston and the Scots Independent itself joined the campaign/debate. Erskine made common cause in this campaign feeling that it was 'wholly appropriate' that the ancient Caledonian forest, 'should be a National Sanctuary – a sort of serpentless Eden'.[2]

In his own style, he tried to mould the discussion. He felt that it should be called a Forest as of its original name rather than the parochial National Park with its images of park keepers, and 'keep off the grass signs.' Though it sounds and reads the opposite, Marr's tongue was not in his cheek. This was a spiritual argument in keeping with his Celtic gospel while keeping his activist's approach that this was about the Highlands and its land. He suggested a scenic road for the tourists from Inchrory to Braeriach hill, peaking at almost 1300 feet, 'in the very bowels of the hills'.[3] This was radical and imaginative. It did not, of course come to fruition and tourists would still find themselves driving for over two hours through Tomintoul and Coylumbridge but at least the Munro is now situated in a national park; the Cairngorms National Park. The campaign in time would be successful.

This is a lovely little detour in Erskine's journey and shows his real skills as a publicist and his ability to reach out to a wider audience. As we have witnessed, he had been doing just that over the last two years in promoting the National Party and raising the banner of Home Rule. He was no sectarian. His stand on abstention from Westminster and rejection of the 'childlike faith' of the NPS did take him out of the Party but not out of the wider Movement. Rejection of the Party led him into a period of reflection which would see him drawn to the Modern Scot with its notions of cultural renaissance. It would lead him toward exploration of the 'English ascendancy' as a concept and enemy to political progress in Scotland and ultimately, frustration; a parting with politics and a renewal as a writer and historian. Quite a path travelled was the journey undertaken by Erskine.

Contrary to the view of Hanham, his 'melancholy note' got even more melancholic. His period of political reflection led to a quite remarkable book, *Changing Scotland*.[4] This was, in effect, his 'Myself Alone' manifesto for Scotland: well written yet thoroughly eccentric, cogent yet off the wall. Radical and reactionary in equal measure, it is a gauge as to where his own head was at after splitting with his Party. As a brief comparison, his old, late friend John MacLean had formed his own party after splitting with the Communist Party of Great Britain in the early twenties with like-minded Scottish Marxian republicans.[5] Even then, MacLean was still isolated. Erskine was in an even worse predicament – no real supporters or base and no alternative Party and it didn't look as if he particularly wanted one. He did want to engage on his notion of a 'Celtic State' and this was the inspiration behind his book.

Seldom will you see such a breathtaking, incredible and completely unrealistic beginning to any political work. His style was usually to start with history, and in keeping with this style, he considered the state of the 'Three Kingdoms'. One remarkable section was entitled, 'Why Kings should govern Ireland'. Erskine contended that the Treatyites were now united and the Republicans were divided. The period of transition for the country will pass, 'in a blaze of national prosperity let us hope... but what will happen to the Treaty and the Treatyites?' His solution:

It is plain from history, as well ancient as modern, that the principal distemper of the Irish State has ever been internal disunion. It is reasonably sure that a King (whose symbol, as whose interest, is unity) would cure the distemper. Therefore, the monarchy should be re-erected in Ireland.[6]

We could confidently infer that nobody, even in the Emerald Isle itself, was talking about resurrecting the monarchy in Ireland. The last King of Ireland was a Scotsman; Edward Bruce back in the fourteenth century. Charles Stewart Parnell was labelled, 'the uncrowned king of Ireland'. Apart from these, monarchist references are hard to find within the Irish nationalist narrative. We can only imagine the response of any Irish readers of the book – especially those who had been acquainted with him.

However, it did fit in with an evolving narrative within Erskine's politics. Separate kings for the separate kingdoms providing unity and, for Scotland and Ireland, a Celtic ethos. This really was the main thrust of the book – the political landscape in his own country. None of the political parties were up to the task. Erskine was not prone to political tributes or eulogies yet in the book he pays tribute to Keir Hardie. Scotland would be a socialist country if the socialists resembled Hardie. Alas, he argued, no one has taken his mantle. The reality, for Marr, is that just like the Liberals and the Tories, the Labour Party in Scotland, 'are thirled to London, are financed, and by consequence, ruled from thence'.[7] The truth of that observation would be cemented over the next few decades as Labour abandoned its long-held belief in Home Rule and looked to establishing an all-Britain socialist government in London.

No salvation would come from the Nationalist Party; a Party with 'no sense of history or ancestry'.[8] This view was based on the Party's rejection of the Celticism of the Scots National League with its supposed modernism and electoralism. Erskine held out no hope for the Party. In returning to the theme of participation at Westminster, Erskine imagined 30 nationalist MPs:

What then? Is it not obvious on the suppositions allowed, that either the Scots must at once return to their own country, no better off as regards their object in leaving it than when they went, or they must complete a pact with someone or other of the English parties, and thus stultify at once themselves and their programme.[9]

Not a single nationalist was listening in 1931. Erskine was in the wilderness and the House of Commons was a means to an end for the Party; a means that would not be experienced until Dr Robert McIntyre was elected as the first Nationalist MP for Motherwell in 1945. Erskine's imagination, however, of a squadron of nationalists in Westminster was intended as a warning for Party managers as, 'they do but resemble the girl who went for a ride on a tiger, and finished it, not astride but inside, her smiling palfrey.'[10]

As I write, there are almost 50 elected SNP MPs in the House of Commons. The means are not in doubt but the end looks a long distance away and, without a second independence referendum, they look trapped. Erskine's warning is now very pertinent for those same Party managers.

These political observations are the pretext for his own manifesto to change Scotland; the manifesto of the Celtic State. The State would have a king; provincial assemblies, in other words devolution within Scotland; Gaelic as the first language; a 'Celtic economy' that would 'diffuse money' and 'tap wealth at its source.' There would be no army but a defensive national militia. The big selling point was that Erskine's Scotland would be 'cheap to run' and banish all the remnants of feudalism once and for all time.[11]

While he respected MacDiarmid's attempts to hoist the banner of the Scottish Renaissance through Lallans, his problem is that most English speakers understand it. It's not that different from English. Gaelic is 'superior' and 'native' and 'with good will and the educational resources of the nation' can be saved.[12] Though he concedes that the language has to 'come down from the hills'.

Changing Scotland was like the bark of an old dog lying on its mat in the corner while nobody pays attention as everything rages on as normal in the household. Political isolation had undermined his contribution. Marr had rejected all the political parties and they, in turn, were hardly likely to listen to him. Scotland was not ready for Sinn Féin style politics of either the old or new variety. This was the root cause of his self-isolation from Scottish nationalism. While he tried to engage with the wider Movement through his book, he was very much yesterday's man. The book was not totally ignored. The North-east press stayed loyal to him and *Changing Scotland* was actually serialised in the *Forfar and Kinecardineshire Advertiser* as well as the *Montrose, Arbroath and Brechin Review*.

Erskine had nowhere to go politically and it was after this book that he started to drift out of politics and any political engagement.

While there were flashes of interest across the thirties, his energy was directed elsewhere. The final hurrah was in 1937 when he formed the Scottish Monarchists and he published a manifesto. No extant copy exists.[13] We will never know if this was a one-man band but we can probably guess that the Celtic State still featured strongly. We do know that the National Party of Scotland was fraught with dissension and early expulsions (including MacDiarmid and MacKenzie) and it is highly likely that Erskine would have been expelled too. The NPS became the SNP in 1934 with the merger with the Duke of Montrose's rightist Scottish Party.

Erskine and the National Party of Scotland were never meant to be. A man in his sixties did what a man in his sixties would usually do and that is revert to type.

Erskine of Marr was a writer, a historian and, of course, an aristocrat. As a decade the thirties were consumed in writing and reflection. As he vanished off the radar of most histories of Scottish nationalism, he did not himself disappear. Nor did he storm off in a fit of pique. There was a period of transition in which he saw his main contribution as being to the Scottish Renaissance that was in full swing. In addition to articles in the *Modern Scot*, Erskine also resurrected *An Rosàrnach*. Fionn MacColla, a fellow Renaissance writer, recognised his work and input: 'For twenty years, in the face of opposition and ridicule and in spite of a total lack of recognition, he almost alone of Gaelic protagonists has consistently regarded the Gaelic in its present form as more than a rustic patois.'[14]

MacColla's only complaint was the lack of fresh blood; all the writers in Gaelic were 'old heroes'.[15] Throughout 1930, Erskine engaged in debate on the state of Gaelic theatre under the combative yet engaging title of 'Comhradh-sgalain', or a 'blast of conversation'. These articles were all in Gaelic and compose his last set of Gaelic writing outside of *An Rosàrnach*. Being the old controversialist, as always, he used his column to praise the Bolshevik approach to drama in Russia.

It was a last hurrah. His life and work were moving in a different trajectory which would see him become a hardback writer of history. Beginning with the publication of *MacBeth* in 1930, he would publish two other history books – *The Stout Adventures of Mary Stewart* and

The Crown of England. He would also publish his closest attempt at autobiography with his *Edward VII and Other Figures.* The last three books all came out over 1936 and 1937, which indicates that he spent a good, few years working on these books as well as organising his moveable, personal life. London and the south east of England would be his home for a couple of years and this showed as there was a discernible change in the intended audience of his output.

Arguably, his first book was his best history book in terms of detail and dates as well as underlying analysis. He proved his credentials as a Gaelic scholar by arguing that the fourth to the ninth centuries constituted a 'Celtic Risorgimento' led by 'intellectual Ireland'. Indeed, this book's agenda was to save MacBeth's reputation as a Celtic king who could have united the kingdom in one Celtic whole. The old Erskine is lining up the Celtic against the feudal or teutonic in his vision of Scotland. While he is not over-critical of England's Bard and his famous 'Scottish play', Erskine believes that Shakespeare's play left a historical narrative around MacBeth:

> ...the whole genius and machinery of Shakespeare's play is feudal, whereas historical accuracy demands that both should be Celtic. He puts thanes in room of mormaers, and his stone-built feudal castles are, archaeologically, laughable.[16]

As a compare and contrast, this book differs from his treatment of another Scottish monarch. His take on Mary Stewart was published in London and certainly seems to have been written for an English audience. There is no passion or fire in his belly as he deals with the themes that he had been writing about since the days of *Guth na Bliadhna* in 1904: the religious reformers and their long-term impact on Scotland. The sentences are overlong; ambling and clumsy. There is a lack of detail to back up his argument. It feels as though he is trying to write as a detached, respectable historian.

Although it would be unfair not to recognise some flourishes of his old self. Auld Alliance with France or Union of Crowns with England? 'For my part I know that had my lot been cast in those times, and had I been indulged a choice suitable to the occasion, I would have unhesitatingly voted for 'France and wooden shoes' in preference to England and boiled potatoes.[17]

He produces few, if any dates which weakens his argument as it all seems conjecture especially as he sought to absolve Mary of Darnley's murder. Erskine does blame Mary (along with Bothwell) for her own fall from Catholic grace and sees this as significant in her own fall. His best flourish, for this writer, was his attempt to bring things right up to date:

> If the doctrine that the end may justify the means employed in order to bring it about be ethically unsound, as I suppose, generally speaking is the case yet of the vast antiquity of this notion, its frequent practice, and its power to seduce minds, warp judgement and corrupt natures – to this effect surely history, as well modern as ancient, bears ample witness.[18]

He was referring to Mary's actions to gain the English Crown from her cousin, Elizabeth – but he could have been referring to Hitler or Stalin. This sense of history, though radically different from the still radical Erskine of 1930, kept him away from any Fascist flirtation which was fashionable among other aristocrats of his time.

In the space of seven years he had detached himself further and the outlook of these two histories of Scottish monarchs is only one example. During the early thirties he had moved back to London and was floating between the metropolis and Hove. One other humorous example shows his detachment. In January 1934 Erskine delivered the Immortal Memory to a Burns supper in Eastbourne.[19] He seemed on form and the local newspaper was very complimentary:

> We all wished that the memory of Burns might endure forever but for ever was a long time. Immortality was a mighty word, which staggered the intellect and baffled the imagination. In what sense could we pledge the immortality of the memory of Burns? The idea of immortality was essentially beyond our grasp, but there was a very particular sense in which the immortality of the memory of Burns could be pledged us, for we could be sure that as long as the Scot existed to encumber, enliven, improve and inspire the earth so long would his memory endure.[20]

The local expats seemed happy. Hugh MacDiarmid, a Burns supper hater, would probably have thrown tomatoes at him. One Scottish observer came back in angry mood. 'Bearsden Man' stated that the crowd sat in 'annoyed silence' as Erskine had the 'temerity' to assert that Burns was only one of many national bards including

Ossian. Ossian must have been flattered, asserted the angry local and that, 'Somebody blundered in selecting the Honourable Ruaraidh'.[21] Erskine had really slumped if he was loved in Eastbourne and disliked in Bearsden!

Perhaps he was jolted by the criticism. The old radical nationalist jumped out of him later in February when he sent a message of support to Wendy Wood, who had organised a conference in the Central Halls, Glasgow under the guise of the Democratic Scottish Self-Government Organisation. There were about 50 in attendance. Wood, too, had clearly fallen out with the Party. She read out Erskine's letter which stated that separatism is the issue that counts. 'Not a single scrap of English rule should be left' and 'all possible action conformable and appropriate thereto should follow and continue till the great end has been gained.'[22]

This was more like his old self. Yet it was short-lived. Erskine was in the process of literally choosing France and wooden shoes. He had written to Muirhead at the turn of the year to inform him that the Erskines would shortly be leaving for Paris. There was still time for a little side swipe at the Party as their, 'meddling in English politics is leading our nation farther into the mire of 1707'.[23] This would be the start of a protracted French exile. Peripatetic as ever, he did not fully settle in France for a couple of years yet as he still had business to attend to in the south of England.

Erskine's last two books would also come out over 1936 and 1937 including his worst, *The Crown of England*. It was a literary and political low point for him although, naturally, he may not have felt that way himself. The idea of the book had germinated back in the days of the *Modern Scot* which serialised in 1931 some articles on 'The Stewart Kings of England'. There is no rationale given as to why he should return to the theme in book form nor, indeed, why he felt the need to write the book in the first place.

'Formal Governance' is the title of his conclusion. Starting by reiterating his Celtic system of government, he ends in a political whirl. Beginning by emphasising a balance of power in the Celtic system as the Celts elected their king, he finishes by railing against the failings of democracy which had given birth, in turn, to Liberalism, Radicalism, Socialism and Communism. Erskine also blames democracy for giving the world Hitler and Mussolini. His greatest ire is for the English Labour Party and their hypocrisy in denouncing Hitler and Mussolini while being silent on Russia. Although he is not defensive of the two main fascist leaders in Europe, the concern is that his rant against democracy displays an aristocratic and monarchic view of the world looking for stability and certainly looking to the right and not to the left. Many fellow aristocrats and men and women of privilege were doing the same thing at this time and were looking to fascism as a bulwark against communism. Erskine was leaving himself wide open to such influences culminating in: ' …but perhaps I mistake, as it is not Englishmen who so object, but some of the Israelitish gentlemen, who in politics, as in commerce, and the public life generally, pull the wires in England today.'[24]

Whatever the contex, it is a distasteful anti-semitic comment that is clearly a cause for concern. Such beliefs were commonly held and led to all sorts of apologetics for the fascist right as they scapegoated the Jewish population across Europe. Erskine of Marr might have known better. It shows how he was regressing back to a London-centred, aristocratic lifestyle and view of the world that was a million miles from the world of *Guth na Bliadhna* and the *Scottish Review*. It couldn't be the same writer, could it? Thankfully, there *were* little flashes of his old self. He did not subscribe to Fascism or to any ideology but to the 'universe of ideas' which obeys the 'divine law of continuous change' and that will take us where we need to go.[25]

This reversion, as he approached 70, coincided with a period of introspection. If the future would look after itself through his divine law of change then what about his past? These reflections produced his near autobiography; *King Edward VII and Some Other Figures*. My reading of these books is that he was cross working on them over a period of a few years. His reflective frame of mind had come out a few years earlier in a magazine as he reminisced about Hyde Park, 'the park of parks'. He concludes that fashion ruled in Hyde Park at one time before it was over-run by the mob (he meant, of course, aristocratic fashion). 'Recollections are ghosts', he proclaimed and his phantoms were Arthur Balfour, Lord and Lady Granville and the Duchess of Leinster, 'the most beautiful of all duchesses'.[26] He was thinking about his past, himself and those he knew in his youth in a way that was perfectly natural. The conclusions, however, were a different story. 'The Destroyer' of the park was none other than his old pal from the Scottish Home Rule Association in London. James Ramsay MacDonald, as Prime Minister, had opened the gates of the park to the mob, 'and straightaway a flood of democracy in shabby little oil-driven vehicles poured in'. It is humorous, irreverent and reminiscent of his old *Whirlwind* days.

Erskine was going back the way at a rate of knots. The politics, the cultural milieu, the characters all swirled about his head and prompted his near autobiography. Eight acquaintances of his youth are portrayed in order to give us a portrait of a young aristocrat. They are: King Edward VII; Gladstone; Redmond; Parnell; Henry Asquith; Lord Granville; Balfour and Lord Roseberry. By far, the most interesting chapters concern the two Irish leaders. There are some interesting, and some not so interesting, anecdotes and reminiscences across the other chapters. Frustratingly, he gives no dates and names are sometimes concealed or generalised. Marr takes great pride in recounting Edward VII's comment to a 'kinsman' concerning himself, 'If he and I had lived in former times I would have had his head'.[27] Erskine seldom spoke or wrote about his kinsfolk at all – so this in itself was revealing.

This book for all its faults – Harry Hanham called it 'arid' – gives us an insight into Erskine's thoughts at this time. Bolingbroke was his inspiration in writing and he did not want to write proper autobiography because he did not deserve it. He recalled saying to a friend in a London cemetery 'recently': 'After all, is not to survive in headstones fame enough for any man, and the tomb the proper burial place for human vanity.'[28]

He reveals an edge to his writing and musing. Men's motives, he argues, are like a bottomless well and as the further down you look, the darker it gets. He dismisses experts such as Sigmund Freud and Carl Jung who are of no use in seeing down this well. It is a powerful analogy to use in his pseudo-autobiography. Among some pretty anodyne reminiscences, this dark well of men's motives comes out of nowhere. There is no elaboration or explanation. Darkness could have resided in the heart of Parnell or Gladstone or even the late king himself. Erskine may have been referring to any of the other figures in his book. Or himself?

What are we to make of Erskine the historian in the 1930s? Those who would be inspired by the Gaelic nationalist of the previous thirty years will be perplexed by a very different output from the same man. His first two offerings were motivated by his thoughts on Scotland. They were published before the end of 1931.

His last three offerings, even the book about Mary Stewart, were very different in their style, content and – most significantly – their intended audience. Madness or mental illness does not offer any explanation. Erskine was his cogent and still his eccentric self: no more eccentric than when he called for the restoration of the Irish crown in *Changing Scotland* in 1931. Observers and friends expected this from him. Likewise, his political outlook did not wholly change as throughout the decade he still made political interventions that were decidedly Scottish nationalist such as his support for Wendy Wood's conference in 1934 or the *Manifesto of the Scottish Monarchists* three years later. A letter to Hugh MacDiarmid in October 1937 is indicative as to his heart's desire:

> Next spring I hope to return to Scotland and then to be of some use there to put things into shape but meanwhile I think that you and I – you in your Shetland and I in my French retreat – might do something to mend our common country.[29]

Up until the last chapter, *The Crown of England* is far more deserving of the 'arid' description as his argument was little more than a quite dull enunciation of the 'great man' theory of history. Something deeper has to describe what was going on in his own mind and heart which leads to the conclusion that he was looking down the dark well of his own motives. This statement seems to have been an apt, autobiographical statement to make that puts in stark context his dark musings on politics and the world and his personal displacement from it.

Outwardly, this will come across as supposition to anybody who has read these books. There are no rants, no pent-up frustration or anger. Even his highly distasteful anti-Semitic comment was made in the most matter-of-fact way. It is the personal displacement that is most pronounced. He should have been in Scotland building the National Party and contributing to the great cause that had taken up most of his adult life; certainly, the most creative part of it. Instead, he is spending his sixties, moving into old age with enough energy left inside of him, writing dull history for a staid, conservative, society audience. It was a wholesale retreat and he knew it. It is this period that wiped him off the radar of most Scottish nationalists then and now as, in their world, he had disappeared into his own 'dark hole'. It was dark for him and as he looked down the bottomless well and saw his dreams slipping away, he blamed democracy, the

Labour Party and those horrible proletarians just as he had done in his youth. Regression helped him make sense of how he was feeling. And it is to his immense credit that he fought back against his darkness.

As much as his books are obscured in the twenty-first century, Erskine was still worthy of review at the time and his book on Edward VII and friends was seen as 'provocative and entertaining' by the Royal institute of International Affairs who saw him as a 'shrewd observer.'[30] If he seemed to be in a dark place and politically isolated, at least he had a plan to get away from it all. From his letter to Muirhead (quoted above) we know that he was in the process of moving to France in 1934. This was a protracted move as he was still getting his hardback histories published in London. Yet he did move. Just when it seemed that he had gone full circle back to his aristocratic life in the south of England, both Erskine and Dona Maria settled in the south-west of France just as war was about to engulf Europe again. It seems a strange move. Surely this would be their final move; a French retirement to see out their final years.

Chapter Thirteen

A Nationalist Once Again!

'Well, what about St. John?'
'There's not one reference to Hell in his Gospel.'
'But surely monsignor, you are not questioning the existence
of Hell?'
'I believe from obedience but not with the heart.'

Graham Greene[1]

Roland Muirhead received a letter through his letterbox one
morning early in November 1946. That letter was a blast from the
past. Ruaraidh Erskine had written to him for the first time in 12
years. The address cited was that of a hotel in Pau in south-west
France and the words reverberated in the style of RAM of old.
The International Trade Society were having a congress on the re-
building of Europe now that the second world war was over and
Erskine wanted Scottish representation at this congress. It sounds
familiar and the fire was back in his belly again.[2] Muirhead, ever the
diplomat, replied on 22nd November that he would make enquiries.

This letter was not the first one sent to old comrades although it
was the most significant as it triggered a series of correspondence.
The little hints of the old nationalist Erskine that seeped through
his writings in the thirties, those hints that seemed to be dying amid
London aristocratic life, came pouring back out unleashed by the
end of six years of slaughter. The Erskines had lived through it
twice – except on the second occasion they were in continental
Europe to witness it first-hand.

We cannot be certain of the exact date when they moved officially
to France. Their move seemed to begin and end in the same itinerant
way as they moved backwards and forwards between France and the
south of England. No doubt they were attending to business and

overseeing the move of possessions and valuables and, it must be stressed, at a time of great crisis on the continent with civil war raging in Dona Maria's home country of Spain and ideological tension all over Europe.

Erskine's work was still popping up in the most unusual of places. This included a published piece in the *British Medical Journal* in May 1939; probably the most unusual publication of any of his written pieces. There was nothing unusual in the subject matter. Erskine used the article to highlight the Celtic tradition in medicine. The article tells the tale of how the Beatons from Fife came to be the physicians to the powerful clan Donald in their capacity as lords of the isles. Beaton is the anglicised form of MacBeth in Gaelic (MacBeatha.)

As a student of Gaelic and its culture, Erskine would have been all too aware of the traditions of the lordship of the Isles as well as the link with the MacBeth clan. The powerful MacDonald clan built their kingdom within a kingdom which became an alternative power base that the kings of Scotland in Edinburgh would not tolerate for too long. This was also a Gaelic speaking, cultural power base with a social network. Various clans took on the role of bards, warriors and musicians. The MacKinnons, for example, were the pipers extraordinaire; the MacBeths were the National Health Service for Gaels. The individuals themselves lived off grants from the clan chief.[3] The defeat of this power base at the hands of the Stewarts was an important part of the overall decline of the language and its culture.

An ancient Celtic source descended to a tradition of 'gentility.' A medical tradition was also present among his own antecedents. Robert Erskine of Alva, we are told, sailed from the port of Leith to Archangel in Russia in 1704 to be the chief physician to Peter the Great. Overall, this is a fascinating article that was totally in place within the journal. As I write, the Royal College of Physicians website also carries a piece on the role of the MacBeths/Beatons as Celtic physicians in the Middle Ages. Their article goes further than Erskine in that they cite Patrick MacBeth as the royal physician to Robert the Bruce no less and also chart the end of the medical dynasty with the death of Fergus Beaton of Islay in 1628 coming at a time when the Beatons influence had waned after the end of the lordship of the Isles.

Erskine had preserved a fine Gaelic tradition in the literary home of British medicine and he would be pleased that the modern-day

College of Physicians preserve the Gaelic saying that described the Beatons as medics and surgeons:

Clann 'ic Beatha a'ghrinn,
Luchd snaidheadth chnamh is chuislean.
MacBeths of the polished ways,
Men who slit bones and veins.[4]

It is hard to say with any certainty where the Erskines spent the war. If their movements after the war are any indicator then it would be fair to say that they floated between Bordeaux, Pau and Biarritz in the south west of the country. After the fall of France and its surrender in June 1940, this area would have fallen under the occupied zone albeit was close to the border with the nominally independent État Francais or Vichy France as history remembers it.

Erskine has left us no memoir of his experience at this time. Both he and his wife may have been allowed to go about their business with Erskine's proficiency in Spanish allowing them to pass themselves off as an elderly Spanish couple. It is also a real possibility that they spent the war in neutral Spain under that Franco, with the protection of Dona Maria's passport. This is merely conjecture. Yet this unknown period of five years of Erskine's life does raise questions.

What did he see? How much collaboration, how much resistance? It is entirely possible that he was cocooned in his hotels or ensconced over the border but even that raises questions as he did not acknowledge the plight of the Basques, Catalans or fellow Celts of Galicia in any of his post-war writings. As late as 1950 he was still going to Barcelona for the winter to escape the cold of Pau – that is, oppressed, Francoist Barcelona. It is sad that none of this registered in his post-war writings. Nor did the plight of those French Jews who were rounded up and sent to their deaths in their thousands in both parts of France. We cannot be too harsh as he may have seen little of this. He may have been in a 'bubble'.

The bubble is a useful analogy for him as this featured in his last two published writings and Scotland was very much to the forefront of his thoughts. In 1940 he published 'The Great Baltic Bubble'. War was raging across the continent and Erskine, ever Erskine, chose to publish a pamphlet on Charles XII of Sweden's attempts to enact a Stuart restoration in Scotland in 1715 by planning to send 8000 foot and 4000 horse. It is a fascinating and well written work but so out of place and time that it is the author who is truly in the bubble. It does show his love-hate relationship with the Stuarts as he believes that they were the best bet to prevent the union of the four nations of the British Isles but blew it through their lack of statecraft and political acumen. No Stuart king is excused as this is true 'from the first even to the last of the race'.[5] His work did receive a favourable review as, insightfully, 'the background was as attractive as its central theme'.[6]

Though he may have been in a bubble of sorts, he did come out the other end with some lessons. Hugh MacDiarmid was the first to receive a letter from Erskine dated 1st September 1945 from Biarritz. He is writing to state that both he and his wife are hoping to leave for London soon and would like to catch up to discuss the political situation in Scotland. He does share some reflections with the poet. How can we make the world safe for peace? That was the priority to build a State committed to peace; committed 'not to use arms'? All the talk of making the world 'safe for democracy' was 'absurd' as the world's militarist-state system had not gone.[7] All states were still subject to the laws of expansion. This was a very observant letter. Although it would have been hard to foresee the Cold War between America and the Soviet Union, he certainly foresaw the grounds for such a conflict.

As western Europe was discussing its rescue package with the United States and various conferences and congresses were being held, Erskine re-found his mojo. This took the form of a fruitful correspondence with Roland Muirhead over the next few years. Two old nationalists trying to plot a course for the movement: one, a fallen angel stuck overseas while the other had stayed true to the Party through its early trials and tribulations. Erskine had always respected Muirhead and the latter had truly devoted his life to the cause of Scottish nationalism. He was also a passionate supporter of world peace and Nan Milton, the daughter of John MacLean, recalls him in his nineties with a long white beard carrying the banner of CND (the Campaign for Nuclear Disarmament) down Glasgow's Sauchiehall Street at a rally in the 1960s.[8] She called him the Grand Old Man of Scottish Nationalism. Wendy Wood also tells a lovely story in her memoirs of how Muirhead had met his young love again, by chance, in his eighties and married.[9]

Some key themes come out of the letters: tactics to take the Party forward; republicanism; peace; the idea of a people's congress; glimpses into the Erskines' lives at that time.

On tactics, Erskine was pushing for Muirhead to use his influence within the SNP to get them to look internationally. Put feelers out to the Dominion premiers like Smuts of South Africa and MacKenzie-King of Canada, Erskine advised Muirhead. Muirhead, at first, pushes back as the Party don't agree on contacting Dominion prime ministers.[10] Erskine came back to the point. The Empire was about to become the Commonwealth, 'then we become, ipso facto, a member of the Commonwealth'.[11] Marr called for more, 'energy and insistence' from the Movement. He believed that the Dominions were sympathetic to Scotland's cause but they just need to know that there is a will in Scotland to 'give the unions the slip.'[12] Interestingly, Erskine is talking about the *two* unions – of Crown and Parliament.

The 'Crown of England' was about to change hands again; the young princess Elizabeth was the heir to the throne. Scotland, of course, had never had any Queen Elizabeth. Both men agreed that any Elizabeth with the second nomenclature (EIIR) was unacceptable. The folk song writer, Morris Blythman, summed it up musically with his song, Coronation Coronach:

Nae Liz the Twa, nae Lillibet the wan,
Nae Liz will ever dae.
For we'll mak' oor land republican
In a Scottish breakaway.[13]

The two old nationalists mused on the subject. Roland was a republican but didn't push it as the need to get self-government first was greater.[14] Erskine replied, dating his letter, 'Feast of St Patrick'. He was not against republicanism and stated that, 'to be a republican is all right no doubt,' but Scotland needs monarchy until she has full sovereignty to choose.[15] Muirhead, for his part, 'swithered' and was tempted to just push for a Scottish Republic now.[16]

Jump ahead six years. Elizabeth has been crowned as EIIR. Erskine came back to Muirhead. What were the SNP going to do about the royal nomenclature now that the young princess was now on the throne? 'For my part, I favour the idea of regarding the Union treaty and Act as now completely dead, after a long sickness from the many injuries inflicted on it by the English. I wish to be bothered by it no longer.'[17]

For her part, Wendy Wood, proclaimed a Scottish Republic at Glasgow Cross and many pillar boxes with the EIIR insignia were blown up by nationalists. Muirhead quickly replied to Erskine stating that his letter was read out at the SNP national executive and Party members were advised not to 'rejoice' in the new monarch.

Hopefully there is a feeling that both men were bouncing off one another, inspiring each other, challenging each other and, in the process, being radicalised all over again. Young at heart and seeing the cause for all it was worth. And soul searching like Sancho and Monsignor Quixote in Graham Greene's novel. The correspondence allowed Marr to open up on his wartime experience. He had been working on a pamphlet on how France could 'stop the rot' and recover her prestige in Europe.[18] This pamphlet was never published and no copy of it exists in Muirhead's papers. A glimpse of his observations can be seen in an earlier letter when he was calling for the SNP to lobby Schumann's conference at the end of 1948. He believed that the Party had driven the 'public spirit clean out of the French people.' There was political apathy and a third world war would 'actively disintegrate them'.[19] This is our only glimpse into his wartime experience. He mentions the Party. Did he mean the Nazis? Or did he mean the one-party state of Vichy which was driving Marshal Petain's 'national revolution'?[20] It is a shame that we do not have more detailed memoirs from that period from Erskine's pen.

Refreshingly consistent is his commitment to peace. Marr was all for challenging the British Army's recruiting drive at the end of the war. He reminisced to Muirhead regarding his experience at the start of the first conflict:

> When the war of 1914 was about to break out I persuaded Hogg, the member at the time of an Edinburgh division in the H of C, to raise the question of Scotland being dragged into that war but, peace to his soul!, he made a bit of a mess of it so that what he urged was just sentiment…[21]

In other words, it was not political and it was not anti-militarist. The SNP, Erskine believed, now have a chance to tap into the anti-militarist wing in Scotland.

Erskine was full of ideas. So too was Muirhead who was proposing that the SNP raise the stakes in their campaigning. Muirhead was inspired by the belief that a third of all SNP members favoured the setting up of a provisional government which was, not surprisingly, rejected by the Party conference as there was no popular will to establish such a government. Marr had sent Muirhead a draft manifesto which the latter had agreed with his Party colleagues was not suitable.[22] Muirhead did not keep a copy of Erskine's document. Muirhead's own process of radicalisation continued as he was fomenting some ideas around the creation of a 'People's Congress' influenced by Gandhi's Congress movement in India.

There was a Scottish background and context to this. The Scottish National Party had failed to woo Eamon de Valera when he was in Glasgow in 1948 to the chagrin of Erskine in particular.[23] As the two old men corresponded on the direction of the Party and the subject returned to Redmond's strategy of securing Home Rule in Westminster, Muirhead showed his true feelings as well as some of his own disillusionment with the direction of the Party. He replied to Erskine that it was 'not practicable' to secure self-government in Westminster although it was 'useful' to contest by-elections. Muirhead believed that the time had come for 'passive resistance' and a People's Congress to force Scotland's demands.[24] This would become the Scottish National Congress a year later coinciding with the time when he ceased to be President of the SNP. The journeys of the two men had coalesced.

John McCormick's SNP were pushing a National Covenant instead, rich in historical connotations in Scotland, which would gain a dubious two million signatories. The Covenant's wording could never gain the support of either of the two:

> …we solemnly enter into the Covenant whereby we pledge ourselves, in all loyalty to the Crown, and within the framework of the United Kingdom, to do everything in our power to secure for Scotland a Parliament with adequate legislative authority in Scottish affairs.[25]

It was as though Scottish nationalism had gone back in a time portal to 1892. This may have had a further radicalising influence on the grand old man. One historian, Keith Webb, believes that Muirhead lost his patience with 'electoralism' which would lead to his founding of the National Congress advocating non-cooperation as the National Party would not get power by parliamentary means.[26]

Harry Hanham goes further by stating that the 82-year-old Muirhead was going back to his ILP roots and this explains the left-wing character of the Congress.[27] In a marvellous way, two men in their late seventies through to their early eighties were travelling full circle. Back home to where they belonged. The honourable

Ruaraidh was a Nationalist once again. His roots were a world away from Muirhead's but ideologically and culturally they coalesced again around the ideas and principles that mattered not out of obedience but with the heart. It was, and remains, a fine connection in letters between two old friends and comrades.

The last part around this correspondence is the insight into the lives of Ruaraidh and Dona Maria. We know that they temporarily moved back to London in July 1950 after Dona Maria had an accident. They were back in Pau later in the year.[28] A year later they were back in Bordeaux[29] which indicates that they stayed in France for the year although 'after a great deal of domestic sore and trouble of late', they were back in London by early 1953.[30] His wife had lost two brothers and they would not be returning to France. At the ripe old age of 84 his nomadic days were now over.

There was one major output from the Erskine-Muirhead letters. From his base in Glasgow's Elmbank Street, near Charing Cross, Muirhead ran the Scottish Secretariat. This was another leftist spin off which published old nationalist classics along with contemporary works. The aim was to fuse the social and national questions in Scotland in a way that Roland had always hoped that the *Forward* newspaper would do. Erskine of Marr would enter the pantheon of Secretariat authors that included Morrison Davidson, Oliver Brown and Douglas Young.

For this pamphlet, published in 1950 although undated, he returns to his 'bubble' motif while on this occasion explaining the rationale. The bubble is, 'the perfect image of all that is empty of thought in life'.[31] This pamphlet would be his final literary output and he returned to the language still close to his heart by declaiming for a final time the Highland-Lowland split. It is not the kilt or the pipes that make the Highlander but the language and that language belongs to Highlander and Lowlander alike. It is the national language of Scotland.

Nothing new. He goes on to cite Gaelic place names from all over Scotland and some historical anecdotes to back his argument. The key thing is that Pict and Scot were closer that many people think but more to the point is the Celtic link. His pamphlet ends by calling for a new declaration on the essential unity of the Gaelic peoples of Scotland and Ireland from a man who had done so much to forge those links. It was a fitting sign off for part one.

Part two of his sign off came in 1956. That year, at the age of 87, Erskine lost his wife, and companion through life. They were back in the south of England. With Dona Maria's death, Ruaraidh would have had the family of his brother around him for comfort and care. The editor of *Gairm*, Derick Thomson, caught up with him as one of Gaeldom's veterans who had done so much to promote the language. *Gairm*, meaning call or cry, would go on to take on the mantle of *Guth na Bliadhna*.

Erskine gave a potted life story informing Thomson that Ireland had taken hold of his imagination: '…agus a dhùisg a dhaingneachd a thaobh na Gàidhlige – daingneachd nach do lagaich riamh agus nach do lagaich fhathast.'[32]

He admits that his Gaelic is rusty but will get better when he returns to Scotland soon. He never did make it back home. His health prevented this. It is fitting that his last public engagement, so to speak, concerned the language that he loved and did so much to cultivate. Just when it looked in the 1930s that he had drifted away back to his aristocratic roots which could have put his political and cultural activities in a different light, the real Erskine of Marr bounced back. The radical nationalist and Gaelic activist who had edited two of the most influential journals over a twenty-year period came back to life. Just in time to pass away from this world: on 5th January 1960, just ten days short of his 91st birthday, he died peacefully in St. Augustine's Hospital in Kent.

Chapter Fourteen

Aristocracy, Nationality and Religion

Compton MacKenzie was a fellow exile and writer. He was born in County Durham and would find fame as a writer through such bestsellers as *Whisky Galore* and *Monarch of the Glen*. He even made it onto *This is Your Life* on Independent Television in 1956 and was given Eamon Andrews's famous red book! MacKenzie had much in common with Erskine although 14 years his junior. They were both founding members of the National Party of Scotland and were both on the fundamentalist, cultural wing of the young Party.

A few years before his best-sellers hit the shelves, MacKenzie brought out the first volume of an exploration of his politics, his faith and his identity. This was nominally a novel and there would be six volumes in all. The title was *The Four Winds of Love*. The main character was John Ogilvie who was not so loosely based on MacKenzie himself. The character's name was the name of the martyred Catholic priest who was executed at Glasgow Cross in 1615 and became a saint. Ogilvie's friend in his youth was Edward Fitzgerald or Fitz. Fitz was a young Irish student and both were in exile studying at a public school in England. Students of Irish history will recognise another martyr's name, this time from the 1798 rebellion in Ireland.

There are some points in MacKenzie's first volume that are pertinent to Erskine's life. Young Ogilvie recalls how he heard his first Gaelic word, *a' bhallaich* or the lenited word for boy, as he listens to a story from old Ardvore. The older man was telling him of how he met a survivor from the '45 rebellion when he was eight years old in 1830. In a later discussion, on Ardvore's estate in Sutherland, the penny drops for Ogilvie. He listens to the older man waxing lyrical about history, culture and Gaelic and draws his own conclusion; namely, independence for Scotland. Ardvore retorts:

'What would be the sense in that?'
'To maintain the traditional habit of life and way of thought of which you were speaking.'

'You won't be dragging politics into it. In any case it is not England we have to worry about up here. It is the south of Scotland...We could not exist materially without England.'

'That remains to be tried', John argued, 'But we could certainly exist spiritual.[1]

MacKenzie sums up in the most glorious way what this question meant for the Celticist exiles. It wasn't about economics or materialism but spirit – and opening up a spiritual dimension to their nationalism that the native-born nationalists, in the main, didn't understand. Gillies did, Erskine did and so too did the South African born Wendy Wood. Naturally, John would look at his own spiritual dimension. Born a Protestant, John gets into a conversation with a Protestant revivalist, Mr Wilbraham about faith. He is unimpressed with the preacher's take and reveals: "The nearest I ever felt to God so far', said John stiffly, 'was in a Catholic Church."[2]

A dual exploration takes place of his nationality with his new found Catholic faith and this faith is re-kindled in the beautiful cathedral of St. Mary's in Cracow.

Simultaneously, Fitz was on a journey. He was back home and travelling through Kerry and Clare, learning Irish and taking in the centenary of the '98 rebellion. He had a vision of his own death as an Irish Republican martyr but could see no date on his headstone. When he met again with Ogilvie, he told him of Ireland's situation. The country seemed at peace:

> But Ireland will not be saved by peace. No, and Ireland will not be saved by a mob of Hibernian playboys in the British House of Commons. No, begod, nor by Nationalist conventions in Chicago or New York. Nor by obstruction of a lot of la-di-da Tories in Parliament. And Ireland will not be saved by a bevy of draggle tailed women with haystacks of hair, stringing away at a harp and warbling about Deirdrie and Grania. And refusal to pay rent will not save Ireland. Nor boycott nor cattle-driving. Dynamite will not do it any more than moaning about dark Rosaleen over a bottle of Johnny Jamieson. A deliberate sacrifice must be offered. Life must come through death.[3]

The Pearseite 1916 language and imagery are striking. Written twenty years later, MacKenzie, while reminiscing, is still looking through the prism of Ireland. John Ogilvie, aka MacKenzie, likes the Irish fixity of nationality and religion and this was true of so many of that generation of Scottish nationalists. Yet he ensured that there was a warning from the Irishman, a kind of reality check. Fitz warns Ogilvie not to rush into converting to Catholicism:

> You want to test your reason and your history before you take a plunge like that. My religion is as much a part of me as the hair on my head; but when you've got to put it on like a wig you want to be pretty certain that it isn't going to blow off with the next change of wind.[4]

Those winds would blow through the rest of MacKenzie's volumes. Ironically, as he wrote the first volume in 1937, Erskine's wig was falling over his eyes as he wrote about Edward VII and the Crown. Faith came natural to Erskine. His feelings toward nationality and language had rocked his aristocratic boat. He had no right to be the revolutionary, Gaelic nationalist that he became. One hundred and twenty years after his birth into the Baronetcy of Erskine in Brighton, a Scottish journalist called George Rosie was also rocking the nationalist boat and raising publicity with his view that there was an 'Englishing' of Scotland. He laid the blame at the door of the Scottish aristocracy who had evolved into an Anglo-Scottish ascendancy over the last 400 years: 'That stratum of society is now almost totally anglicised, Episcopalian in religion, southward looking and politically Conservative.'[5]

That could have been true of the Honourable Ruaraidh Erskine of Marr but for the spiritual pull of his nationality. He had to reject his class, or at least its view of the world, to enter into this new, politically radicalised world. As we have seen he couldn't fully reject his family or his background. It was part of who he was. He did, however, set out on a course that hugely shaped Scottish nationalism and Gaelic language activism.

This may seem a strange statement as most Scottish nationalists today have never heard of Erskine. When he died there was, sadly, no obituary in the *Scots Independent*. The *Times* was the only periodical to carry an obituary for him. It shows that he was a literary force at that time and the author of the obituary complimented his 'highly idiosyncratic' writing style and perceptively commented that this, 'smacked more of the eighteenth century that the twentieth'.[6] Bolingbroke was always his hero, I suppose. While it is true that London society were paying him tribute, they could never understand him and could only see him through the light of his book on Edward VII.

Nationality and language were the driving forces for him. The evolution of his ideas led to a radicalisation that took Scottish nationalism to a different place from the pro- Imperial, pro-Union Home Rule for Scotland type of nationalism that was prevalent at this time. It was an evolution as he chipped away through his language activism, asking the same questions as Ogilvie and finding the answer just as easily. Scotland should be independent. As Catherine Kerrigan observantly put it:

> By putting the stress on linguistic differences as the manifestation of cultural and political problems, Erskine of Marr drew many non-Gaelic speakers and took the nationalist movement into a new phase which was to go well beyond any previous historical attempts to demand the right for self-government for Scotland.[7]

This was his main contribution and why, primarily he is the forgotten hero of Scottish nationalism. Scottish nationalists talk the language of independence today because of the Celticists of the early part of the twentieth century. The other forgotten heroes: Diack, Gillies, McGarry, MacNeil[8] were revolutionary nationalists who forced Scottish nationalism to look in the mirror. Was Home Rule enough? What was the Union's real legacy in Scotland? Could you ignore the language questions and stay true to your identity? Whose side were they on as Ireland took on the might of Britain?

As the early National Party developed, they moved away from this radicalism. John McCormick stamped a pro-Union, Home Rule stamp on the Party and it was probably no accident that he joined the Liberal Party in later years as he always favoured a federal option for the future of Britain. The SNP would make its way back home to a position of outright independence and for this they can thank the Liberty group of nationalists.

It is true that their Celticism was going to hamper the early attempts to form a Party and the modernists among the Scots National League at the time around Tom Gibson would always move away from this position. Yet it is to the fundamentalists' credit, and Erskine was their de facto leader, that they did not descend into racialism. They too had their pragmatic side and after the Irish Treaty was signed, the Liberty group accepted the pro-Treaty position in Ireland which led them to use the language of a Scottish Free State within the Commonwealth. If the prism reflected that it was good enough for the Irish then it was good enough for them too. They ignored the fact that there was battle for the spiritual soul of Irish nationalism too that ended in a bloody civil war. The last word on Ireland should be left to Constance Markievicz, who shared with Erskine some aristocratic baggage and eccentricities and who had fought in 1916 and through the war of Independence. She was a semi-regular visitor to Glasgow and had stayed in John MacLean's house. Writing in a Glasgow newspaper, she wrote that the term Saorstat was the nearest translation of Republic in the Irish Gaelic. Poblacht was a Latinised word turned into Gaelic. The Free Staters were guilty of a cultural theft: 'They stole our name, they stole our uniform, they stole our badges, they stole our Republican flag.'[9]

There is a link to Erskine's other main contribution which is infinitely more problematic but concerns the soul of modern Scottish nationalism. When will they withdraw from Westminster? At the outset, it should be stressed that Erskine was not anti-parliamentary as such although he had his anarchist moments. His problem was with the Palace of Westminster and its reign in his home country. A fellow radical Celticist, Peter Berresford Ellis, summed up the Celtic nationalists' views. Regarding the Union treaties of 1707 and 1801, he writes:

> It should, of course, be pointed out that the English controlled Parliament has continuously ignored the provisions of these treaties and thus the state has continued de facto without a written constitution while it exists de jure. Therefore, the body that sits in Westminster remains an English Parliament in which a small group of representatives from the Celtic periphery, impotent to act on the will of that assembly, and unable to address it in their native languages, are allowed to sit.[10]

Erskine's own views have been well quoted. They did not change and his correspondence with Muirhead in the late forties confirmed this. Scotland's cause would not be won on the floor of the House of Commons in Westminster. Parnell failed, Redmond failed and the SNP would fail too, in Erskine's opinion.

The vast majority of contemporary nationalists would, of course, disagree. Tactically, it would raise massive challenges if the SNP adopted an abstentionist line. It took a special set of circumstances for the Sinn Féin line to win out in Ireland. It would be argued that neither Scotland or her electorate would understand if the SNP MPs withdrew and came back home. They would be marching home, like Charlie's army after the retreat from Derby in 1746, to oblivion.

It seems to be a classic case of principle versus tactics and to political pragmatists, tactics always come first. Idealists and dreamers are for songs and memorial speeches but not for day to day politics. Yet, I believe that Erskine's views offer much for modern Scottish nationalists to ponder. As I write the Scottish National Party has 49 Members of Parliament in Westminster. The SNP also control the devolved Scottish Government in Edinburgh under Nicola Sturgeon as First Minister. They have much to gain and much to lose. Scotland voted against independence in a referendum in September 2014. All of these things would have seemed fantastical to Erskine and Muirhead in the late forties and early fifties.

The starting point for my view is that in principle, Erskine was right if not tactically sound. The referendum came about through a strong nationalist base in a devolved Scotland leading to the then Conservative Prime Minister, David Cameron acceding to a referendum. The strong showing of the SNP in Westminster came about, bizarrely, as a reaction to the No vote in that referendum. In the general election of 2015, the SNP won 53 out of 56 seats. The current 49 Nationalist MPs are in limbo. The UK has left the European Union after another referendum in 2016 while the majority of the electorate of Scotland voted to remain. The British Government are refusing to grant another referendum on independence as Scotland had the vote in 2014. Simply put: where do the SNP go?

Ruaraidh Erskine of Marr, the founding member and dissident who left the Party over the issue, can be held up as a mirror to the modern SNP. When are you going to leave Westminster? It is not a reflection that many in the Party would want to see. In their heart of hearts, they know that they will need to withdraw sometime. The best-case scenario is that they withdraw after winning a second independence referendum. This is problematic, being dependent upon the British Government agreeing to a referendum and then the tricky task of taking on the might of that State and its resources and media to win that referendum. In this situation, the lone voice of Erskine of Marr will not be heard. The worst-case scenario is to stay in limbo; politically impotent within a parliament that they do not believe in. They would have to play the Westminster game even harder to keep their seats and their political reputation as a mainstream party. They would be Scotland's version of the Irish Party.

There may be a middle ground. To withdraw gently and by stealth and concentrate on running the Scottish Government in Edinburgh: to become Scotland's party of government – especially as the Labour Party in Scotland is so weak. They may be able to concentrate on building a movement for independence back here in Scotland and win the Scottish electorate over to the notion that they do not belong in Westminster. This position is also fraught with danger. Parties of government become cosy and complacent. They also govern; they don't protest. Many grassroots campaigners for independence are critical of the SNP's efforts to push a second referendum. Their very existence as a mainstream party may overshadow their very reason for existence in the first place.

So, there is no easy answer. We should remember that the discussions to form a National Party were delayed by this very question. Dissidents such as Erskine and MacDiarmid were arguing an uncomfortable truth that the then Party managers (as perhaps would be the case with today's Party managers) didn't like. Only dissidents tell the truth. If nothing else, modern Scottish nationalists should re-engage with the argument and re-engage with the revolutionary earl.

Another critical factor in his spiritual sense of nationality was language. He took language activism to a different level as we have seen and infused his nationalism with it just like the fictional Ogilvie. His Hebridean nanny played her part, of course, but not as much as he would have liked us to believe; a young English born aristocrat thinking about his own sense of identity was the real factor. Gaelic defined him and *Guth na Bliadhna* was the measure by which later publications would be assessed. It would be unfair to say that Gaelic scholars have not tapped into its riches yet there is more that could be done to open up its contents to a wider audience. The author attended a superb lecture by a young Czech academic, Petra Johana

Poncarová, in Glasgow University which compared Erskine with Derick Thomson.[11] More such interventions would raise Erskine's profile in the Gaelic world of letters.

Both Erskine and Thomson resisted the cosiness and even laziness of the mainstream Gaelic world; looking to energise and enthuse people with the dynamism and creativity that the language could offer. Erskine himself summed this up in a letter to Malcolm MacFarlane. MacFarlane had been a member of An Comunn Gàidhealach, who run the traditional, annual Mòd competition. Erskine was no fan of this staid format. He wrote to MacFarlane in 1911 praising his new editor, Eneas MacKay: 'He seems an energetic sort of man and that is just what is required in the Gaelic field where so many are sleep prone, not dreaming dreams or seeing visions, but in the dull dead slumber of ignorance and indifference.'[12]

Thomson would perhaps agree. He himself was such a driving force of Gaelic literature and met Erskine in his old age in 1956. Thomson paid a fine tribute from one Gael to another:

> Although Ruaraidh Erskine's Gaelic publishing work was not very successful in a commercial sense, it had a positive influence on Gaelic writers, and helped to lay the foundations for a resurgence in Gaelic writing (in fiction, poetry and journalism) which was to come when he had retired from active work in the field.[13]

Erskine was very much a modernist in the Gaelic language. The first all-Gaelic newspaper; four periodicals and he was the author of a Gaelic play as well as a creative short story writer and political polemicist in his own right in his adopted language. While he may have facilitated others to do this also, it must be stressed that Erskine led from the front. He was also a translator and translated Neil Munro's *The Old Tribute* into a book with some other pieces of writing in 1929. Marr had translated a Gaelic translation of Munro's *Ivis Primae Noctis*. Erskine had brought it back into English and earned this compliment from the original author: ' ...and I think you have been most happily inspired to re-tell them in English that is not merely a literal translation, but unquestionably has the spirit and blas of the Gaelic.'[14]

It was a perceptive comment as Erskine did have the spirit of the language and he saw, better than any of his political peers, the importance of Gaelic to Scotland. Economically and materially, Scotland will unquestionably live on if Gaelic dies. Spiritually and culturally, Scotland will not be the same; a piece of Scotland will die with it. I attended a Gaelic play in 2020 with my daughter, Lucy, in Glasgow's Tron Theatre entitled *Maim*. This means 'Panic'. The cast were from a Gaelic band, Whyte, led by the fine Gaelic singer, Alasdair Whyte. It was a fine piece of Gaelic language activism with energy, anger, passion. One thing stuck with me: every Gaelic word that we use is a thread to link the language's past and future together. Erskine provided much thread to the beautiful cloth of the language. Modern activists have much to learn from him.

Political Gaeldom certainly honours their hero. No language, no nation still inspires modern Gaelic nationalists. It is in this light that the writer, Seumas Mac A' Ghobhainn wrote of Erskine. Mac A' Ghobhainn, with Peter Berresford Ellis, wrote the defining book on the 1820 insurrection in Scotland.[15] Just as he reclaimed a forgotten working class rising, so too did this particular author look to reclaim a 'forgotten Gaelic patriot' and 'gentle Scottish revolutionary' whose 'innate humanity' shone through.[16] Mac A' Ghobhainn was right to acknowledge Erskine's contribution while conceding that most Gaels and Scottish nationalists have probably never heard of him. That contribution has to be introduced to that constituency in Scotland.

Scottish Nationalists, as I write, now have political power in a devolved Scotland. They have an opportunity to do something radical to save the language. Prior to the independence referendum, the Scottish Government published a White Paper with a commitment to Gaelic:

> Our aim as a government would be to continue to reverse the decline of Gaelic in Scotland. The most recent Census has demonstrated that initiatives in support of Gaelic have significantly slowed down the decline of the language. Policy and resources would continue to be directed to the priority of increasing the numbers speaking, learning and using the language.[17]

There is still much to be done and the Party of nationalism in Scotland could be doing much more. There are positive signs. The first all Gaelic speech was made in the Scottish Parliament by the Member for Skye, Kate Forbes. There is also a Gaelic language development officer in the Parliament, Alasdair MacCallum, who has produced a Gaelic leaflet, *A' Phàrlamaid Albannach Agadsa/ Your Scottish Parliament*.[18] MacCallum has been a fine activist for the language himself. Whether the modern nationalists have heard of them or not, the stamp of Erskine, Gillies, MacGarry and MacNeil are all over such initiatives.

Neither Erskine's commitment to the language or the nation were fads. His revolutionary nationalism was genuine. He went through a crisis of identity in the thirties but came out of that as the same Erskine of Marr, the 'quintessential romantic' as James Hunter called him.[19] His fad was his flirtation with the Left. This has hoodwinked many scholars who see a proto-socialist in his association and collaboration with John MacLean. Erskine was no socialist albeit he was 'Citizen Marr' for a short period. Citizen Marr may have been a flirt but his influence was felt.

Reading the list of left wing heavyweights whom he enticed on to his National Committee in 1919 is nothing short of impressive; all battle-hardened class warriors who warmed to Erskine's argument that Scottish self-determination was a principle to be fought for in its own right. This came at a time when socialist revolution was in the air all over Europe and Erskine's Committee could be seen as a nationalist distraction. Erskine, for his part, retained a lifelong admiration for those socialists who were friendly to the Scottish cause including Keir Hardie and Jimmy Maxton.

Yet his relationship with MacLean invites the most attention. Every biography of the Red Clydesider, and there are many, all mention his relationship with the eccentric aristocrat. I have touched on this above. The main point is that in influencing John MacLean, the eccentric aristocrat had a real influence on the history of the Scottish Left. The two men's meeting in MacLean's house in July 1920 had a direct bearing on MacLean's leaflet calling for national independence in his own Marxist style: a Scottish Workers Republic. The timeline is inescapable.

I was unaware of this meeting when I wrote my own biography of MacLean. Knowledge of this meeting gives a timeline. By August, MacLean was able to articulate what he had been thinking about for the last couple of years. His advocacy of independence and that it was consistent with both socialism and Scotland's historical development marked his break with British socialism. He did not look back and rejected the nascent British Communist Party and its London line. Hugh MacDiarmid would describe this position, a Scottish Workers Republic, as the 'John MacLean line.' This 'line' would be a minority tradition largely among the nationalist left and also the poets and songwriters. This 'line' was worked out in discussion with the Honourable Earl of Marr.

As someone who has researched the life and influence of the Marxist as well as his influence on the Left, it is quite a revelation to understand the part played by Erskine. Their collaboration was significant enough and they both played an active role in supporting Ireland's struggle for independence. I can only come to the conclusion that Erskine, and his troubadors in the *Liberty* journal, understood something that it would take Scottish socialism another seventy years to understand. Erskine understood that the Left could be autonomous and internationalist. There was no contradiction. Whether it was the Labour Party chasing government power in Westminster as a leverage to socialist change or even the name of the 'Communist Party of Great Britain', Erskine could see that the Left in Scotland – and its activists and trade union supporters – felt that their internationalism was defined by being British. The *Liberty* group saw this as imperialist and a suppression of the traditions and roots of the Left in Scotland. In this *Liberty*, arguably, was more politically advanced than their friends in the traditional left-wing organisations.

The Irish Left understood this and this understanding was crystal clear to Erskine. When the Irish trade unions were feeling pressure to merge with the British organisations in the name of unity, even as the Treaty negotiations were taking place, Cathal O'Shannon penned an open letter reminding his British comrades that it would be for Irish workers to decide the form of organisation that they should choose, be it a closer political unity with Britain, a unity of consent as existed in the Dominions or, 'an entirely separate political entity free to work out its own destiny untrammelled by political ties.'[20] The Scots never asserted that organisational self-determination. When they came close to it, as witnessed by Tom Johnston's activity and cooperation with the SHRA into the late twenties, they fell in line with the British organisation that they were part of as they were expected to do. Erskine pushed for an autonomous Scottish left organisation and deserves to be recognised for doing so.[21]

Nothing cemented Erskine's world view together more than his faith. We do not know if he was born a Catholic but it is highly probable. His clan connections were with the north east where pockets of Catholic worship survived. To use Compton MacKenzie's analogy, cited above, his Gaelic and his nationalism may have been well fitted wigs but his faith was intrinsic to him. His faith imbued his politics and language activism with the spirituality that his comrade MacKenzie, a fellow Catholic, also saw in his semi-autobiographical self as John Ogilvie.

We know that *Guth na Bliadhna* was launched as a Catholic periodical. Even as it evolved, it evolved into a Catholic Nationalist journal. A strong sense of positive faith is in the journal with strong contributors including priests, Fathers Kent and Pollen, who were both politically astute, and writers such as Mòrlamh who contributed pieces on the Saints, especially Columba. As I write, Gaelic Christianity is struggling in general and especially in its Catholic variant in its heartland in the southern Hebridean islands. There is a shortage of Gaelic speaking priests which puts the practice of the faith in Gaelic in real danger. Erskine's treasure trove of faith will probably go unplundered.

At the time he did receive much criticism for the faith line that was taken by the journal. He did not help himself by some intemperate remarks against Presbyterianism and lack of contrition for these remarks. William Gillies' grandson commented in his lecture on his grandfather's contribution, that this was the one thing about Erskine which made Gillies angry.[22] Gillies was not alone and there were letter writers who raised their objections. Erskine was on stronger ground when he defended the positive aspects of his faith. He kept this with him even to the time of the *Pictish Review* which again combined the old themes with some of the old writers. When faced with the rebuke that his journal was promoting 'medievalism', he recounted with a radiant reply that will resonate with any person of that faith: 'Holy Mass is the most beautiful thing on God's earth: it is the supreme act of worship of the human world: it is the noblest piece of spiritual architecture ever planned and raised.'[23]

Faith wasn't just personal. Neither was it esoteric or mystical. There were noble ideals involved in saving a language and a nation: his Gaelic nationalism was a kind of spiritual architecture itself. Underpinning his critique of Scots Protestantism lay a political and historical critique of the Reformation. Scotland turning away from the old faith was probably the one single event that led to political union with England in Erskine's opinion. He wasn't alone and it wasn't just a Catholic viewpoint. I will use two examples.

The first takes us back to 1903. In a letter in Waddie's *Scottish Nationalist,* coincidentally at a time when Edward VII was on a State visit to Scotland, the contributor, D J MacKinnon, was raising a 'Highlander's Protest'. A silver coin from the reign of Henry VIII had been unearthed at Kirkintilloch Waterworks near Glasgow. The reason being that England's Reforming king had bribed the Reforming Scottish nobility. Knox received £20 per annum, we are told, and the nobles who held St Andrews for the cause of Reform received £2480 plus provisions from England. The Archbishop of St Andrews, James Beaton, and his soon to be assassinated nephew, Cardinal Beaton, had the 'moral courage' to resist these bribes.[24]

The second takes us forward to 1970; ten years after Erskine's death. Wendy Wood, who was not a Catholic, used her autobiography to berate John Knox. She cites the figure of £1500 that Knox received from English agents at a tower just outside Berwick. She believed that that represented treachery and underhanded deceit. Wood states that she is all for Luther and Calvin but not, 'Knox and his destructiveness, the enemy of the aristocracy of beauty'.[25] Two examples almost seventy years apart that may be seen to paint John Knox as a kind of pantomime villain for Scottish nationalists, and perhaps allowing Erskine to square his faith with the national cause of Scotland. Of course, the argument could be seen as a big 'what if' of history, ignoring any potentially positive contribution that Knox and the Reformation may have made to Scottish life.[26] On the other hand, this historical strand of nationalism offers a counterpoint to the main narrative that runs through Scottish history.

On Saturday 4th March 1933, Art O'Brien returned to the National Party of Scotland's London branch to deliver a lecture entitled 'The Complete Nationalist'. The subject was his dear friend and colleague, Liam Gillies, who had died in July 1932. Gillies had all the attributes: the culture, the radicalism, the zeal and passion as well as the language to be the complete nationalist. O'Brien spoke from authority as he had watched the National Party grow from its inception with 'sympathy and interest.' O'Brien himself was still the old Celticist. Language was key:'

As a language develops it becomes the repository, both in its spoken and written manifestation, of the mental treasures, the philosophy, the inner spirit, the outlook, the activities, the yearnings, the urges – in a word: all the inherited tradition of the people and the nation.[27]

At this particular time, it is unlikely that Erskine would have been in O'Brien's good books after calling for the restoration of an Irish monarchy! However, the term 'complete nationalist' would also apply to Erskine. According to Professor William Gillies it was Erskine who was the inspiration for his grandfather as Liam Gillies saw in Erskine, 'idealism and erudition and international horizons'.[28]

With this Erskine touched all whom he came into contact with and his first principles never changed: 'gun chànain, gun chinneach! 'His last written words in his pamphlet for the Scottish Secretariat summarise this:

As to the language, on whose prosperity that of the Gael himself depends according to ancient ways of thinking about the matter I recall to mind in this connection the Reverend Lambert Daneau, a famous Calvinist preacher in France, who, talking about his creed affirmed that the duty of the civil magistrate was to maintain if it existed, establish if it existed not, and revive if were anywhere perished the Calvinist religion. With the assistance of what remains of our language in Scotland it should not be difficult to restore to it in time its former supremacy.[29]

When your last words tie in with your first principles then you have achieved something. He even seemed to have made his peace with Calvinism. Like any writer he appeared to grapple with the big questions of his own identity; in his own case that of class, nation and religion. From the opposite end of the class spectrum, James Connolly (the socialist martyr of the 1916 Rising) grappled with similar questions from a working-class perspective and Connolly's views challenged an assumption regarding the atheism and internationalism underpinning the identity of a socialist.[30]

The subjects are powerful indicators of personal identity. Connolly was no Celticist but he was an exiled Irishman. He came at the subjects by way of debate with a Catholic priest about socialism and grappled with his own sense of faith and nationality. Such subjects were, and are, easily dismissed by pragmatists and native-born nationalists who scorn any romantic illusions about their cause. James Joyce summed this up vigorously in his *Portrait of the Artist as a Young Man* through the thoughts of his autobiographical hero, Stephen:

Stephen, following his own thought, was silent for an instant – The soul is born, he said vaguely, first in those moments I told you of. It has a slow and dark birth, more mysterious than the birth of the body. When the soul of a man is born in this country there are nets flung at it to hold it back from flight. You talk to me of nationality, language and religion. I shall try to fly by those nets.[31]

For Joyce, the subjects were still important and they related to the soul and yet he still saw them as stifling and inhibiting; a 'net' that will entrap you. The exiles had no such worries about being trapped in any net and they flew and soared and created with their sense of personal identity at the heart of what they did. This doesn't, of course, mean that Joyce was wrong. He, too, was challenging assumptions.

In his own way, Erskine of Marr also challenged long-held assumptions. A Brighton-born, aristocrat proved his credentials as a revolutionary nationalist and won over many on the Scottish and Irish Left because he was genuine. He grappled with the great questions, the spiritual questions and came out sure as to his own sense of self and what he believed in. He wobbled in the 1930s but in the end he held firm.

I personally received a lovely reminder of Erskine's aristocratic credentials from the current Earl of Buchan in a postcard. He told me that he remembers his grandfather's brother from when he was a small boy. Erskine was a small man and the current Earl still has one of his kilts.[32] This is a reminder of who Erskine was, as seen by his family, and it raises all sorts of questions and contradictions in itself. These questions and contradictions go to the heart of the notion of personal and national identity.

Ruaraidh Erskine of Marr deserves to be re-discovered by Scottish nationalism and he has something to offer. Yes, he will frustrate, inspire, perplex and amuse in equal measure. Party managers and bureaucrats of any hue may never understand him. He leaves us with interesting and sometimes difficult questions about Scotland and her sense of nationality as do many of the women and men mentioned in this book. Looking for those answers is a positive and energising quest.

REFERENCES

Introduction

1. H J Hanham, *Scottish Nationalism*, Edinburgh, 1969, p. 10.
2. See also D S Thomson, 'Erskine, Stuart Richard (known as Ruaraidh Erskine of Marr), 1869–1960', *Oxford Dictionary of National Biography*, September 2004.
3. Seumas Mac A' Ghobhainn, 'Ruaraidh Arascainn is Mhàirr', *Stornoway Gazette*, 19/2/1972.
4. Andrew Marr, *The Battle for Scotland*, London 1992, p. 65.
5. H J Hanham, *Scottish Nationalism*, Edinburgh, 1969.
6. Gavin Kennedy, *The Radical Approach: Papers on an Independent Scotland*, Edinburgh, 1976, p.5.

Chapter One

1. Ian Grimble, *Scottish Clans and Tartans*, London, 1973, p. 77
2. Roddy Martine, *Scottish Clan and Family Names: Their Arms, Origins and Tartans*, Edinburgh, 1987, p. 91.
3. E P Thompson, *The Making of the English Working Class*, 1980, p. 148
4. Eric J Evans, *The Forging of the Modern State: Early Industrial Britain 1783–1870*, New York, 1983, p. 50.
5. The following information comes from *Cracoft's Peerage* – online edition.
6. See the profile in *Gairm*, An Aireamh 16, 1956 p. 367, as captured by the Gaelic scholar, Derick Thomson.
7. See https://www.uppingham.co.uk
8. *Northampton Mercury*, 21/1/1888.
9. Evans, ibid, p. 351.
10. *The Honourable R Erskine of Marr, King Edward VII and Some Other Figures*, London, 1936, p. 38. In the original text, Erskine uses the English, James III.
11. For example, 'An Interesting Biography', *Derby Evening Telegraph*, 11/10/1889.
12. Manifesto of the Scottish Home Rule Association, Edinburgh, 1/12/1887, in the Special Collections, University of Glasgow, MS 1484/11/1-3.
13. Manifesto, ibid.
14. Manifesto, ibid.
15. Nathan Kane, 'A Study of the Debate on Scottish Home Rule, 1886–1914', PhD thesis, University of Edinburgh, 2015.
16. See https://www.electricscotland.com/history/hardie/chapter3.htm
17. Sydney and Olive Checkland, *Industry and Ethos: Scotland 1832–1914*, London, 1984, p. 168.

Chapter Two

1. *The Whirlwind – A Lively and Eccentric Newspaper*, University of Edinburgh Special Collections, Vol 1, number 1, 28/6/1890, p. 1.

2. *The Whirlwind*, ibid.

3. Honourable Stuart Erskine, 'Gusts', *The Whirlwind*, ibid, p. 2.

4. Honourable Auberon Herbert, *The Whirlwind*, ibid, p. 6.

5. *The Whirlwind*, Vol 1 number 2, 5/7/1890 p. 29.

6. See HRH Prince Michael of Albany, *The Forgotten Monarchy of Scotland*, London, 2002, pp 273-274.

7. 'A True and Real State of Prince Charles Stuart's Miraculous Escape after the Battle of Culloden', *The Whirlwind*, Vol 1, number 13, 20/9/1890, p. 197.

8. *The Whirlwind*, Vol 1, number 5, 26/7/1890, p. 67.

9. 'Letters to Absurd People', *The Whirlwind*, Vol 1, number 12, 13/9/1890, p.181

10. 'Revolution', *The Whirlwind*, Vol 1, number 13, 20/9/1890.

11. *The Whirlwind*, Vol 1, number 5, 26/7/1890, p. 68.

12. Ibid, p. 68.

13. Herbert Vivian, 'Reminiscences of a Short Life – chapter 8', *The Whirlwind*, Vol 1, number12, 13/9/1890, pp 188-189.

14. 'The National Convention', *The Standard/ Bratach na h-Alba*, July 1922.

15. This account comes from *The Honourable R. Erskine of Marr, King Edward VII and Some Other Figures*, London, 1936, p. 97.

16. Ibid, p. 101.

17. Ibid, p. 102.

18. John J Horgan, *From Parnell to Pearse*, Dublin, 1948, p. 48.

19. H J Hanham, *Scottish Nationalism*, Edinburgh, 1969, p. 93.

20. *The Whirlwind*, Vol 1, number 6, 2/8/1890, pp 86-87.

Chapter Three

1. *The Whirlwind*, Vol 1, No. 1, 28/6/1890.

2. Alasdair MacMhaighstir Alasdair, 'Oran do'n Phrionnsa' ('A Song to the Prince') written prior to the Rising. Quoted in John Lorne Campbell (ed.), *Highland Songs of the Forty-Five*, Edinburgh, 1997 edition, p. 48.

3. MacMhaighstir Alasdair, 'Tearlach Mac Sheumais' ('Charles Son of James'), in Campbell, ibid p. 53.

4. Campbell, ibid, p. 279.

5. William Ross, 'An Suaithneas Bàn, 1788' quoted in Campbell, ibid, p. 290: 'Farewell to the White Cockade, Till Doomsday he in death is laid, The grave has ta'en the White Cockade, The cold tombstone is now his shade.'

6. *Huddersfield Daily Chronicle*, 29/10/1891. Many regional newspapers carried the story.

7. *Glasgow Herald*, 29/10/1891, p. 6.

8. *Sheffield Evening Express*, 15/1/1891, p. 10.

9. *Dundee Courier*, 30/9/1891, p. 4.

10. Naomi Lloyd-Jones, 'Liberalism, Scottish Nationalism and the Home Rule Crisis, c1886–93', *English Historical Review*, Vol. CXXIX, No. 539, August 2014, p. 882.

11. *Rothesay Chronicle*, 23/4/1892, p. 3.

12. *Manchester Courier*, 18/2/1892.

13. Reprinted in the *Lancashire Evening Post*, 17/10/1892, p. 3.

14. *Home News for India, China and the Colonies,* 30/12/1892.

15. *United Ireland*, 8/7/1893. The piece was entitled, 'Revival of Jingoism.'

16. Political Diary, *York Herald*, 17/9/1893.

17. No definitive date is given on the death certificate. See https://www.Ancestry.co.uk .

18. *Northampton Mercury,* 3/5/1894. No details are given other than that the death occurred in Torquay.

Chapter Four

1. The Honourable Stuart Erskine, *Lord Bolingbroke: Being Extracts from the Political Writings of Henry St. John Viscount Bolingbroke*, Westminster, 1897.

2. Erskine, ibid. p. 25.

3. *Sir Charles Petire, Bolingbroke*, London and Glasgow, 1937, p. 11.

4. *The Honourable Stuart Erskine, Lord Dullborough: A Sketch*, Bristol, 1898, p. 26.

5. Erskine, *Dullborough*, pp 120–121.

6. The Honourable Stuart Erskine, Braemar: *An Unconventional Tour Guide and Literary Souvenir*, Edinburgh, 1898, p. 22.

7. Erskine, *Braemar*, p. 100.

8. *Dundee Advertiser*, 18/3/1897. Review of Erskine's article, 'Lord Mar's legacy to his Son.' This appeared in the *Scottish History Society Journal.*

9. Patrick Witt, Connections Across the North Channel: Ruaraidh Erskine and Irish influence on Scottish Discontent !906-20, *The Irish Story*, Irish History Online.

10. The following account draws on the report, 'The Pan-Celtic Visitors', *South Wales Daily News*, 19/7/1899.

11. The Gaelic Revival, *The Highland News,* 29/9/1900, p. 2.

12. 'In Town and Out', *The Tatler*, 14/1/1920. Erskine stated in a profile for a fashionable society magazine that his father had given him his Gaelic Christian name. I have found no evidence of this.

13. 'The Irish Language: Agitation in Scotland and Ireland to Save It', *Dundee Evening Post*, 4/5/1900, p. 2.

14. The Honourable Stuart Ruadri Erskine, *The Kilt and How to Wear It*, Inverness, 1901, p. 1.

15. Erskine, *The Kilt*, p. 5.

16. Donald John MacLeod, 'Gaelic Prose', *Transactions of the Gaelic Society of Inverness*, Vol XLIX, 16/1/1976, p. 203.

17. MacLeod, *Gaelic Prose*, ibid, p. 210.

18. *Am Bàrd*, Vol 2, number 1, An Ceitein/May 1902, p. 25.

19. Ibid, p. 8.

20. Ibid, p. 8.

21. *Am Bàrd*, Vol 2, number 2, An t-Òg Mhios/June 1902.

22. *Am Bàrd*, Vol 2, number 3, An t-Iuchar/July 1902, p. 6.

23. *Am Bàrd*, Vol 1, number 2, ND.

Chapter Five

1. D Thomson, 'Erskine, Stuart Richard [known as Ruaraidh Erskine of Mar], 1869–1960, *Oxford Dictionary of National Biography*, September 2004.

2. Donald John MacLeod, 'Gaelic Prose', *Transactions of the Gaelic Society of Inverness*, Vol XLIX, 16/1/1976, p. 211.

3. 18th June 2019 to be precise.

4. *Aberdeen Press and Journal*, 7/8/1902.

5. *The Scottish Nationalist*, Vol 1, No.1 March 1903 p. 1.

6. Ibid, p. 2.

7. Ajax, *Highland Patriots*, 1909, p. 31.

8. See H C G Matthew, 'Davidson, John Morrison', *Oxford Dictionary of National Biography,* 23rd September 2004.

9. J Morrison Davidson, 'Juvenescat Scotia Invicta!' *The Scottish Nationalist*, Vol 1, No. 1, March 1903, p. 5.

10. 'Socialism – the Only Hope of the World!' was the banner on a hired bus that toured London at the turn of the century.

11. J Morrison Davidson, Ibid, p. 5.

12. Erskine, 'The Church and the Highlands', *Guth na Bliadhna*, Vol 1, Book 1, An t-Earrach/Spring, 1904, p. 1.

13. Erskine, ibid, p. 11.

14. Erskine, *Guth na Bliadhna*, Vol 1, Book 2, p. 128.

15. *Guth na Bliadhna*, Vol 2, No 1, 1905 p.103. 'Iona of my heart, Iona my love. The place where the voice of the monks meets the bellow of the cows; but before the coming of the rising of the world Iona will be as she was in the beginning.'

16. Erskine, 'On language', *Guth na Bliadhna*, Vol. 1 Book 1, 1904, p. 82.

17. From a piece on Andrew Carnegie, Guth na Bliadhna, Vol 3 No. 1, 1906, p. 163.

18. M H Dzlewicki, *Poland's Struggle for Existence*, Vol 2, No 1, 1905.

19. R Erskine of Marr, The Passing of Unionism, Vol 2, No 3, 1905.

20. R Erskine of Marr, ibid, p. 206.

21. B Purdie, 'Crossing Swords with WB Yeats': Twentieth Century Scottish Nationalist Encounters with Ireland', *Journal of Irish and Scottish Studies*, Vol 1, Issue 1.

22. R Erskine of Marr, 'Sword and Pen', *Guth na Bliadhna*, Vol 1, No.4, 1904, p. 315.

23. P H Pearse, "Education' in the West of Ireland', *Guth na Bliadhna*, Vol

2, No 4, 1905, p. 377.

24. See, for example, Erskine's pieces on 'A' Ghàidhlig agus na sgoilean' ('Gaelic and the Schools'), Vol 3, No 1, 1906 and Education and 'Atmosphere', Vol 3, No. 4 1906.

25. P H Pearse,' O' Donovan Rossa – Graveside Panegyric', *Political Writings and Speeches*, Dublin 1952, p. 135.

26. Editorial, *Guth na Bliadhna*, Vol 2, No 4, 1905, p. 308.

27. *Northampton Mercury,* 18/11/1904.

28. *Bail' A Bheolain*, Argyll.

29. R MacDonald, *Parliament and the Gael*, Vol 3, No1, 1906, p. 184.

30. Editorial, *Guth na Bliadhna*, Vol 3 No 4, 1906, p. 321.

31. Joseph E A Connell Jr, 'Arthur Griffith and the Development of Sinn Féin', *History Ireland*, Issue 4, July/August, 2011.

32. R Erskine of Marr, 'Ireland and Scotland', *Sinn Féin*, 13/7/1907. I am indebted to Máirtín Ò' Catháin for allowing me access to his notes through Stephen Coyle to whom I also owe a debt of gratitude. Both are fine scholars and authors on the Irish experience in Scotland and who fit Erskine's description as the sort of people to undertake the task.

33. *Guth na Bliadhna*, Vol 4, No 1, 1907, p.12 Translated: ' …and when we do that business that we were supposed to do regarding this encouragement (of Ireland), if we had let them forget anyhow one thing about the English Parliament, or those that were chosen for to improve our own affairs and take these forward at Westminster.'

34. *Guth na Bliadhna*, Vol 4, No.4, 1907, p. 406.

35. *Guth na Bliadhna*, Vol 4, No 4, 1907, p. 373.

36. RAM, Bruadar, An Sgeulaiche, *An Naodhamh Mios,* September, 1909, p. 84.

37. Anja Gunderloch, *The Gaelic Manuscripts of Glasgow University: A Catalogue*, 2007, p. 116.

38. Erskine to Charles Loch, 24/7/1909, Charles Loch papers, University of Glasgow, Gaelic Collection, Gaelic Correspondence I.

Chapter Six

1. Madeleine Bunting, 'Gaelic: The Secret Language of Revolution', *Sunday Herald,* 25/9/2016.

2. B Purdie, "Crossing Swords with WB Yeats': Twentieth Century Scottish Nationalist Encounters with Ireland, *Journal of Irish and Scottish Studies,* Vol 1, Issue 1.

3. See Naomi Lloyd-Jones, Liberalism, Scottish Nationalism and the Home Rule Crisis c 1886-1893', *English Historical Review,* vol CXXIX, No 539 for a thorough analysis of nationalism of this type. Thanks to Dr Catriona MacDonald for this source.

4. See Richard J Finlay, 'Gillies, William (Liam Mac Gille Iosa), 1865–1932,' *Oxford Dictionary of National Biography*, September 2004 for a short, excellent introduction to his life.

5. Purdie, ibid, p. 193.

6. Fear an Réidhlein, Modh-Sgriobhaidh, *Guth na Bliadhna*, Am Foghar/ Autumn, 1910, p. 351.

7. AME, 'An Sluagh Chunntas (The Census)', An Samhradh/Summer, 1911. Scotland's population was 4,759,521 with 287,418 Gaelic speakers.

8. Eamon O'Flaherty, 'The Abbey Theatre – the first hundred years', *History Ireland,* Issue 1, Spring 2004, Volume 12.

9. *Guth na Bliadhna*, An Geamhradh/Winter 1912, p. 96.

10. Seumas Mac A' Ghobhainn, Ruaraidh Arascainn is Mhàirr, *Stornoway Gazette*, 19/2/1972; Alasdair MacCallum, 'Ruaraidh Arascainn is Mhàirr,' *Scottish Workers Republic*, Spring 1997.

11. For a good insight into Sinclair's work, see Aonghas MacLeòid, 'The Historical Plays of Donald Sinclair', accessed online.

12. Erskine of Marr, 'Gaelic Drama', *Guth na Bliadhna*, Volume 11, An Samhradh/Summer, 1914, p. 219.

13. Erskine, ibid, p. 215.

14. *Guth na Bliadhna*, Am Foghar/Autumn, 1912, p. 494.

15. Ibid, p. 495.

16. This was a footnote on p. 497.

17. *The Thistle – A Scottish Patriotic Magazine*, Vol 3, September, No 38, p. 156.

18. A good example would be 'A Scottish Conservative', The Scottish Elections of 1895', *The Scottish Review*, July and October 1895, Vol XXVI.

19. Ruaraidh Araiscainn is Mhairr, 'Dealachadh nan Rathad' ('Parting of the Road'), *Guth na Bliadhna*, Am Foghar/Autumn, 1914. 'We laboured for our world, believing that the day of the little states had passed; that there wasn`t anything else we needed to find in it; and that it (the British Empire) was the Empire of light, the saviour of the whole world. These deceived thoughts of ours lasted as long as the whole night of our ignorance; but, at the break of the day, we saw a form of change on matters that we didn`t all know properly before this. We finally understood that the day of the little states hadn`t passed, instead, the axe of men was put against the old branches of the tree of the Empire.'

20. R Erskine of Marr, 'Celt, Slav, Hun and Teuton', *Scottish Review*, Vol 37, Autumn, 1914.

21. ''A Scottish Artisan', Round about a pound a week', *Scottish Review*, Vol 37, Spring 1914, p. 40.

22. William Diack, 'Scotland and the War', *Scottish Review,* Vol 37, Winter 1914, p. 491.

23. James Maxton, 'The Working-Class Movement', *Scottish Review*, Vol 37, Winter,1914, p. 566.

24. Editorial, *Highlander*, 29th May, 1875.

25. I M M MacPhail, 'The Highland Elections of 1884–86,' 27/10/1978, *Transactions of the Gaelic Society of Inverness*, Volume L, 1976-78 p.383.

26. Quoted in Ewen A Cameron, *Land for the People? The British Government*

and the Scottish Highlands, c1880–1925, East Linton, 1996, p. 141.

27. The Highland Land League: *Objects and Constitution – Council and Annual Report for 1916*, p. 13.

28. Ibid, pp 12-13.

29. See Iain Frisor Grigor, *Highland Resistance: The Radical Tradition in the Scottish North*, 2000, p. 185 where the author cites such a meeting in Greenock.

30. 'Mar sin, chan e an Dia beò, thoiribh an aire, is còir a bhi prìomh cùspair ar na achainaichean na's mo tuilleadh, ach a mhain 'the force called God.' – Ruaraidh Arascainn is Mhàirr, A' Chriosdachd agus an Cogadh, *Guth na Bliadhna*, An Samhradh/Summer, 1916, p. 173.

31. ;Ceartas!; *Guth na Bliadhna*, Am Foghar/Autumn, 1915, p. 296.

32. RAM, 'Sith an t-Saoghail agus an Ceann Suidh Wilson' ('World Peace and President Wilson'), *Guth na Bliadhna*, Am Foghar/Autumn 1916, p. 301. Eadar-theangachadh: 'They are beautiful, also, our beloved can take them and use them for ever, if we so wish to correct (put an end) to hurt, and the age of miracles can move forward as they always have done.'

33. Erskine of Marr, 'Ireland and Scotland at the Peace Congress', *The Scottish Review*, Winter 1917, p. 424.

34. William Diack, 'Scotland's War Bil'l, *The Scottish Review*, Winter 1917, p. 456.

35. *The Derry Journal*, 25/1/1918.

36. *The Dumfries and Galloway Standard* the next day.

37. *The Celtic Annual*, 1918–19, Hew Morrison Collection, National Library of Scotland digital collection, p. 15.

38. 'Achd An Fhoghluim Neo-Albannaich', *Guth na Bliadhna*, An t-Earrach/Spring, 1918, p. 107.

Chapter Seven

1. Citing MacLean's reply to Erskine's invitation to sign a petition to President Woodrow Wilson for Scottish self-determination.

2. Art O' Brien papers, National Library of Ireland, MS8427/18. Letter from Erskine to O'Brien, 17/7/1920.

3. Erskine to O' Brien (ibid).

4. John MacLean, 'All Hail, the Scottish Workers Republic!' In Nan Milton (ed), *John MacLean: In the Rapids of Revolution*, London, 1978, p. 217 – 218.

5. I was not aware of this meeting when I wrote my own biography of MacLean. See G Cairns, *The Red and The Green – A Portrait of John MacLean*, Glasgow, 2017.

6. John MacLean, 'Irish Stew,' in Milton (ed), ibid, p. 218.

7. Andrew Marr, *The Battle for Scotland*, Penguin, 1992, p. 65.

8. Erskine, 'The Celtic and Labour Movements,' *Guth na Bliadhna*, An t-Earrach/Spring 1918, p. 97.

9. Erskine, ibid, p. 101.

10. Erskine, 'The Dictatorship of the Proletariat', *The Scottish Review*, Vol 42, Spring 1919, p. 10.

11. Editorial, 'Scotland and the Peace Congress', *The Scottish Review*, Vol 40, Autumn, 1917, p. 289.

12. Editorial, 'Scotland and the Peace Congress', *The Scottish Review*, Vol 41, Summer 1918, p. 149.

13. Erskine, 'Chronicles of the Quarters', *The Scottish Review*, Vol 41, Autumn 1918, p. 396.

14. Erskine, 'The National Memorial', *The Scottish Review*, Vol 41, Winter 1918, p. 430.

15. 'Chronicles of the Quarters', *The Scottish Review*, Vol 41, Winter 1918, p. 536.

16. Cathal O' Shannon, 'John Maclean and President Wilson', *The Voice of Labour*, 25/1/1919.

17. 'Chronicles of the Quarters', *The Scottish Review*, Vol 42, Spring, 1919, p. 115.

18. The full committee is listed on page 449 in the winter edition of Volume 42. In line with Marr's male chauvinism, there are, unsurprisingly, no women on the Committee.

19. Erskine to O'Brien, 10/5/19/, O'Brien Papers, MS 8427/18.

20. Francis Stuart to O'Brien, 23/5/19, O' Brien Papers, ibid.

21. Quoted in Alfred Cobban, *The Nation State and National Self-Determination*, London and Glasgow, 1969, p. 66.

22. Cobban, ibid, p. 66.

23. Memo, 9/2/20, O' Brien Papers, ibid.

24. Erskine to O'Brien, 20/6/20, O'Brien Papers, ibid.

25. William Diack, 'Scottish and Irish Labour Colleges', *The Scottish Review*, Vol 42, Winter, 1919, p. 399.

26. William Diack, 'Scottish TU's and Industrial Unrest', *The Scottish Review*, Vol 40, Autumn 1917, p. 338.

27. Review, Vol 42, Summer 1919, p,139

28. R Erskine of Marr, 'Celtic Communism', *The Vanguard*, No XIII, December 1920, in the Brenda Bennie Papers, John Maclean Collection, Glasgow Caledonian University.

29. James Connolly, *Labour in Irish History*, Dublin, 1956, p. xxx.

30. R Erskine of Marr, 'Celtic Tribal Communism', *The Socialist*, December 1922.

31. Erskine, ibid.

32. That is why I spell John MacLean with the capital 'L'. His father, Daniel, hailed from Mull. John himself spelled his surname Maclean with one exception: a postcard of himself around 1922. This is not common among his other biographers.

33. R Erskine of Marr, 'Celtic Tribal Communism', *The Socialist*, January 1923.

34. R Erskine of Marr, 'Cuisean Politiceach' ('Political Issues 34) *Guth na*

Bliadhna, An Samhradh/Summer 1921, p. 82.

35. 'Cuisean Politiceach', *Guth na Bliadhna*, An t-Earrach/Spring, 1921, p. 5. Karl Marx is dead, but the Celtic gospel lives on.'

36. William Diack, 'The Scottish Mines', *The Scottish Review*, Vol 43, Spring 1920, p. 41.

37. Erskine's letter and the reply from the Mines Commission, CJS Middleton papers, LP/JSM/MIN/1-3, Peoples History Museum, Manchester.

38. R Erskine of Marr, 'Russian Sovereignty'. *The Scottish Standard*, March 1922. He had made a similar point in a letter to Forward on 9th October, 1920.

Chapter Eight

1. Text taken from the website: https://ireland-calling.com/mise-eire.

2. *The Scottish Review*, Vol 39, Autumn 1916, p. 355.

3. Quoted in Peter Berresford Ellis, *Celt and Saxon – the Struggle for Britain, AD 410–937*, London, 1993, p. 248 for Britain, AD 410 – 937, London, 1993, p. 248.

4. Erskine, ibid, p. 369.

5. Erskine, ibid, p. 374.

6. Erskine to Charles Loch, 6th June 1916, Charles Loch papers, University of Glasgow Gaelic Collection, Gaelic Correspondence 1.

7. Erskine to Loch, 16th December, 1916, Charles Loch Papers, ibid.

8. Erskine, 'Chronicles of the Quarters', *The Scottish Review*, Vol 41, Spring 1918, p. 145.

9. *R Erskine of Marr, King Edward VII and Some Other Figures*, London, 1936, p. 59

10. Ibid, p. 61.

11. H C MacNeacail, 'The Celt in Ireland', *The Scottish Review*, Vol 42, Spring 1919, p. 93.

12. MacNeacail, Ibid, p. 94.

13. Erskine, 'Chronicles of the Quarters', *The Scottish Review*, Vol 42, Spring 1919, p. 117.

14. Alexander McGill, MA, 'The Case for Ireland: an appeal to Scottish fair play', *Liberty*, June 1920.

15. This rally was reported in the *Scotsman* (16th August – 'Archbishop Mannix: Sinn Féin Demonstration in Trafalgar Square') and the *Glasgow Herald* (19th August – 'A Scottish Sinn Féin.') The Glasgow newspaper passed comment that Erskine was an 'irritant' and a 'diversion' away from real consideration of home rule.

16. Liam Mac Gille Iosa, 'A Most Seditious Paper', *Liberty*, September, 1920.

17. *Liberty,* 9th October, 1920.

18. Richard J Finlay, 'Gillies, William (Liam Mac Gille Iosa), 1865–1932', *Oxford Dictionary of National Biography,* September 2004.

19. Liam Mac Gille Iosa, 'Toirdhealbhach Mac Suibhne (Terence MacSwiney)', *Liberty*, 6th November 1920.

20. Seumas MacGaraidh (McGarry), Open Letter to the Stornoway Gazette, *Liberty*, 13th November 1920.

21. R Erskine of Marr, 'The True Character of a 'Terror'', *Liberty*, 20th November, 1920.

22. Honourable R Erskine of Marr, 'The Problem of Physical Force', *Welsh Outlook*, March 1921.

23. R Erskine of Marr, 'New Worlds for Old', *Liberty*, 4th December, 1920.

24. For an excellent short account of O'Brien's life see Owen McGee, Collection List No. 150, The Art Ó Briain Papers, National Library of Ireland, 2009. There is financial scandal, withdrawal from public life, involvement in music publishing and political redemption in the Free State as an ambassador to France.

25. Darragh Gannon, 'Celticism in Exile: the London Gaelic League, 1917-21', *Proceedings of the Harvard Celtic Colloquium*, Vol 30, 2010.

26. Gannon, ibid, p. 98.

27. O'Brien to Erskine, 30/3/1921, The Art Ó Briain Papers, National Library of Ireland, MS 8428/21.

28. Letters exchanged over 23rd and 24th October 1921 in the Ó Briain Papers, MS 8429/16.

29. O'Brien to 'Mrs Erskine', 27/8/21 with a reply from Dona Maria's on 5/10/21, MS 8428/21.

30. Ibid, MS 8427/18. O'Brien has a hand written note 'write to Dublin for SF consent.'

31. Stephen Coyle, *High Noon on High Street*, Glasgow, 2008; Máirtín Ó Cáthain, Michael Collins and Scotland, Frank Ferguson and James McConnel (ed.), *Ireland and Scotland in the Nineteenth Century*, Dublin, 2009.

32. Letters from Erskine to O'Brien, 1/7/20 and 7/7/20, ibid. MS 8427/18.

33. O'Brien to Erskine, 21/12/20, Ibid. MS 8428/21.

34. Memo from O'Brien to Collins, 6/7/19, ibid. MS 8433/28.

35. Memo from O'Brien to Collins titled 'Scotch affairs', 22/7/19, ibid. MS 8433/28.

36. Erskine to O'Brien, 19/8/20, Dáil Éireann files, National Library of Ireland, DE2/435. O'Brien sounded out Seán Milroy, a Glasgow based Republican.

37. Memo from O'Brien to Collins, 15/9/20, enclosing John MacArthur's two 'newsbills' – one on Ireland and the other on Scotland as well as other solidarity leaflets including MacLean's provocative Proposed Irish Massacre. Ibid DE2/435.

38. Collins to O'Brien, 21/3/21, ibid. DE2/435.

39. Collins to O'Brien, 8/4/21, ibid. DE2/435.

40. De Valera to 'Minister of Finance' (Collins), 2/4/21, Ibid, DE2/435.

41. 'A very genuine man.' Memo entitled 'Scottish Friends' from Collins to O'Brien, 3/4/21, Ibid, DE2/435.

42. In one of his earlier letters to O'Brien, Erskine gave out his phone number, Mayfair 4723 to be precise, which would have raised security concerns. 23/6/19, Art O'Brien Papers, MS8433/28.
43. Memo from O'Brien to Collins, 29/3/21, Dáil Éireann files, DE2/435.
44. C. Desmond Greaves, Liam Mellows and the Irish Revolution, London, 1971, pp 231–232.
45. Gerard Cairns, *The Red and the Green – A Portrait of John MacLean,* Glasgow, 2017, p. 125. The discovery of the papers of Seamus Reader, archivist of Scots-Irish republicanism, Republican liaison between Dublin and Scotland from before the 1916 Rising as well as a gun runner for the Irish revolution has given us the only real on the ground evidence of any such activity in Scotland but he makes no reference to Fianna na h-Alba. My thanks to Stephen Coyle for information from the Reader papers.
46. Memo from O'Brien to Collins, 31/8/21, Ibid, DE2/435.
47. Patrick Witt, 'Connections Across the North Channel: Ruaraidh Erskine and Irish Influence in Scottish Discontent, 1906-20', *The Irish Story,* Irish History Online.
48. Máirtín Ó Cáthain, ibid. p. 171.
49. De Valera to 'Minister of Finance' (Collins), 2/4/21, Ibid, DE2/435.
50. Erskine to O'Brien, 13/5/21, O'Brien Papers, MS 8428/21.
51. Report on London Branch of the SNL, *Scottish Standard,* December 1921.
52. H C MacNeacail, 'The Anglo-Irish Treaty', *Scottish Standard,* January 1922.
53. Liam Mac Gille Iosa, 'England's Offer', *Scottish Standard,* January 1922.
54. Library of Ireland, MS18005/2/4.
55. Patrick Witt, ibid, *The Irish Story,* Irish History Online.
56. Hansard Online, Vol 52, cc 6-48. 23/11/1922.
57. Cathal Brennan, 'The Tailteann Games, 1924-1936', *Irish History Online* gives an entertaining account of the first Games.
58. *Aberdeen Press and Journal,* 23/7/1924.
59. Christopher Harvie calls Erskine and MacDiarmid the 'Embassy' who were 'critical in establishing Celtic credentials of Scottish literary and political nationalism'. See Harvie, *A Floating Commonwealth: Politics, Culture and Technology on Britain's Atlantic Coast, 1860 – 1930,* 2008, p. 126.

Chapter Nine

1. The following description comes from 'Comunn nan Albannach, Lunainn, Syllabus 1909-10', Paipearan Calum MacPhàrlain/Malcolm MacFarlane Papers, National Library of Scotland, MS 9736, Printed material.
2. Ibid.
3. *Comunn nan Albannach, A Manifesto to the Scottish People,* Kensington, nd (1910), p. 10.

4. Ibid, p. 11.

5. Ibid, p. 14.

6. Comunn nan Albannach, Lunainn, The First Annual Scottish Bi-Lingual Concert, *A' Bhliadhna Ùr*, 1912.

7. 'Scots National League: Great Protest Demonstration at Arbroath', Liberty, October 1920,

8. Ibid.

9. Ibid.

10. 'Scots National League – Great Meeting in London', *Liberty*, April 1921.

11. The Reverend J Stuart Barr, Famous Scots, Liberty, March 1920.

12. HC MacNeacail, Liberty, January 1921.

13. See, for example, James D Young, *The Rousing of the Scottish Working Class*, London, 1979 and James D Young, *John Maclean: Clydeside Socialist*, Glasgow, 1992. In both books Young argues convincingly that this historiography strongly influenced MacLean.

14. Liam Mac Gille Iosa, 'How the Republic Went Down', *Liberty*, 20/11/1920.

15. E P Thompson, The Making of the English Working Class, London, 1980 edition, p. 13.

16. R Erskine of Marr, 'New Worlds for Old', *Liberty*, 4/12/1920.

17. R Erskine of Marr, 'Praise Bull from Whom all Blessings Flow', *Liberty*, January 1921. The journal went back to being a monthly publication.

18. R Erskine of Marr, 'Scotland and the 'New World'', leader article, *Liberty*, July 1920. A month earlier Roland Muirhead had engaged on the subject in *Forward* (19/6/1920) accusing the MP and his parliamentary colleagues of prevaricating. 'Scotland has demanded a National Parliament by a majority of its parliamentary representatives, time after time… Why is she still without a National Parliament?'

19. *Liberty*, June 1920.

20. This part of the Red Clydeside MP's story has only come to light thanks to huge collection of clippings of Roland Muirhead.

21. Clipping from 27th March, 1922 in the Roland Muirhead papers, National Library of Scotland, Acc 3721, Box 124, No. 19.

22. 'The Fiery Cross, London Branch' in *The Standard* (as *Liberty* was re-named), February 1922.

23. *The Daily Record*, 24th June 1922.

24. The Honourable R Erskine of Marr, 'The Scots National League', *New Witness*, 4th August 1922.

25. *Scotsman*, 16/10/1922,

26. SNL General Election leaflet (n.d), Tom H Gibson papers, National Library of Scotland, Acc 6058, Box 4/1.

27. 'Scots National League Manifesto', *Leinster Reporter*, 4/11/1922, p. 3.

28. *Dundee Courier*, 31/10/1922, p. 8.

29. Lewis Spence, *The Scottish Nation*, 19th June 1923, advertising the League's national convention of 1923.

30. Lewis Spence, 'The Scots National League', *The Scottish Nation*, 22nd May, 1923.

31. *Glasgow Herald*, 25th June, 1923.

32. Ian Donnachie, Christopher Harvie and Ian S Wood, *Forward! Labour Politics in Scotland 1888–1988*, Edinburgh, 1989, p. 36-37.

33. Lewis Spence, *The Scottish Nation*, 19th June 1923.

34. The Hon R Erskine of Marr, The Revival of Scottish Nationalism, *The Scottish Nation*, 9th October, 1923.

35. Richard J. Finlay, Gibson, Thomas Hill, *Oxford Dictionary of National Biography*, 23rd September, 2004.

36. Gerard Cairns, *The Red and the Green: A Portrait of John MacLean*, Glasgow, 2017, p. 180.

37. Roland Muirhead to Tom Gibson, 17th April 1924, Muirhead papers ibid, Box1/1.

38. See Richard J Finlay, *Independent and Free: Scottish Politics and the Origins of the Scottish National Party 1918-45*, Edinburgh, 1994, pp 46-53 for a lively and informative narrative of these events.

39. *Scotsman*, 20/6/1925.

40. H J Hanham, *Scottish Nationalism*, London, 1969, pp 142-143 lists the points with some interesting background.

41. "Exile', Ireland and the Outside World', *The Irish Worker*, 22nd December 1923.

Chapter Ten

1. The Honourable R Erskine of Marr, *Bordology – being the science of determining character according to what a man eats and drinks*, London 1925, p.9. This pamphlet first appeared as an article in the *London Evening Standard*.

2. *Shields Daily News*, 17/6/1925.

3. C M Grieve, 'The Honourable Ruaraidh Erskine of Marr', *Scottish Educational Journal*, 19/2/1926, reprinted in Hugh MacDiarmid, *Contemporary Scottish Studies*, Stockport, 1995, p. 284-5.

4. R Erskine of Marr, Mr. Grieve's Studies, *Scottish Educational Journal*, 25/9/1925, in MacDiarmid, op. cit., pp 130-131.

5. R Erskine of Marr, letter, 13/11/1925, MacDiarmid, op. cit., p. 187.

6. MacDiarmid, op. cit., p. 193.

7. R Erskine of Marr, 'History in Schools', 21/5/1926, in MacDiarmid, op. cit. p. 336.

8. *Edinburgh Evening News*, 20/2/1925.

9. Erskine to Gibson, 29/4/1926 in the Tom H Gibson papers, NLS, Acc 6058, Box 1/1.

10. Gibson to Erskine, 1/5/1926, Gibson papers, ibid.

11. Quoted in C Desmond Greaves, 'Father Michael O'Flanagan; Republican Priest', A Connolly Association pamphlet, 1954.

12. Erskine to Gibson, 9/5/1926, Gibson papers, ibid. Erskine offers

to help out in the West and states that he has been active in Inverness, Aberdeen, Perth and Stirling.

13. Erskine to Gibson, 20/3/1926, Gibson papers, ibid.

14. Erskine to Gibson, 7/7/1926, Gibson papers, ibid.

15. Mr Baird is never fully named and within a year or so Erskine had found him to be a disappointment.

16. Gibson to Gillies, Jr., 26/7/1926, Gibson papers, ibid.

17. Erskine to Gillies, 20/10/1926, Gibson papers, ibid.

18. The Honourable R Erskine of Marr, 'The Importance of History', *Scots Independent*, Volume 1, No. 1, November 1926.

19. The Honourable R Erskine of Marr, 'The League and its Journal', *Scots Independent*, Volume 1, No. 5, March 1927.

20. Editorial, 'A National Convention', *Scots Independent*, Vol 1, No. 2 December 1926.

21. Murray G H Pittock, *A New History of Scotland*, Stroud, 2003, p. 269.

22. Richard J Finlay, *Independent and Free: Scottish Politics and the Origins of the Scottish National Party 1918-45*, Edinburgh, 1994, p. 46-53.

23. Erskine to Spence, 11/1/1926, Lewis Spence Papers, National Library of Scotland, Acc. 5916/1.

24. Erskine to Gibson, 25/3/1927, Gibson papers, Box 1/2.

25. Erskine to Gibson, Easter Monday 1927, Gibson papers, Box 1/2.

26. Erskine to Gibson, 25/3/1927, Gibson papers, Box 1/2.

27. Erskine to Gibson, Easter Monday 1927, Gibson papers, Box 1/2.

28. Erskine to Gibson, 6/5/1927, Gibson papers, op. cit. Spence was a 'coxcomb.'

Chapter Eleven

1. For an interesting and informative discussion see Catherine Kerrigan, *Whaur Extremes Meet: The Poetry of Hugh MacDiarmid, 1920 – 1934*, Edinburgh, 1983, Part 3.

2. P H Pearse, *The Separatist Idea, Political Writings and Speeches*, Dublin, 1952, p. 263.

3. The Hon R Erskine of Marr, *Pictish Review*, February 1928, p. 38.

4. The Hon R Erskine of Marr, 'Celticism', *Scots Independent*, Vol 3, No. 1, November 1928.

5. The Hon R Erskine of Marr, 'Scottish Nationalism and the 'World State'', *Scots Independent*, Vol 3 No. 4, February 1929.

6. James D Young, *The Rousing of the Scottish Working Class*, London, 1979, p. 208.

7. Editorial, 'Scotland and Fascismo', *Pictish Review*, April 1928.

8. Erskine to Gibson, no date, January 1928, Tom H Gibson papers, NLS, Box 1/2.

9. Erskine to Gibson, 18/1/1928, Gibson papers, ibid.

10. R E Muirhead, *Fèin-Riaghlaidh airson Alba*, Oban, 1927. The title can

mean home rule but is self-government for Scotland in direct translation.

11. Erskine to Gibson, 17/3/1928, Gibson papers, ibid.

12. Gibson to Erskine, 24/3/1928, Gibson papers, ibid.

13. Erskine to Gibson, 18/4/1928, Gibson papers, ibid.

14. 'SCOTTISH NATIONAL PARTY – Inaugural Demonstration at Stirling', *Scottish Home Rule*, Volume 9, No. 2, August 1928, p. 14

15. Muirhead to Erskine, 21/7/1928, Roland Muirhead papers, National Library of Scotland, Acc 3721, Box 9, File 181.

16. Erskine to Muirhead, 25/7/1928, Muirhead papers, ibid.

17. Erskine to Muirhead, 25/3/1929, Muirhead papers, ibid.

18. Leader, 'North Midlothian Election', *Scottish Home Rule,* Volume 9, No. 8, 1929.

19. The Hon R Erskine of Marr, 'Scots and Welsh Demand for Home Rule', *Current History* (New York), 1/12/1929, Volume 31, No. 3, p. 542.

20. Erskine, 'Scots and Welsh Demand for Home Rule', ibid, p. 542.

21. Erskine, 'Scots and Welsh Demand for Home Rule', ibid, p. 543.

22. The Hon R Erskine of Marr, 'That Which Today Stands Roofless', no date (1930 as advertised in the *Scots Independent*) p. 40.

23. Erskine, op. cit. p. 31

24. Erskine to Gibson, 10/10/1929, Gibson papers, ibid.

25. Reverend Malcolm MacColl, Leader, *Scots Independent*, Volume 1, No. 12, 1927.

26. Leader article and report, *Scottish Home Rule*, Volume 8, No.6, December 1927.

27. Leader article, ibid., p. 174.

28. Leader article, ibid., p. 175.

29. Leader article, ibid., p.176.

30. Leader article, *Scottish Home Rule*, Volume 8, No. 7, January 1928, p. 186.

31. Honourable R Erskine of Marr, 'Unrealities', *Modern Scot,* Volume 1, No. 1, Spring 1930, p. 31.

32. Erskine, 'Unrealities', ibid., p. 32.

33. Erskine, 'Unrealities', ibid., p. 32.

34. H J Hanham, *Scottish Nationalism*, London, 1969, p.145.

35. Erskine, 'Unrealities', ibid., p. 33.

36. Erskine did have one defender at the time. Joseph McDonell, from the Irish community in Scotland, wrote a piece on 'Ourselves Alone: A Practical Policy' in the *Scots Independent*, Volume 4, No. 8, June 1930. This did not elicit any movement wide response and the political notion of Sinn Féin remains Irish.

Chapter Eleven

1. See Hayden Lorimer, 'Your wee bit hill and glen: The Cultural Politics of the Scottish Highlands c. 1918-45', Doctoral thesis, Loughborough University, September 1997 for an engaging discussion of Erskine's

intervention in the discussion. Erskine is cited as, 'an ageing Nationalist provocateur and publicist.' The original articles quoted come from the *Scots Magazine*.

2. Lorimer, ibid. p. 151.

3. Lorimer, ibid. p. 154.

4. The Honourable Ruaraidh Erskine of Marr, *Changing Scotland*, Montrose, 1931.

5. This was the Scottish Workers Republican Party (SWRP) in February 1922. Scotland's first pro-independence political party.

6. The Honourable Ruaraidh Erskine of Marr, *Changing Scotland*, Montrose, 1931, p.1 4.

7' Erskine, ibid, p. 19

8. Erskine, ibid, p. 20.

9. Erskine, ibid, p. 21.

10. Erskine, ibid., p. 22.

11. Erskine, ibid, p. 63.

12. Erskine, ibid, p. 34.

13. The copy in the National Library of Scotland has disappeared!

14. Fionn MacColla, Review of 'An Rosàrnach', *Modern Scot*, Vol 1, No. 4, Winter 1930, p. 72.

15. MacColla, ibid, p. 74.

16. The Honourable Ruaraidh Erskine of Marr, *MacBeth – being a sketch of the historical figure as opposed to that of some Tradition and the Drama*, Inverness, 1930, p. 90.

17. The Hon Ruaraidh Erskine of Marr, *The Stout Adventure of Mary Stewart*, London, 1937, p. 24

18. Erskine, *The Stout Adventure of Mary Stewart*, p. 161

19. The Eastbourne and District Scottish Association.

20. *Eastbourne Gazette*, 31/1/1934.

21. Bearsden Man's Notes, *Milngavie and Bearsden Herald*, 2/2/1934.

22. 'Treaty of Union Broken', *Scotsman*, 19/2/1934.

23. Erskine to Muirhead, 8/1/1934, Roland Muirhead papers, National Library of Scotland, Acc 3721, Box 9, File 181.

24. The Honourable Ruaraidh Erskine of Marr, *The Crown of England*, London, 1937, p. 175.

25. Erskine, *The Crown of England*, p. 180.

26. Honourable Ruaraidh Erskine of Marr, 'When Fashion Patronised the Park', *The Saturday Review*, 15/9/1934, p. 116.

27. The Honourable Ruaraidh Erskine of Marr, *King Edward VII and Some Other Figures*, London, 1936, p. 27.

28. Erskine, ibid, p. xi.

29. Erskine to MacDiarmid, 25/10/1937. Quoted in John Manson (ed.), *Dear Grieve*. Edinburgh, 2011.

30. 'IFDM', The Royal Institute of International Affairs, Vol 15, No. 6, (Nov – Dec 1936), p. 925.

GERARD CAIRNS

Chapter Thirteen

1. Graham Greene, *Monsignor Quixote*, London, 2006, p. 67.
2. Erskine to Muirhead, 26/10/1946, Roland Muirhead papers, National Library of Scotland, Acc 3721, Box 9, file 181.
3. Ruaraidh Erskine, Tradition and the Physician in Scotland, *British Medical Journal*, Vol 1, No 4088, 13/5/1939, p. 995.
4. Dr Ross Mitchell, Hereditary Physicians in Celtic Medicine at www. rcpe.ac.uk/heritage/hereditary-physicians-celtic-medicine The author has studied the distance learning An Cùrsa Adhartais at Sabhal Mòr Ostaig on Skye and this Celtic tradition is covered as part of Gaelic cultural traditions and its decline.
5. Honourable Ruaraidh Erskine of Marr, *The Great Baltic Bubble*, London, 1940, p.122.
6. *Aberdeen Press and Journal*, 27/4/1940.
7. Erskine to MacDiarmid, 1/9/1945, Hugh MacDiarmid papers, National Library of Scotland, Acc 7361, Box 1.
8. Nan Milton, *John Maclean*, London, 1973, p. 41.
9. Wendy Wood, *Yours Sincerely for Scotland*, Bristol, 1970.
10. Muirhead to Erskine, 7/3/1947, Muirhead papers, Box 9, file 181.
11. Erskine to Muirhead, 31/3/1947, ibid.
12. Erskine to Muirhead, 4/7/1947, ibid.
13. The tune was the Orange favourite of the Sash. Morris loved the idea of a republican song to an Orange tune.
14. Muirhead to Erskine, 7/3/1947, ibid.
15. Erskine to Muirhead, 17/3/1947, ibid.
16. Muirhead to Erskine, 11/4/1947, ibid.
17. Erskine to Muirhead, 6/6/1953, ibid.
18. Erskine to Muirhead, 15/10/1949, ibid.
19. Erskine to Muirhead, 11/8/1948, ibid.
20. This was the RNP – Rassemblement National Populaire created by Marcel Déat. For a highly readable account see Rod Kedward, *La Vie en Bleu: France and the French since 1900*, London, 2006, chapter 11.
21. Erskine to Muirhead, 21/7/1947, ibid.
22. Muirhead to Erskine, 4/9/1947, ibid.
23. Erskine to Muirhead, 28/9/1948, ibid.
24. Muirhead to Erskine, 10/1/1949, ibid.
25. Quoted in Keith Webb, *The Growth of Nationalism in Scotland*, Glasgow, 1977, p. 65.
26. Keith Webb, op. cit. p.67
27. HJ Hanham, Scottish Nationalism, London, 1969, p. 177.
28. Erskine to Muirhead, 20/10/1950, ibid. Erskine informed his friend in this letter that they were going to Barcelona for the winter.
29. Erskine had sent MacDiarmid a postcard on 26/10/1951 praising his latest work and a letter to Muirhead dated 21/2/1952 was postmarked

from Bordeaux.

30. Erskine to Muirhead, 31/3/1952, ibid.

31. The Honourable Ruaraidh Erskine of Marr, *The Great Highland-Lowland Bubble*, Glasgow, nd, p.2

32. *Gairm*, 16, 1956, p. 367. '…and it awakened a resolve regarding the Gaelic – a determination that will never weaken and hasn't weakened yet.'

Chapter Thirteen

1. Compton MacKenzie, *The Four Winds of Love – Book 1: The East Wind of Love*, London, 1937, p. 272.

2. MacKenzie, ibid, p. 291.

3. MacKenzie, ibid, p. 563.

4. MacKenzie, ibid, p. 564.

5. George Rosie, 'The Englishing of Scotland', fourth lecture to the annual SNP Conference in Dunoon, 1989, p. 6.

6. *The Times*, 8/1/1960.

7. Catherine Kerrigan, *Whaur Extremes Meet: The Poetry of Hugh MacDiarmid 1920 – 1934*, Edinburgh, 1983, p. 141

8. For an excellent account of Seumas MacGaraidh's contribution, see Steve Jackson, From Arbroath to San Francisco – Poet and Visionary, Soldier and Patriot, the unpublished biography of James Carr Hay aka Seumas MacGaraidh. Steve links the stories of Seumas and Ruaraidh well and gives some excellent examples of MacGaraidh's own language activism including a protest against the singing of 'God Save the King' at the 1913 Mòd in Dundee pertinent as the King was due to attend!

9. Constance Markievicz, 'Ireland: Her Struggles Past and Present' *Unemployed News*, 5/2/1923, p. 2

10. Peter Berresford Ellis, *Celt and Saxon – the Struggle for Britain, AD 410 – 937*, London, 1993, p. 229.

11. 'Ruaraidh Erskine and Derick Thomson: Gaelic Innovators', a lecture by Petra Johana Poncarová in the University of Glasgow, 18/6/2019.

12. Erskine to MacFarlane, nd, Malcolm MacFarlane papers, National Library of Scotland, Acc 9736, Box 50. Chronologically, the letter seems to be from late January 1911.

13. D S Thomson, Erskine, Stuart Richard (known as Ruaraidh Erskine of Mar), 1869 – 1960, *Oxford Dictionary of National Biography*, September 2004.

14. Ronald Renton, Editorial, Paragraphs – The Neil Munro Society Journal, Issue 19, Spring 2006, p. 3

15. Peter Berresford Ellis and Seumas Mac A' Ghobhainn, *The Scottish Insurrection of 1820*, London, 1989 edition.

16. Seumas Mac A' Ghobhainn, Ruaraidh Arascainn is Mhàirr, *Stornoway Gazette*, 19/2/1972.

17. *Scotland's Future – Your Guide to an Independent Scotland*, Edinburgh, 2013, p. 449.

18. A' Phàrlamaid Albannach Agadsa, Dùn Èideann, 2016.

19. James Hunter on Erskine in Derick S Thomson (ed.), *The Companion to Gaelic Scotland*, Oxford, 1983, p. 238.

20. From Irish Labour to British Labour – An Open Letter across the Channel, *The Voice of Labour*, 19/12/1921.

21. Erskine was popular among the Irish Left. One example: in a report of a fundraiser to aid the creation of an Irish Labour College, named after James Connolly, in the St Andrews Hall in Glasgow, the reporter informed his home based audience, quite out of the blue, that, 'Ruaraidh Erskine will be glad to see the spontaneous re-union of the sea-divided Gael and proud that the initiative has come from Scotia minor.' (Watchword of Labour, 11/10/1919.) Connolly's daughter, Nora, was the main speaker.

22. Prof. William Gillies, 'Liam Macgill'Iosa: A Friend of the Gael', 23/2/1990, *Transactions of the Gaelic Society of Inverness*, Vol LVI, 1988-90.

23. Erskine, *Pictish Review*, February 1928, p. 45

24. DJ MacKinnon, 'A Highlander's Protest', *The Scottish Nationalist*, Vol 1, No. 3, May 1903.

25. Wendy Wood, *Yours Sincerely for Scotland*, Bristol, 1970, p. 196.

26. It should be noted that in the early 1990s certain writers argued that there was a revolutionary, republican Presbyterian tradition from Knox down to the Cameronians in the late seventeenth century that opposed Stewart/Jacobite autocracy and reaction. See *Jacobites or Covenanters: Which Tradition? A Scottish Republican Debate*, Glasgow, 1992 especially the contributions by Mark Stewart and Allan Armstrong. Mark has written an unpublished history of Scotland ('Scotland 84 – 1689, Our Buried Past') and Allan has written and debated extensively on the revolutionary Covenanting tradition in Scotland.

27. Art O' Brien, 'The Complete Nationalist', 4/3/1933, p. 5 in the Art O' Brien papers, National Library of Ireland, Acc 8436/19.

28. Professor William Gillies, ibid, p. 528.

29. Erskine, *The Great Highland – Lowland Bubble*, p. 8

30. James Connolly, 'Labour, Nationality and Religion: Being a discussion of the Lenten discourses against Socialism by Father Kane, SJ, in Gardiner Street Church, Dublin, 1910', in James Connolly, *The Workers' Republic*, Dublin, 1951, p. 191 – 264.

31. James Joyce, *Portrait of the Artist as a Young Man*, 1992, Ware, p. 157.

32. Postcard from the Earl of Buchan to the author, 31/1/2019.

SOURCES

Primary Sources:

Brenda Bennie papers, Glasgow Caledonian University.
John Devoy papers, National Library of Ireland.
Tom H Gibson papers, National Library of Scotland.
Charles Loch papers, University of Glasgow.
Hugh MacDiarmid papers, National Library of Scotland.
Malcolm MacFarlane papers, National Library of Scotland.
Roland Muirhead papers, National Library of Scotland.
Art O' Brien papers, National Library of Ireland.

Newspapers/Periodicals:

Alba
Am Bàrd
An Ròsarnach
An Sgeulaiche
Birmingham Daily Gazette
British Medical Journal
British Newspaper Archive
British Union Catalogue of Periodicals
Burke's Peerage
Call
Catholic Historical Review
Celtic Annual
Cencrastus
Cracroft's Peerage
Current History
Derby Evening Telegraph
Dundee Courier
Dundee Evening Post
Dundee Evening Telegraph
Edinburgh Evening News
Forward
Freeman's Journal
Gairm
Glasgow Herald
Guth na Bliadhna
Hansard
Highland News
Highlander
History Ireland
Huddersfield Daily Chronicle

Irish History Online
Irish Radical Newspaper Archive
Journal of Irish and Scottish Studies
Journal of Modern Literature
Lancashire Evening Post
Leinster Reporter
Liberty
London Daily News
Modern Scot
Montrose Standard
North Down Herald
Northampton Mercury
Oxford Dictionary of National Biography
Paragraphs: The Neil Munro Society Journal
People
Perthshire Advertiser
Pictish Review
Press and Journal
Rothesay Chronicle and Buteshire Advertiser
Royal Institute of International Affairs
Saturday Review
Scots Independent
Scotsman
Scottish Home Rule
Scottish Nation
Scottish Nationalist
Scottish Review
Scottish Studies Review
Sheffield Evening Express
Sinn Féin
Socialist
Standard
Stornoway Gazette
Strathearn Herald
Sunday Herald
Tatler
Thistle: A Scottish Patriotic Magazine
Transactions of the Gaelic Society of Inverness
United Ireland
Vanguard
Voice of Labour
Welsh Outlook
Whirlwind
Who's Who
York Herald

Articles:

Brennan, Cathal – The Tailteann Games, 1924 – 36, *Irish History Online*.
Bunting, Madeleine - Gaelic: The Secret Language of Revolution, *Sunday Herald*, 25/9/2016.
Finlay, Richard J – Gillies, William (Liam Mac Gille Iosa), 1865 – 1932, September 2004, *Oxford Dictionary of National Biography*.
Finlay, Richard J – Gibson, Thomas Hill, September 2004, *Oxford Dictionary of National Biography*.
Fox-Davies, Arthur Charles – Armorial Families: *A Directory of Gentlemen of coat-armour online*.
Gannon, Darragh – Celticism in Exile: The London Gaelic League, 1917 – 21, *Proceedings of the Harvard Celtic Colloquium*, Vol 30, 2010.
Gillies, Professor William – Liam Macgill' Iosa: A Friend of the Gael, *Transactions of the Gaelic Society of Inverness*, Vol LVI, 1988 – 90.
Hunter, James – The Gaelic Connection: The Highlands, Ireland and nationalism, 1873 – 1922, *Scottish Historical Review*, 1975.
Lloyd-Jones, Naomi - Liberalism, Scottish Nationalism and the Home Rule Crisis c 1886-1893, *English Historical Review*, vol CXXIX, 2015.
Lyall, Scott – The Man is a Menace: MacDiarmid and Military Intelligence, *Scottish Studies Review*, 8.1, Spring 2007.
MacCallum, Alastair – Ruaraidh Arascainn is Mhàirr, *Scottish Workers Republic*, 1997.
Mac A' Ghobhainn, Seumas – Ruaraidh Arascainn is Mhàirr, *Stornoway Gazette*, 19/2/1972.
Purdie, Bob – 'Crossing Swords with WB Yeats': Twentieth Century Scottish Nationalist Encounters with Ireland, *Journal of Irish and Scottish Studies*, Vol 1, Issue 1.
Thomson, DS - Erskine, Stuart Richard (known as Ruaraidh Erskine of Mar), 1869 – 1960, September 2004, *Oxford Dictionary of National Biography*.
Witt, Patrick - Connections Across the Channel: Ruaraidh Erskine and Irish Influence in Scottish Discontent, 1906 – 1920, The Irish Story, *Irish History Online*.

Books:

Bell, Henry – *John Maclean: Hero of Red Clydeside*, London, 2018.
Berresford Ellis, Peter – *Celt and Saxon – the Struggle for Britain, AD 410 – 937*, London, 1993.
Black, Ronald (ed.) – *Eilein na h-Òige: The Poems of Fr Allan McDonald*, Glasgow, 2002.
Brown, Gordon – *Maxton*, Edinburgh, 1988.
Cairns, Gerard – *The Red and The Green: A Portrait of John MacLean*, Glasgow, 2017.
Cameron, Ewen A – *Land for the People? The British Government and the Scottish*

Highlands c. 1880 – 1925, East Linton, 1996.

Campbell, John Lorne (ed) – *Highland Songs of the Forty-Five*, Edinburgh, 1997.

Checkland, Sydney and Olive – *Industry and Ethos: Scotland 1832 – 1914*, London, 1984.

Cobban, Alfred – *The Nation State and National Self-Determination,* London and Glasgow, 1969.

Connolly, James – *The Workers' Republic*, Dublin, 1951.

Connolly, James – *Labour in Irish History,* Dublin, 1956.

Coyle, Stephen - *High Noon on High Street,* Glasgow, 2008.

Coyle, Stephen and Ó Catháin, Máirtinn (ed.) – *'We Will Rise Again': Ireland, Scotland and the Easter Rising,* Glasgow, 2018.

Diack, William – *The Moral Effects of Socialism, being a lecture delivered in Greyfriars Hall on the evening of 12th February, 1893 under the auspices of the Aberdeen Socialist Society*, 1894.

Diack, William – *History of the Trades Council and the Trade Union Movement in Aberdeen,* Aberdeen , 1939.

Donnachie, Ian, Harvie, Christopher and Wood, Ian S (ed.) – *Forward! Labour Politics in Scotland 1888 – 1988,* Edinburgh, 1989.

Douglas, Dick – *At the Helm: The Life and Times of Dr Robert McIntyre*, nd.

Dressler, Camille and Stiubhart, DW – *Alexander MacDonald: Bard of the Gaelic Enlightenment*, Isle of Lewis, 2012.

Dudley Edwards, Owen – *How David Cameron Saved Scotland and May Yet Save Us All*, Glasgow, 2015.

Erskine of Marr, The Honourable Ruaraidh – *MacBeth: Being a Sketch of the historical figure as opposed to that of some Tradition and the Drama,* Inverness, 1930.

Erskine of Marr, The Honourable Ruaraidh – *Changing Scotland*, Montrose, 1931.

Erskine of Marr, The Honourable Ruaraidh – *King Edward VII and Some Other Figures*, London, 1936.

Erskine of Marr, The Honourable Ruaraidh – *The Stout Adventure of Mary Stewart,* London, 1937.

Erskine of Marr, The Honourable Ruaraidh – *The Crown of England*, London, 1937.

Erskine of Marr, The Honourable Ruaraidh – *The Great Baltic Bubble*, London, 1940.

Erskine, The Honourable Stuart – *Lord Bolingbroke: Being Extracts from the Political Writings of Henry St John Viscount Bolingbroke,* Westminster, 1897.

Erskine, The Honourable Stuart – *Braemar: An Unconventional Guidebook and Literary Souvenir*, Edinburgh, 1898.

Erskine, The Honourable Stuart – *Lord Dullborough: A Sketch*, Bristol, 1898.

Erskine, The Honourable Stuart Ruadri – *The Kilt and How to Wear It,* Inverness, 1901.

Evans, Eric J – *The Forging of the Early Modern State: Early Industrial Britain*

1783 – 1870, New York, 1983.

Ferguson, Frank and McConnel, James (eds) – *Ireland and Scotland in the Nineteenth Century*, Dublin, 2009.

Finlay, Richard – *Independent and Free: Scottish Politics and the Origins of the Scottish National Party 1918 – 45*, Edinburgh, 1994.

Gouriévidis, Laurence - *The Dynamics of Heritage: History, Memory and the Highland Clearances*, 2010.

Greene, Graham – *Monsignor Quixote*, London, 2006.

Grigor, Iain Frisor – *Highland Resistance: The Radical Tradition in the Scottish North*, 2000

Grimble, Ian – *Scottish Clans and Tartans*, London, 1973.

Hanham, HJ – *Scottish Nationalism*, London, 1969.

Harvie, Christopher – *Scotland and Nationalism: Scottish Society and Politics, 1707 – 1977*, London, 1977.

Harvie, Christopher – *A Floating Commonwealth: Politics, Culture and Technology on Britain's Atlantic Coast, 1860 – 1930*, 2008.

Hobsbawm, Eric J – *Industry and Empire*, Middlesex, 1968.

Horgan, John J – *From Parnell to Pearse*, Dublin, 1948.

Howell, David – *A Lost Left: Three Studies in Socialism and Nationalism*, Manchester, 1986.

HRH Prince Michael of Albany, *The Forgotten Monarchy of Scotland*, London, 2002.

Jackson, Steve – *From Arbroath to San Francisco – Poet and Visionary, Soldier and Patriot. The Untold Story of James Carr Hay aka Seumas MacGaraidh; campaigning for an independent 'Gaelic Scotland.'*

Kedward, Rod – *La Vie en Bleu: France and the French since 1900*, London, 2006.

Kee, Robert, *The Green Flag: A History of Irish Nationalism*, London, 1972.

Kennedy, Gavin (ed.) – T*he Radical Approach: Papers on an Independent Scotland*, Edinburgh, 1976.

Kerrigan, Catherine – *Whaur Extremes Meet: The Poetry of Hugh MacDiarmid 1920 – 1934*, Edinburgh, 1983.

McCombes, Alan and Paterson, Roz – *Restless Land: A Radical Journey through Scotland's History, Volume 1 (500 AD – 1914)*, Glasgow, 2014.

McCulloch, Margery Palmer – *Modernism and Nationalism: Literature and Society in Scotland 1918 – 39*, Glasgow, 2004.

MacBean, Lachlan – *The Celtic Who's Who*, Kirkcaldy, 1921.

MacDiarmid, Hugh – *Contemporary Scottish Studies*, Stockport, 1995.

MacKenzie, Compton – *Catholicism and Scotland*, London, 1936.

MacKenzie, Compton – *The Four Winds of Love – Book 1: The East Wind of Love*, London, 1937.

MacKinnon, Kenneth – *Gaelic: A Past and Future Prospect*, Edinburgh, 1991

Manson, John (ed) – *Dear Grieve*, Edinburgh, 2011.

Marr, Andrew – *The Battle for Scotland*, London, 1992.

Martine, Roddy – *Scottish Clan and Family Names: Their Arms, Origins and*

Tartans, Edinburgh, 1987.

Marx, Karl and Engels, Frederick – *Selected Works in One Volume*, London, 1980.

Milton, Nan – *John Maclean*, London, 1973.

O'Donnell, Ruán – *Patrick Pearse*, Dublin, 2016.

Pittock, Murray GH – *A New History of Scotland*, Stroud, 2003.

Petrie, Sir Charles – *Bolingbroke*, London and Glasgow, 1937.

Ryan, Ray – *Ireland and Scotland: Literature and Culture, State and Nation, 1966 – 2000*, 2001.

Thompson, EP – *The Making of the English Working Class*, London, 1980.

Thomson, Derick S – *The Companion to Gaelic Scotland*, Oxford, 1983.

Tuckett, Angela – *The Scottish Trades Union Congress – The First Eighty Years, 1897 – 1977*, Edinburgh, 1986.

Watson, Moray (ed.) – *Edinburgh Companion to the Gaelic Language*, Edinburgh, 2010.

Webb, Keith – *The Growth of Nationalism in Scotland*, Glasgow, 1977.

White Paper – *Scotland's Future: Your Guide to an Independent Scotland*, Edinburgh, 2013.

Wolfe, Billy – *Scotland Lives*, Edinburgh, 1973.

Wood, Wendy – *Yours Sincerely for Scotland*, Bristol, 1970.

Young, James D – *The Rousing of the Scottish Working Class*, London, 1979.

Young, James D – *John Maclean: Clydeside Socialist*, Glasgow, 1992.

Pamphlets:

'Ajax' – *Highland Patriots*, 1909.

Bell, Stan – *Robert Bontine Cunningham Graham: The First President*, Glasgow, 2002.

Erskine of Marr, The Honourable Ruaraidh – *Bordology–being the Science of Determining Character according to what a man eats and drinks*, London, 1925.

Erskine of Marr, The Honourable Ruaraidh – *That Which Today Stands Roofless*, nd (1930)

Erskine of Marr, The Honourable Ruaraidh – *The Great Highland – Lowland Bubble*, Glasgow, nd (1950)

Greaves, C Desmond – *Father Michael O 'Flanagan; Republican Priest*, Connolly Association, 1954.

Mac Gille Iosa, Liam – *Some Arguments for Scottish Independence*, 1922.

MacQueen, Hamish – *A Short History of the Scottish National Party and the National Movement* (Prior to 1979), Glasgow, 1992

Oban and Lorne branch, *Highland Land League – Tiree Food Producers sent to Prison at the Instance of the Duke of Argyll*, 1918.

Pàrlamaid na h-Alba – *A' Phàrlamaid Albannach Agadsa*, 2016.

Rosie, George – *The Englishing of Scotland*, Edinburgh, 1989.

Spence, Lewis – *Freedom for Scotland: The Case for Scottish Self-Government*, Edinburgh 1928.

Scots Independent – *The Wit and Wisdom of Oliver Brown*, Stirling, 1992.

Academic Papers

Gunderloch, Anja – The Gaelic Manuscripts of Glasgow University: A Catalogue, 2007.
Kane, Nathan – 'A Study of the Debate on Scottish Home Rule, 1886 – 1914', PhD thesis.
Lorimer, Hayden – "'Your Wee Bit Hill and Glen': The Cultural Politics of the Scottish Highlands c.1918 – 45', Doctoral thesis, Loughborough University, September 1997.
MacLeòid, Aonghas – 'The Historical Plays of Donald Sinclair', Online.

INDEX

HOG'S BACK